HOW WAS
IT FOR YOU?

Eve Smith has worked for over twenty years in almost all areas of the sex industry: in a brothel, as an escort, in a strip club, online and as a dominatrix. She lives and works in the north of England.

EVE SMITH

HOW WAS IT FOR YOU?

The Lives and Loves of a Sex Worker

PICADOR

First published 2024 by Picador

This edition first published 2025 by Picador
an imprint of Pan Macmillan
The Smithson, 6 Briset Street, London EC1M 5NR
EU representative: Macmillan Publishers Ireland Ltd, 1st Floor,
The Liffey Trust Centre, 117–126 Sheriff Street Upper,
Dublin 1, D01 YC43
Associated companies throughout the world
www.panmacmillan.com

ISBN 978-1-0350-2453-7

1 3 5 7 9 8 6 4 2

A CIP catalogue record for this book is available from the British Library.

Typeset in Garamond Premier Pro by Palimpsest Book Production Ltd, Falkirk, Stirlingshire
Printed and bound by CPI Group (UK) Ltd, Croydon, CR0 4YY

Visit **www.picador.com** to read more about all our books
and to buy them. You will also find features, author interviews and
news of any author events, and you can sign up for e-newsletters
so that you're always first to hear about our new releases.

To all the sex workers out there. This is my story and, as we all have very different tales to tell, I only speak for myself. But my hope is that this book will go some way towards making our working lives safer from both the police and the clients who seek to harm us.

CONTENTS

AUTHOR'S NOTE

As I was writing this book, I attempted to change as many of the details as I could regarding locations and people, while staying true to the heart of the story, as I really do not want to become a household name. I never wanted that as an actress, and I don't want it now. My editor went one further and removed some details about things that have happened in my life to protect me, as they are stories that are pretty weird and unforgettable and can't have happened to many people. But, even with a careful eye on my anonymity, I want this book to be read by some of the bigger pricks it features. They will know who they are. But I doubt it will be them who out me. No, unfortunately, if I am outed it will probably be by another sex worker, a disgruntled client or a git from my family. But sometimes a story has to be told, whatever the risk.

PROLOGUE: WHO AM I?

There is a lot of power in a name. Using someone's name suggests that you see them, and that you know them. Or you want to get to know them. Maybe you like them, so their name plays softly, gently on your lips. Perhaps it's used as a term of endearment. You use it as often as you can.

But it's also possible that you might use a name against someone. You might use a person's name when you're angry, punctuating every sentence with it. Spitting it out. A name becomes a weapon.

Let's take it further.

A name might be used to find out more about someone. To dig into who they are. To stalk someone. To find out where they live, who they're friends with on social media, who their family is. Where they hang around. Where they work. What they do for a living.

A name might be used to contact someone's workplace and reveal information about them. Report them for sex working, perhaps. I know that's possible because I'm a sex worker. And in my job, I can all too easily imagine a scenario in which a client thinks we have a connection but I've said I won't see him again because he's too clingy, or perhaps because I don't have the time. He's devastated. But he knows my name. He knows the address I do business from. He has my bank details, because that's how I get paid.

Imagine what he could do with that information to fuck with my life.

The way I see it, you don't want a man – or anyone, really – to know your real name and have that kind of power over you. For this reason, sex workers advise other sex workers never to give a client their real name. And I think that's wise. So I have many names. My name is Hope. My name is Angel. Some people call me Emma. Others call me Milan or Natasha. A few call me Charlotte. I'll answer to all of them.

When I transitioned from escort work to domination, ten years ago, I chose a final name for myself. And I'm still using it. I won't reveal it now because I don't want my clients to know too much about my life; no more than they need to know. If they recognize themselves here, they might be proud or excited to be a part of my story. It's also possible they might not like it. Or, worse, they might pity me. I can't stand being pitied. One look of pity and I have the urge to pluck out an eye. I would much rather be hated than pitied, and I can tell you there's no shortage of people who hate me and all the other sex workers out there.

So, who am I?

Very few of my clients know exactly who I am. And that privacy works both ways. I won't look up a client's name unless they piss me off – maybe they don't treat me well, maybe they're reluctant to pay. If that happens, then I want to know exactly who they are. If you're ever my client I suggest you try very hard not to piss me off. Don't stiff me for money. Don't bombard me with emails. Don't push my boundaries. I can see you on Facebook with your family. I can see you on LinkedIn with your colleagues . . .

Avoiding my wrath is very simple.

Don't be abusive. Be nice. Always.

And, if you're a sex worker, my advice is that you use a pseudonym.

It's not easy to live and work under a false name. The banks are now clamping down so that if there isn't an exact name match on a bank transfer when a deposit is paid, an automated message about fraud is generated. This freaks out clients, men who are already twitchy about paying a sex worker in a transaction that's recorded. But I need that deposit for my services. Firstly, because there are so many timewasters out there and, like anyone, I have to be paid for the work that I do. Secondly, and more importantly, I need it because I want there to be a correspondence trail if the client decides to kill me. Account number, sort code and the name Miss D is all they get from me and this is, at present, enough for a bank. It means I can see my clients. But they can't see me. That seems like a fair exchange.

So it's deposit by bank transfer, please, and the rest of the money paid in cash when the client and I finally meet. Then I attempt to find a bank so that I can pay it in, remembering that cash amounts over a certain value are flagged as a potential money-laundering transaction.

Some savvy sex workers now use crypto currencies in order to be paid, but I can't get my head around imaginary money. Others take deposits via Amazon, accepting gift certificates in lieu of cash. The obvious catch is that you can only use the gift certificates on Amazon. No, thank you. I am not working in the sex industry to make Jeff Bezos more money. I don't want things I can get next day on Prime. I want money to pay off my mortgage. Believe it or not, I want to bank all of my money as it makes it easier to work out what I need to pay in tax. I actually want to pay tax unlike – in my opinion and according to the reams of serious investigative reporting on the subject – Amazon.

But you can see why some women in the industry don't do things above board; they're asking, with louder and louder voices, why should we pay tax when we have no workers' rights?

When you have no rights you're driven to aliases. To anonymity. To feel fear about sharing a name.

A couple of my names were chosen by me. Some of my names were chosen for me by pimps. Some men are daft enough to believe that the name a sex worker goes by indicates our class and by extension our character, and that that will dictate our behaviour. Grace? Hope? It's the exact opposite of how I might be feeling at the time. But do the clients know that? Of course not. Sex workers are very good at showing only what we want to show. We are very good at being the person the client needs us to be. And it all starts with a name.

For you, my name is Eve.

Brothels

When people think about the sex industry, they usually imagine women working on the street or working from dingy flats. While I haven't done the former, I have worked in many a flat. These brothels are everywhere. Sometimes they are obvious, with huge neon signs in the windows or positioned above doorways that tell you the venue is a sauna, but most of the time you won't know they are there. They're a flat swallowed by a huge apartment block with no nosy porters to wonder what's going on. They're a house on a short lease on a suburban street, because the madam knows there is only a limited amount of time before she has to move her girls out fast. They're luxurious basement flats with private entrances. And they're pungent, pokey flats with the neighbours' shoes piled up in the hallway.

You may have even been in a brothel and not realized. Perhaps when viewing a flat that was newly on the market you were surprised to find a long, floor-length curtain separating the kitchen from the living room. That's curious, you might have thought, before dismissing it. Then, further into the tour, you were delighted to find that each bedroom had a shower in the corner and noticed the many white towels neatly folded on a nearby shelf. You didn't give much thought to the cheap Argos bedside drawers that didn't quite fit with the sturdy, solid oak bed displayed proudly in the middle of the room. You don't know that an Ikea bed isn't up to the job of accommodating a banker, a trader and two sex workers all in one go. Believe me, I know.

But the biggest giveaway that a place is a brothel is the Johnson's Baby Oil. If you ever book a massage and find some Baby Oil on the shelf, you have probably booked a hooker by mistake.

Brothel Creepers

What kind of man goes to a brothel? It's a simple question to answer. Almost every type of man. There is only one type that doesn't and that is the type who says, 'I don't need to pay for it.' You know the type. They're the ones who buy you half a shandy on a date at the pub and expect to get into your knickers. The ones who buy you a nice meal and then feel as though they have earned the right to come on your face.

Give me the brothel creepers over that entitled lot any day of the week.

Of course, you get boundary pushers in all brothels. If your boss doesn't have your back, then in an ideal world you would just quit and move to another brothel where you feel safer, happier. Which is the same as in any job, right? If a manager, whether in a shop, a restaurant or a bar, refuses to deal with rude customers, preferring to take the money rather than look after their workers, you quit. You find another place to ply your trade. But the better places – where we have more agency to do what we want, to see who we want, and to charge more for the service we provide – are always being closed by police raids. More bad bosses leads to more punters who try it on in any way they can.

Back when I did brothel work, in the sitting area where men and women would relax and chat while waiting for a bedroom to become available, we would have lawyers in Savile Row suits sitting next to men who were celebrating coming out of prison. We would have a policeman twitching nervously next to a man who was on stage in a West End show. I became so friendly with a few that I saw them outside of work, just for fun.

Then there were my three favourites. The stockbroker and the banker, who have both become great friends over time and who have enriched my life. And the wonderful man I have settled down with and built a life with.

Let's call him Adam.

A Beautiful Love Story

Yes. I met my partner at work. I think it's a beautiful story. A story of overcoming the odds.

We met. He paid me. We fucked. And then slowly we grew into each other's lives in a way that I don't know where I end and he begins. If it sounds romantic it's because it is. I have never judged him for visiting sex workers, and he has never judged me for being one. The real *Pretty Woman* story, I like to call it.

People ask if there is a difference between the men who visit hookers and men who visit dominatrices and my answer, which will probably infuriate both types of client, is no. Some are more kinky, certainly. Some want pain to precede the pleasure. Or to be humiliated while they worship their 'goddess'. But the truth of the matter is they all want to get off. It's how they get there that informs whether they book a domme or a hooker.

What they probably don't expect is to find a wife.

Do the Hustle

The more interesting question is what type of woman goes into sex work? Women who need money, of course. It helps if you like men and like sex, but that isn't essential or necessary. Money drives us women, just as the cock drives a client.

The sex industry is somewhere that women can always find money, should they need it. And, with benefit cuts, the cost-of-living crisis, energy and food prices increases and wage stagnation, we need it. So, we sell sex. That sounds simple enough, but the reality isn't that easy. These days, sex workers often have to look at different ways to earn enough money because a normal brothel service (that is, condom for sex and condom for blowjob) is now charged at a lower rate than it was twenty years ago. It seems to be the only area of the economy where prices have gone down. And, as in every industry, whether profit is being made or not, there are always bosses waiting to pounce and who will push their workforce to perform for them just that little bit more. All those pressures mean that in some brothels the women now make their main money from extras such as kissing, oral without, CIM (come in mouth) and anal. Not brilliant for us and not brilliant for the wives at home.

We do our best with what we've got. I have worked with women who will charge extra for anal, blindfold the client or turn the lights down really low and then tighten up their pussy as much as possible, squealing when the client's penis goes in to convince the man that it's the other hole. You can take from that little story that many sex workers are good hustlers. I have watched with awe as those women have worked men over for every penny they can get, but I have never been very good at extracting extra funds from a man's wallet myself, even though at times I really needed to.

Market conditions dictate that brothel workers now have to give the whole performance, complete with fluttering eyelashes and parted lips. The girlfriend experience. The porn star experience. Giving of themselves more and more, and they might then make the same money as they would have done years ago, when a man was often happy with a simple handjob. Then, thanks to the risks they're forced to take, it's off to the sexual health clinic to check for chlamydia, syphilis and gonorrhoea. Very sexy.

Ladies, a word of advice. Always inspect a man's todger before giving him head. Even if he's your husband. Actually, especially if he's your husband.

Make no mistake. Women do not want to be doing extras.

But if it's what the male customer requires, and we don't offer it, he will find another brothel and a girl who does. That is not good business.

Other ways to hustle and make more money out of a client could include encouraging the man to buy drugs so he stays around longer. By becoming a party girl yourself, you can get and keep clients – it's a USP on your CV, as it were. Because, generally, if a client likes cocaine, he wants you to do it too.

Some women might be capable of robbing a client (or even their own colleagues). Or they might record the clients and use the footage to blackmail them. That's a hustle with a side of scumbag. Other women might offer discounts to stop men from choosing other girls. And while undercutting each other is certainly a way to get more clients in the short term, in the long term those women will have fucked themselves and every other girl in the place, because once you lower a price it is very hard to raise it again. Punters will start to haggle with you. And maybe you need the cash right now so you agree to the lower rate too but, the thing is, the girl in the next room won't be so hard up next month, and maybe you won't be either; from now on, though, you are both stuck at the lower price.

Then there are the women who will deliberately get pregnant by a wealthy client. Some sex workers will deny that that happens. But it does. One hooker I used to know was shagging both a lawyer and a banker bareback, 'Because I trust you!' she would say to them. They both bought it because, in my experience, when the cock is hard and the booze is flowing, men are not capable of thinking with their big brain. In this case, neither man knew about the other and the banker was horrified when he discovered 'his' girl was shagging the lawyer bareback too. Some clients can develop a misplaced sense of ownership, which is a no-no for me.

But all's well that ends well. The last time I saw this particular woman she was on the Tube with her baby and was in a relationship with the lawyer.

They tell people they met at church.

Keeping Hold of Yourself

Most of my female friends' partners were also punters once upon a time and there shouldn't be any surprise about this. Admittedly, it's not your average nine to five, but lots of couples meet through their work, so why should we be any different? Perhaps the problem is that it's harder to hold on to a relationship when you're a sex worker, because working in this industry can change you into someone you don't recognize, or even like. Not because of the soul seepage which comes from being prodded by a little old man penis, which is what the radical feminists or deeply religious – who pity and loathe us in equal measure – would have you believe. But because of all the shit you have to put up with from everyone else.

From the police who rob and arrest you on a regular basis and the MPs who solicit your services while voting to pass laws that make your life harder, to the doctors who will look at you like you're shit on their shoe during the routine screenings that are in place to keep you well, and the lawyers who clearly despise you, even as they bill you by the hour. Then there are the landlords who will try to get a discounted shag but keep your deposit when you move out. And finally, there is the general public, who all have an opinion on sex work. And this can sometimes be good but is often bad and ugly, because they've never done it so they really don't know what they're talking about.

The moralist view, which is still incredibly common, is that we are all drug-addicted to cope with being raped and unloved as children. Another popular view is that we are filthy rich because people actually believe what they see posted on social media: pictures of immaculate women in their stylish penthouse apartments surrounded by ostentatious wads of cash or an artful screenshot of a £20,000 bank transfer. All of that is a load of bollocks. The vast majority of us are grinding to buy food, to pay rent, to support our kids. Because we can't rely on men. And we certainly can't rely on the government.

All of these things are far more wearing than shagging ten men in a day. These are the things that chip away at your self-esteem and your mental health and which harden you. These are the things that could turn you into someone it may be difficult to love. I'm so grateful to be loved by my partner, because I catch myself sometimes saying and thinking mean-spirited, ugly things I wouldn't have years ago. I'm still soft as shit when it comes to children and animals, but these days if I see a pretty woman asking for change on the street I can't help but think, *Go suck a cock.* And I'm not entirely sure that's nice.

I didn't think that way before I became a hooker.

Deep down I'm soft enough to want to be able to pick all the homeless up off the streets. But I'd want to deposit them in the homes of the people who I see giving them change and advising them 'Don't buy drugs with this money', as the homeless person nods subserviently and eagerly grabs the fifty-pence piece the prosperous, patronizing prick is handing over.

I'm an angrier person these days, but my wrath is almost solely aimed at the privileged. Not only the rich men firmly and comfortably rooted in the establishment but the advantaged women too. The ones who proclaim themselves feminists are arguably the very worst. A few years ago, Amnesty International stated that they were for decriminalization of sex work. 'Decrim' is the legal model that sex workers want. It would allow us to work together in safety and without the fear that we will end up either in prison or dead – which is currently the choice in England. But the actresses didn't agree. Meryl Streep, Ann Hathaway, Emma Thompson, Lena Dunham and many others signed a letter telling Amnesty to rethink their stance. The sex workers, in no uncertain terms, told the actresses to fuck off. Then in New York another group of actresses tried to interfere with waitresses' earnings by campaigning to end tipping and to replace that system with higher wages. The waitresses also told them to fuck off. There is nothing more dangerous than a liberal, middle-class white woman with a moralistic agenda. If you don't live our lives, don't tell us that you know better than we do. And while you might have played a fucking hooker in a film it doesn't mean you know what it is like to actually be a hooker.

I know what it's like.

And I think my partner has a bit of an idea, too.

Hell, he has had to put up with ten years of me talking about it. And, unlike most people with a view on it, he listens. He really listens. The problem for us is everyone else thinking they know best. That's the kind of shit that will either pull you apart as a couple, or push you closer together. It makes me glad every day that we are tight. We are good.

I was told once by another hooker that I wouldn't stay nice if I stayed in the industry. But I have. Or at least I hope I have. Fuck the people who think we're unlovable.

Shame on You

If we're thinking about the people who make life harder, then there are also those who expect me to feel shame about what I do for a living. I feel no shame. I have a few small regrets about how I treated some people when I was younger, for which I have a sense of shame. Those people may have forgotten how I behaved, but I haven't. I'm thinking about when I worked in a factory with a drug user who was a good mate, but I was embarrassed to know him when he showed up at my house because my friends were there. Back then I really thought I was better than him. That makes me feel disgusted with myself, but being a sex worker doesn't. When it comes to my jobs and life choices, I feel no shame. None. You will never find me apologizing for selling sex. Fuck the people who apologize.

'Well, you might be happy ... but would you want *your* daughter doing it?' is a question always asked by people who want to erode the rights of sex workers even further. And they ask the question with a sneer, as if they're so dreadfully clever to make this point, and the first person ever to make it. We see straight through them. They don't give a monkey's about us or our daughters. If they did, they would be on our side, supporting us in our fight to work as safely as possible, which means one thing: decriminalization.

Charm Not Included

I have worked as a hooker in a brothel. I have worked as an independent escort. I have worked as a hostess in a strip club, as a dominatrix and on the sex chatlines. I have only earned real money as a hooker and as a dominatrix; I earned fuck all in the other jobs. But, I have to admit, the poor pay could have been more about me being a bit shit at those jobs rather than them not paying well if you're good at them.

Escorts, hostesses and chatline operators have to ooze charm at all times and I just don't have that in me. Clients want more and more for less and less. Some chatlines charge as little as thirty pence a minute now and men still object to the price. I once told a guy who spent his time and money complaining to me that he should 'fuck off and call the Samaritans instead', and I got fired. No surprises there, perhaps. I can turn the charm on when I need to, and when I want to. No problem at all. The problem is that I have no patience for dickheads, you see. And the world of sex work is full of dickheads.

When I was a hooker the men were 'punters' or 'johns'. Why johns? Well, I don't know for sure, but I assume it's something to do with how many clients tell us their name is John. As a dominatrix they are known as 'subs' – short for submissives – 'clients' or 'slaves'. But all these different words to describe our paying clients amount to the same thing: a man with the permanent horn is an easy man. There is a reason why the sex industry is the oldest profession; men want to get off. Always have, always will. Whether that is sex and a cuddle or a fist in the arse while they're dressed as a fairy, it amounts to the same thing.

Of course, there will be differences among them; the worst of them might be clingy, needy, demanding or boundary pushing. But if you have been in this game long enough you know how to control them . . . unless, of course, you have the misfortune to meet one who can't be controlled. Any wannabe young hooker who thinks that it's a cool job with no dangers is kidding herself. Sex workers get killed every year by clients. You might think that street sex workers get killed more than indoor workers, and that was certainly the case before 2010 in the UK. But now indoor workers get killed more, probably due to us working alone because of an increase in police raids.

In the UK we are more likely to be killed than women in any other industry by men who are angry because they can't get it up. Or because they hate women. Or because we are easy targets as the police don't give a fuck.

All that said, generally, if certain men are too much of a handful it is easy enough to discard them, as long as you haven't let them into your life. And, of course, that starts with not giving them your real name. If they do know a lot about you, there are other ways to put them off. Burping, farting, scratching your arse and talking about raising your rates will soon make them lose interest.

If you work in the sex industry for long enough, you will deal with every type of man. The good, the bad, the ugly. The dangerous. Clients are replaceable. Get rid of the bad ones as quickly as you can. The trick is to hold on to the good ones and keep them coming back for more.

Easy Peasy

I used to find the typical full-service sex-work session as easy as riding a bike. I'll show you.

The client enters the room. You greet him with a huge smile and say, 'How are you? It has been ages!' Two cups of tea and a brief chat later you remove your dressing gown, which will be silk or satin, not a huge fleece number, to reveal something flimsy underneath.

'Fancy warming me up?' you ask, and away you go.

Little back rub for him followed by kisses on his back to show that you're ready. He rolls over, oral for him, oral for you, and a breathy exclamation of: 'Oh my God, you're gonna make me come!'

This is followed swiftly by a shag that lasts about five minutes and finishes with the client coming. As they left I used to say something like, 'Oh I needed that. Thank you for coming.' A little laugh. 'Pun intended! See you next time!'

The trick is to split up the hour with different focuses and, because everything is separated – a little bit of this, a little bit of that – he feels as though he has been in your company for longer. He feels as though it was fun for you and well worth his money. He leaves feeling great and already looking forward to his next visit.

Like I said, easy peasy.

Of course, it takes a little while for it to feel so easy as there is no guidebook for a woman stepping into sex work for the first time. She may be lucky enough to find a mentor, as I did, but that is rare. Generally, it's expected that she will know how to have sex, as not many virgins seek out a career in prostitution, so she will just be left to learn on the job.

Newbie hookers, if you don't want future boyfriends to know about your work, you need to muddy up your blowjob skills. We are fucking amazing at giving head. Deep throat with no gagging, no teeth, better suction than a Dyson, with opposite hand twisting that makes a man's eyes roll back and his mouth speak in tongues. Lastly, don't get drunk and slip the condom onto your boyfriend's cock with just your mouth. Most women can't do that.

But here's the thing that people can find surprising. When I was a hooker I generally enjoyed the session, unless the guy was a prick. I like earning money and I like sex. I have never faked an orgasm; I don't see the point. One man once rubbed my belly in circles and, when I looked confused, he said he had made a woman come like that before. Poor sod. So naive. He'd obviously had a rather sheltered time of it up until he met me. So, I gave him a lesson on the clit and after that he became a regular client.

It's worth making the point that he was a Muslim who

exclusively wore traditional Islamic clothing. Never make the mistake of thinking it is only the 'toxic' masculine white male that visits a sex worker. Religious beliefs are no barrier to the need to do something with a hard cock.

Borrowed Time

Clients have come in all shapes and sizes. Which leads me to a memory of Douglas and the sun gently warming my skin as I looked out onto paradise. To my left, a luxurious outdoor sauna. And, just past that, a rippling turquoise lake. A croquet lawn was laid out on the other side of the house, an immaculate square of green situated by a small waterfall.

My sub shuffled out of the house with a bottle of good champagne and two crystal flutes. The word 'submissive' creates an illusion. The sub is very often a man born into vast wealth and, in this particular story, was the owner of the gorgeous house. I was – I am – the submissive one. The servant. The one who is paid to indulge Douglas's fantasies, and the fantasies of men like him. I am the one who leaves the big house with the pool and the private tennis courts at the end of the session and goes home to something rather different.

If this makes me sound a little bitter, as though I am coveting what Douglas has . . . well, I am. I can push it to one side while we spend time together, but I know that, however hard I work, and whatever I do, I will never have any of this. I can only borrow it for a while. And then I have to hand it back.

In the early days of domination when I first gained access to the lives of rich men, I would fool myself that I would one day achieve that kind of wealth, that kind of luxury, too. Then a year passed, and I was no further forward. Then another year and another, until I finally realized with staggering clarity that, if I worked hard, if I got paid well for these jobs, I might put together a bit of money that gave me access to certain nice things in life, but I would never have wealth.

In a moment of flaring anger, I once said to Douglas that, no matter what I did, I would never end up with money. He'd laughed and told me I was talking nonsense.

'Look at where you are!' he'd exclaimed, his arms spread wide, gesturing to the beauty that surrounded me. 'This is paradise!'

But it wasn't mine and it never would be.

I could, perhaps, have married into it. That's a thought that comes back time and again. Though it was my looks that first got me business, it has been my personality that has given me my regulars. Personality, I've learned, keeps a man hooked even when the lines start to show and tits start to sag. Indeed, this particular wealthy man tried to woo me into being his lifelong companion. But, fiercely independent and much younger at the time, I didn't even consider it.

To be so close to wealth, to see it, taste it, but not own it, nor to have any hope of ever owning it can make you resentful. I do try not to be bitter but I let my mask slip all the time now that I'm older. When a rich man tells me he has worked hard all his life to have what he has, I tell him how I used to clean toilets or work on factory lines for eighteen hours at a stretch, the most menial of jobs. He will invariably look at me with pity and tell me that he is impressed with how far I have come. But the point these men are missing when they talk about my supposed ascension to the upper class, complete with all the trimmings, is that it's not my life I'm experiencing. It's theirs.

So I would quaff champagne with a smile on my face, and get ready to pee into Douglas's mouth, while my soul was fucking seething.

As you get older and your patience wanes at the same pace as your body, the opportunities to make money become fewer and further between. That's a fact of life for most women, not just sex workers, and it's not without some truth for men too. So, I have to admire a woman who marries a rich man in the hope he dies first and leaves her something worth having as a thank you for all her hard labour. Because the job she's doing as his wife is exactly that: hard work. Difficult, stressful and often unrewarding slog. Spending just a weekend with a demanding, controlling man is challenging. I've done that often enough and have come away exhausted. Whether you're an escort, a dominatrix or a trophy wife, you are there because you are being paid for your sexiness, for your company, for your feminine compliance.

My thinking is that any woman who marries solely for status is also a full-time sex worker. So, a woman who marries an aristocrat in order to become a member of the aristocracy is, in my mind, a sex worker. Look at how 'The Prince William Effect' caused St Andrews to become the most popular university for degree applications while he was in attendance. I doubt the ladies were solely after him for his looks.

Love may develop over time but, the way I see it, it may at least initially be an exchange of companionship and sex for the assurance of a comfortable or even lavish lifestyle. Life can be hard for women. You do what you have to do. But a ring on the finger and a title to go along with it command the sort of respect that a hooker can't begin to imagine.

But at least I can walk away at the end of the day.

The 100-Million-Pound Tosser

When I left hooking behind and became a dominatrix, the class of client who wanted my services completely changed. For the first time, I regularly met very wealthy men like Douglas. I got taken on trips to Monaco, Saint Lucia, Milan, Barbados, Gibraltar and Bermuda, which opened up to me a world of money, luxury, agency and a totally different outlook on life. One of entitlement and privilege. From that point on, it was very rare that I met a working-class man, even though my rates were exactly the same as in my last few years as a hooker. These wealthy men were more likely to want to take me for dinner, to spend a weekend with me, to talk with me and enjoy my company, as well as enjoy a little sexual titillation. They bought me designer shoes and dresses. Oh, and they were also some of the most demanding, controlling and difficult men I have ever met.

There was, for example, the owner of a large restaurant chain who emailed me from his work address. 'Send me photos,' he wrote.

I sent him a photo that was readily available on my website

– I don't do bespoke unless clients cough up some cash. If he was expecting any special favours just because of who he was he had chosen the wrong domme. He emailed me back immediately, a furious, panicked shout in angry capital letters. 'DON'T SEND IT TO MY WORK EMAIL!'

He wanted to arrange a meeting but didn't understand that I couldn't see him on a particular day. 'What do you mean, you have another client? I will make it worth your while,' he messaged.

If he hadn't been worth £100 million, I would have told him to fuck off then and there. Instead, I managed to charm him into considering another day.

'OK, Wednesday could work,' he conceded. Then, 'I know you don't offer it, but eight grand for a blowjob?'

It was at that point that I told him to sod off.

It's a funny thing. If he had known me as Charlotte four years earlier he could have had a blowjob for forty pounds. But he wouldn't have been interested in Charlotte. This man wanted something, and someone, that wasn't available. He thought, mistakenly, that his money could buy anything. That he could buy me. What he failed to understand was that the decision was mine. And I decided that he could stick his money up his arse.

The Root of All Evil

Although you can't buy everything, if you find yourself in court, have a health condition, want to educate your child, or simply take a break, we all know that money makes those things easier. My subs who are in their seventies and eighties are all in better health than my dad in his sixties because they've always had the money to make sure they are looked after. The tragedy is that so many working-class people don't realize how badly they've been had because they don't get the same glimpse of other people's lovely lives that I do. I've heard them compliment the Queen for being in good health and working until her dying day, without seeing the sheer irony of that statement. Work? People like that don't know what work is. Being ferried in a car from fete to factory and cutting ribbons does not compare to collecting varicose veins on a factory line.

A lot of working-class people will never see the scale of the injustice that is still happening in our society, and they don't appreciate that it will continue to be this way until we come up with a fairer system, a safety net which actually supports people. I've seen systemic failures at first hand. When my dad, a stonemason, had a stroke in his early sixties, he was left unable to do calculations, and his mobility and balance were off. Stonemasons need to work on their feet and to work out figures, so what followed as he tried to continue managing his business despite his new disabilities was a log jam of dissatisfied customers. Things were not going well.

He tried to claim disability benefits. After all, he had worked since he was fourteen and had never stopped slogging away. I was sure he could get some help now he was in need. But no. Apparently, according to the government, my dad was still fit to work. It was a tragedy to watch this once strong man bested by a system that had just been waiting to fuck him. We fought back – I'm a fighter and was firmly in his corner – but it took three years for a court to decide what we already knew. That he was not fit to work.

We are often so busy squabbling across political divides that we fail to see what is staring us in the face. Money causes inequality. And those who have it will do all they can to hold on to it, and those who don't have it will use any tools at their disposal to get it. We all need money to live. Society says it's OK to use your mind to make money, and that it's OK to use your body in certain ways. It has rather different views on using your body to make money if it involves sex work. But I use both my mind and my body in the work I do. It's what I have done for a long time now. It's what I still do on a regular basis to make money. And it's not me who's evil.

Childhood Innocence

As a kid you don't know about money until you are made aware of it – you have what you have, and, unless you're struggling with truly desperate poverty, you don't miss what you don't have. But I do think you are always aware of the presence or indeed the absence of love. There was a constant stream of love in our house during my early childhood. My parents adored each other, and they adored me and my sister too. Mum made our clothes, often creating matching outfits from whatever material she had around at the time. While she didn't have the money to buy herself nice clothes, she always made sure that my sister and I looked lovely. It was the same with food. We never went to bed hungry and never once suspected that Mum would sometimes go without because there wasn't always enough to go around. If we noticed her empty plate at dinnertime, she would say she wasn't hungry and we'd believe her. It was something I didn't think anything of at the time but I know now it was a lie.

My childhood was almost perfect, then. And I don't use that word lightly. It was pretty much the dream that I wish every child could live. Every day an adventure – meeting up with the kids from the village after school and getting hopelessly lost in the countryside, jumping in brooks, balancing on fallen trees over small ravines, bike rides and exploring woods that farmers were desperately trying to keep us out of. And things were just as fun at home. Each day full of laughter and happiness. Perhaps some Christmases were sparse, though my sister and I would hardly notice, and at others we had so many presents that it made my head spin when I rushed downstairs on Christmas morning to see what was under the tree. We weren't skint but the truth is that Dad never managed his business very well and we lived with a constant boom, of sorts, and quite a lot of bust. We didn't care. Days were filled with reading, playing in our tiny garden, day trips out to farms, walks, zoos, country houses, caravan holidays in Wales, flying kites in the park, my dad teaching me how to ride the bike that I was so proud of and, as I got a little older, pitching our wits against each other in endless games of chess. It sounds too good to be true but I've got the photographs to prove it.

Our annual day trip to Morecambe for some seaside fun would begin when the coach finally came to a stop in the terminal around midday. All the other families would jump off and head to the pier; we'd stay on to eat our tinfoil-wrapped salmon and vinegar sandwiches. It was a way to save money. Not only did Mum and Dad not have the means for us to eat out, but we couldn't afford to go on all the pier rides either, so delaying us on the coach meant we wouldn't have as much time and spending opportunities would be limited. We visited country houses just to see the gardens, as they offered free entrance. We never took the costly house tour but would look and marvel from the outside – a sort of metaphor for the rest of my life, in many ways.

Although Mum and Dad were always working out ways to cut corners and make ends meet, they also made sure that as little people we were nourished in every way. They had made the move to the countryside when I was three, to ensure we had healthy air and were near nature. They both smoked like chimneys, of course, but it was the eighties. If in doubt, they'd crack a window. But I was fine. I soaked it all up. I learned to love the soft feeling of grass under my feet, the sound of the wind whistling through the branches of the trees, and to savour being able to look around and not see a single house or another person. I loved my parents so much and I loved the life they gave me and my sister. They made me feel as though anything was possible and at Sunday School I would wonder what the point of Heaven was when nothing could be better than the life I had on earth.

All of which completely shatters the broken-home-to-prostitute pipeline that is persistently portrayed in the movies and spewed out in the media, doesn't it?

The Word 'Prostitute'

I can only assume that media writers, producers and presenters want as many as possible of us sex workers killed. Characters on TV are often brilliantly written. They're nuanced, layered and complicated – it's why they linger in our minds and become real to us. But give a writer or director a sex worker to bring to life and immediately the reductive narrative is 'sold herself to pay her rent' or the classic 'nobody loves her, so she seeks it from men on the street, but they just use her'. Prostitutes are often portrayed as disposable; they simply don't matter. That's the message you receive. If you have the hero or heroine of a much-watched, much-loved drama describing us in that way to the viewing public – who, let's face it, often have a hard job identifying the difference between characters on TV and real people – then many people will fall in line with that way of thinking. It means that when a sex worker gets killed on screen people both are titillated and feel something, but at the same time do not give a single fuck when one of us is killed in real life. Let's remember that there are still walking tours for ghouls to see where Jack the Ripper cut and killed those women. It took *The Five*, a book published in 2019, to make me – a sex worker – aware that not all of the Ripper's victims were sex workers. Would there be walking tours and restaurants if the women who were killed were widely known to be impoverished mothers with addiction issues? I doubt it. That story doesn't sell as well as the 'prostitute' victim, where the reductive narrative is that she had it coming.

The *Oxford English Dictionary* specifies that the term 'prostitute' is most usually employed with reference to women. We all work to pay for the things we need to survive; we all exchange our skills and labour for money in some form. 'Prostitute' could have been a neutral term to describe the act of selling sex – just as the term 'greengrocer' describes someone who sells vegetables. But 'prostitute' is instead a word designed to subjugate women who sell sex. There's an ugliness around it and people who use the word, who are not working in our industry, wield it like a weapon.

Yet when I was a hooker, almost all of my feelings at work were the same emotions I'd have in any of my minimum-wage jobs. I was bored at times, degraded or humiliated at others. Occasionally, I was amused and content and pleased with the way things were going. And sometimes I was downright angry. Depending on the day. Depending on my interactions. Hooking is just a job, like most jobs. The common consensus, however, is that sex work is dirty and the worst job of all, the lowest of the low. In fact, so poorly regarded is it that many people refuse to call it a job. Sex workers are accused of being abusers or victims, of being ruined and damaged people, products of child abuse with mental health and addiction issues. It's an absurdly one-dimensional perspective, just like those badly drawn TV characters.

You know what would make me want to take smack and to lean into the role of victim? Cleaning toilets in a club for the rest of my life, as one clubgoer asks me why I didn't bother to get an education while another pukes on my shoes.

You can stick that job right up your chuff.

For me, working for peanuts for bosses who don't care has

always been the worst job of all. The lowest of the low. I would rather work for real money for bosses who don't care because at least the money affords me the luxury to be able to leave. If things aren't what I want them to be, I can say, 'Goodbye, and fuck off.' Sex work gives me options.

Only once have I felt truly powerless as a hooker, and that was when the police barged into my working life – overjoyed to have found another brothel to pull apart because, of course, there aren't far worse things going on in the world every day, everywhere – and shat all over me. But I felt powerless every single day that I worked in retail and in other minimum-wage jobs because I knew that I was on a treadmill going absolutely nowhere.

When I was hooking, I was actively paying off debt and saving to buy property. I was able to pursue an acting career, which is almost impossible to do with no money behind you. As a glass collector in a club, a sales assistant, a waitress, a cleaner – the feeling of powerlessness never went away. It was with me every day. There might have been a token promotion that gave me another twenty pence an hour but, in terms of career prospects, that really was as good as it got. It's when you're in a minimum-wage job with no education behind you that you are well and truly fucked. Not when you're a prostitute. It's in those jobs that you are undervalued and viewed by people around you as inferior, lazy, as someone who has failed at life. That's the message delivered loud and clear from the father who informed his daughter as I cleaned their table, 'This is why you have to work hard at school. So you don't have to do jobs like this.' And if you don't manage to get out, you breathe in that toxic air every day until you finally retire, your mind and body exhausted, your self-esteem shattered.

Next time you hear the word 'prostitute', think about all the things you have done to make money and what you will be doing every day to make a few pounds until ill health takes you away in a wooden box. And next time you're watching TV and you see a one-dimensional, judgemental portrayal of someone who sells sex for a living, think about the many times you have had to drop your morals or kiss goodbye to your dignity for money – the only difference being that you had your clothes on at the time.

Think about all that and change the channel.

Freak

By the time I was twelve things were changing at home and had definitely changed at school. Not for the better. My glasses resembled the bottom of a jam jar and, along with heavy braces on my teeth, they meant I was called all the usual unimaginative names that kids reach for. 'Freak' was the most common. I wonder now if some people make it their mission in life to snuff out other people's light, to stamp and stamp until all hope is gone. For me, the bullying at secondary school was immediate and relentless. Every single day. The happy, hopeful eleven-year-old who had radiated such positive vibes disappeared almost overnight.

The teachers witnessed everything but did nothing. Even when I was punched on the nose by one of the boys. Even when I had chewing gum rubbed into my hair. Even when they kicked, kicked, kicked the back of my chair until it broke with me still sitting on it, spilling me onto the floor to everyone's amusement. Those careless teachers ruined lives one school day at a time.

Back at home Mum and Dad would often be working until six, so the first time we all saw each other was when we sat down for tea together around our table. I always answered the questions about school with brief, non-committal answers. I was embarrassed, ashamed, and I didn't want my problem to become theirs.

After a year of hell our class was introduced to a new pupil. A boy of colour. The only person of colour in our school year. There was part of me that thought, *Finally, here's someone else who will get picked on for being different.* He could share my burden, I thought, and maybe even become a friend in such a lonely place. But I was very wrong about that. He looked at me, at how the others singled me out and saw an in, a way to take the heat off himself. And so he viciously joined in and became one of the worst abusers, screaming 'Freak' into my face, pushing me, hitting me, or pulling at my tie until I choked. But given the choice of conforming with the vicious pricks or being a freak, I will always choose to be a 'freak'.

Orcs and Elves

I've had a lot of things shouted at me.

'No dignity!'

'No morality!'

'No sense of family values!'

People often say these things about sex workers, spitting them at us with venom through the fire-stoking media or, given half a chance, face to face. It hardly touches the sides now. I find it tedious, if I'm honest. I've heard it too often. Behind the words is the idea that to be touched by a man makes you less human – less worthy, less deserving of respect – and that's ridiculous. That servicing someone's sexual needs for money means you lack a moral compass doesn't stand up to logic. I've cleaned old cocks in care homes and I have wanked old cocks in brothels. Neither was a big deal.

When the public think of sex work, they often cite the degradation of beautiful young women and how sad it is that they are being prodded and poked by fat and ugly old men. What they're saying is that prostitution is disgusting because it often features physically unappealing clients. This idea that appearance denotes your character should have died out with Tolkien. Shouldn't we, by now, have got past judging people by how they look? Meanwhile, in perhaps more salubrious surroundings, the handsome young son of a Russian oligarch gets a free pass despite getting his kicks from beating escorts half to death, because he can pay for their silence. It's the kind of thing that, protected by a sheen of glamour and complete respectability, has happened under everyone's nose in a fabulous penthouse in London.

Don't make the mistake of thinking that the men who look like ogres behave like ogres. I am much more likely to be wary of the flashy handsome banker who tells me he's got a big knob and unlimited cash than old sweaty Albert in his grubby raincoat. It's the men who have got away with shitty behaviour all their entitled lives that give sex workers trouble. Gorgeous young women fucking old men isn't the problem.

Teenage Dirtbags

My mum and dad were completely oblivious to what was happening to me, but it was not their fault. I was an expert at pretending I was OK. Pretending I was strong. Besides, Mum had unknowingly given me the tools to cope with the mess I had found myself in. She has always loved reading and she shared that love with me. So, as a bullied child, I retreated into a world of books and imagined that I was anywhere but school. I was on a farm. I was on a pirate ship. I was in a forest. Sometimes, in my school exercise books, I would write adventure stories that never had an ending. And that strategy worked, up to a point.

As the bullying got worse, I started to imagine not running away from the pain, but towards it. I began to think I could fight back. I would daydream for hours that one day, having been pushed too far, I would pull out my devastating karate moves – moves I simply didn't possess – and in a blur of nimble limbs hustle all the boys into a weeping pile on the floor. They would beg for forgiveness. The teachers would pay, too, in fantasies that became more and more violent. In dreams I could punch, punch and punch harder still, and I would wake up feeling at peace, until I realized that it was just a dream and that I still had to go to school. But the memory of the fantasy would give me an occasional moment's respite, and I would smile a little, just for a second, as the name-calling battered me once again. Now, I can see that schools have got to do better, because children fantasizing about how they're going to fix the problem often leads to two things. Self-harm or harming others. And neither is acceptable.

Sometimes the memories of school appear from nowhere and hit me – even now. I'll blink and, suddenly, I'm twelve or thirteen and on my way back from a school trip. My triple-glazed glasses are somewhere at the back of the bus, in someone else's hands, but I'm in the middle, and I can't see. I need to get them back. The boy who started this cruel game of 'Where are my glasses?' thought it would amuse every other kid on the bus. He was right about that. My classmates whoop as they pass the specs around, row by row, and I desperately chase after them, trying to get them back. I reach out for them, my face stricken, before giving up and stumbling back to my seat, my damp face turned blindly to the window.

The Grafter

I got some of my power back by working and making money. I landed a paper round as soon as I was legally able to, aged thirteen. On the first Saturday morning the bag was so heavy that the paper shop owner said I'd probably be needing a trolley.

'The last girl did,' he told me. 'It's why I usually go for the boys.'

No freakin' way, I thought, as I huffed the sack over my shoulder.

I was proud of my fluorescent orange bag, and I smiled at neighbours as I posted their newspapers through letterboxes. I worked the papers six mornings a week throughout the rest of my school years, without a trolley. By the time I was fifteen I was also working after school in a greasy spoon on a Friday and, from sixteen, I added a pot washing job on a Saturday and another job as a cleaner in a care home on a Sunday. I loved having money in my pocket. I loved the feeling it gave me.

I soon learned, however, even as a money-making teenager, that I would never be 'up' financially. Mum would borrow a bit of money from me now and then when I got paid. When I pointed out to her that she never paid me back she started a little book so that all the borrowed money could be noted down and kept track of. Of course, despite the diligent book-keeping, the money was never repaid and the notebook was forgotten. By her. Never by me.

I was busy. But it didn't affect my schoolwork as our teachers had already given up on us. We weren't expected to succeed at my school, and we didn't let the teachers down by doing so. My education, which amounted in the end to just a few GCSEs, didn't matter to me all that much because I was a worker. I was going to work my way up, right to the top, with nothing but hard graft. One day, I'd daydream, I would buy my parents a house, which I hoped would allow them to stop working, and perhaps even stop them from borrowing my paper-round money. I would have glorious holidays in exotic places and return to my own house, which would be huge, with a pool and tennis court. I'd sit by the pool sipping champagne from crystal flutes in the sunshine . . . Most of all, I would move away from the area and never again see this bunch of losers I'd been thrown together with at school.

Eventually, as life chips away at you over the years, you learn that without an education it's difficult to claw yourself out of minimum-wage penury. Jobs in retail. Jobs in care homes. In bars. But I wasn't bright enough or wise enough to know that then, as an ambitious teen. I thought success was all about hard work, and perhaps that is the way it works for a few exceptions – but I've found it's not the rule for most people. Back then, though, as the coins jangled in my pocket I felt rich and hopeful. And, sometimes, even just a little bit of hope can keep you going for a long time.

Pregnant

I am pregnant. I haven't felt any movement yet, it's too early, but I know that they – whoever they are – are in there, slowly growing and being nurtured by my body. My bloody brilliant body.

There are many thoughts and feelings that go along with this new state. But for the first time in my life what I'm feeling is real fear. I am utterly terrified for my physical safety, which is so very important now because my safety is the baby's safety too. As a dominatrix I have multiple weapons hidden around my dungeon: screwdrivers, scissors, hammers, all tucked away but easy for me to access quickly should I need to. I would never call the police to help me, so I have to be ready to defend myself as much as I possibly can.

Adam also worries. He thinks I should stop sex work. And not just while I am carrying the baby, but for ever. He worries for the right reasons. He worries because I have filled his mind with stories of sex workers who have been criminalized and brutalized, and with stories of children who have been ripped by the state from their sex worker mothers. That's all horribly relevant to us now. The system – our entire society – relies on people who have the power to be able to punish those who don't have power. The idea that we are completely vulnerable should those people in social services get involved in our lives scares us both. Middle-class doctors who neglect their children keep custody, even if their negligence leads to one of their children dying. A working-class sex worker wouldn't be treated so kindly.

There is fear, but there is also joy. Importantly, my mum and dad are happy too. When I give them a photo of the first scan, they peer at the murky grey shapes with disbelief. My dad blinks and blinks and blinks. It's a wonderful moment. And this is what I'm thinking: I might finally get the photo of me that's barely visible at the back of the piano upgraded to join the numerous photographs of my sister and her children, all proudly perched at the front.

Everybody is so pleased for me, my mum says. That's lovely, I know. But at the same time it irritates me that carrying a baby has, in their eyes, finally given my life purpose. Mum has never had great ambition for me. She just wanted me to settle down with a family and be happy, while I wanted to get as far away as possible – to be a strong, independent woman.

I think, what about the achievement of being the first in my family to get accepted, eventually, into university? What about going to drama school and often financially supporting them, when times were hard? For a long time, they didn't know that I was a sex worker … but how did they think I was making enough money to bail them out? Over the years, my work has enabled them to keep their house and to pay off the workers Dad couldn't afford to pay when his business failed. My work has kept the bailiffs at bay. Sometimes, my work has kept food on the table. But now that I'm having a baby it's as if this act of reproduction is the only work a woman's body can do that's worthy of their approval.

I bite my tongue, smile and prop the scan up right at the front of the wholesome display.

My Mum

As a teen I came to realize that there was something wrong with my mum, but at the time I didn't quite know what it was. I couldn't put a name to it. I couldn't work out what had happened to her, why she had changed and become someone I couldn't talk to any more, someone I could hardly be in the same room with any longer.

When I was really young, Mum didn't drink, but she was always either up or down. She operated at the extremes of the emotional scale. That was fun as a small kid. Her total commitment to us having a great family day began with her throwing back our duvets with a shout of 'Good morning, sunshines!' She would beam at us, her face lit up, and we would jump out of bed laughing. Her gleaming happiness was infectious. We couldn't wait for the adventure we were about to embark on. But as I edged into my teens I began to notice the cracks. She demanded absolute obedience from us all – even Dad. When I didn't obey her there were a few coping mechanisms she'd turn to. She would either ignore me for days, or scream at me about having 'respect for your mother', while telling Dad to 'sort out your daughter'. Of course, screaming back didn't help, but I did it anyway. I couldn't help myself. She couldn't take any criticism of her behaviour, but neither could she hit me – for my disobedience or my vicious words – because I was too big, too strong. I would laugh at her sometimes, which made her incandescent with rage. When I realized that mocking her really got to her, I laughed even harder. But, perversely, it was when she was happy that she really pissed me off. Because we were all supposed to be up there with her, floating along somewhere on Cloud Nine. I just couldn't keep up. She was so unpredictable. I couldn't understand the violent swings from joy to rage, from feeling carefree to feeling utterly despondent. Then she would take to her bed. There were bouts of medication and counselling, searching for a cure for her moods. Then when that didn't get anywhere, she self-medicated with alcohol instead.

By the time I was a fully fledged teenager and quite moody myself, her manic highs grated and I grew to prefer the lows, which took her deep into herself and out of my face. The chance I had had to tell her about the bullying was gone. She'd have taken it as a personal attack if I'd told her how I felt about my life. Anyway, she didn't seem even to notice my pain, she was so wrapped up in her own issues. I think now that depressed people often wear a cloak of narcissism. They have to, to enable themselves to get through to the next day. But when I was young all I knew was that she really, really got on my tits. When I was fourteen my dad lost his business, and not for the last time. He was a talented tradesman who trusted the wrong people. With no money and lots of debt, my mum took a job in a factory. She worked a lot and, as there was always overtime to be had, she took all of it. She had to. She worked and she worked – until she had a nervous breakdown.

She blamed me for that. God knows how a teenager is responsible for their mother's breakdown. It made me hate her.

I am stubborn. I speak my mind. And I can't stand bullshit. I looked at her when she was having a mad moment and I couldn't help but reveal what I thought of her. If it wasn't on my lips, it was in my eyes. And it was in hers, too. I could see that my mum just didn't like me any more. She was always more comfortable with my sister, who was tactful and soothing, rather than confrontational and provocative. Their relationship worked.

Questions

After the initial shock had worn off, I called my GP.

'Congratulations,' said the unenthused receptionist, who told me that a midwife would call 'in due course'.

Three weeks later, a woman phoned and introduced herself

as my midwife. She said she had a few questions to ask that would take around forty minutes to answer. I gestured to Adam and we sat on the bed together. I put her on speaker phone.

The questions were as I expected. Health concerns, how I was in myself, how far along I thought I was. The family history took a while. Mental illness, stomach cancer, stroke, heart disease, prostate cancer, Crohn's disease, pneumonia, gangrene, asthma. Then it was Adam's turn to talk about his family.

Next came questions about lifestyle. Alcohol consumption, caffeine consumption, smoking, and if I had ever used any illegal drugs. Adam shook his head vigorously at me, but it was too late. 'I have done cocaine in the past but not in the last few years,' I told her.

There was a pause and the midwife said that she had written down 'occasional user'.

I gasped as I imagined social services and the police turning up to our house, mob handed and carrying my little baby away as I cried and Adam tried to console me.

'Please don't put that,' I said. 'I did, like, two lines, over two years ago.'

But it was too late. It was down, she said. I put my hand on my belly and felt real fear. I thought of what I would and must do to protect my baby.

So, I was ready for the next question.

'What's your job?' she asked.

'Writer,' I said. 'I am a writer.'

First Kiss

School and home made me so miserable that I became angry and withdrawn. The only things that kept me from giving up on life were my various little jobs and a local drama group that I had joined, weekly meetings where I would hang out with grown-ups and learn the mechanics of what it took to put on a play. Actors were needed, obviously, but I also experienced the hard work of the lighting and set team, and got to know about the sound and the props and the costumes. There were the directors, who always had a meltdown the week before our first performance. And there was the excitement backstage as the auditorium filled with chattering people on opening night.

When I was little, Mum had introduced me to lots of old films starring the likes of Jimmy Stewart and Cary Grant, Ava Gardner and Ingrid Bergman. I would look at the glamorous women in black and white and want to be them. All of them. From the age of four, if anyone asked, I would proudly respond that I wanted to be an actress. For me, for a long time, there was nothing else. But then, in one of Dad's boom years, we booked our first package holiday to Benidorm, and I got kissed for the very first time.

All the girls at school had been dropping their knickers for a couple of years by this stage, but I was a freak and no boy would come near me. The boy who kissed me on that holiday was called Barry. He was from Scotland and was utterly beautiful. He didn't care about my jam-jar glasses or my train-track braces. And, when he kissed me, I found a confidence that I'd never had before. It came from nowhere and it felt incredible. With my newfound self-belief I kissed two more boys that week. Their names and faces are seared into my brain because I knew, even in the moment, that they were undoing all the damage the high-school boys had caused.

I felt desired. I felt beautiful. I felt wanted.

And I loved it.

The Immaculate Conception

Adam and I decided to roll the baby dice at the beginning of 2020, but just as I was about to have the procedure to take out my contraceptive implant, Covid hit. No more family-planning appointments until further notice. By midsummer, with everything, especially the NHS, still in crisis, I was panicking. We wanted at least to try for a baby and the idea that we couldn't until the pandemic was over, and I was older and less fertile, made me feel powerless. I was thirty-nine and I didn't know if my eggs would work at that age, and no one knew when the pandemic would end. The implant was just a little rod in my arm, which I had seen nurses and doctors pop in and out over the last decade. Surely it wouldn't be too hard to take out myself, I thought.

Adam came home that day to find me on the sofa, swearing wildly, with blood streaming down my arm. I was screaming to myself, to anyone who'd listen, that I couldn't get hold of the little fucker, while unsuccessfully trying to tweezer the implant out.

'You mad bastard,' he said gently as he took the tweezers from my shaking fingers.

We conceived on New Year's Eve. A drunken fumble, I think, while the fireworks exploded outside our bedroom window. I can't quite remember the details. But it was an immaculate conception. Perfect, planned, wanted.

What I Want for My Child

I have stopped watching true-crime serial-killer shows. I worry that as the baby develops and can hear more and more of their environment, they might think that the torture of animals and the sexual abuse of women is normal behaviour. Instead, as the baby books advise, I listen to classical music, sing softly to my bump, read edifying books and watch old movies, which take me on a glorious trip down memory lane.

I want this child to have everything. I want them to go to a good school and have teachers who care. I want them to have a loving and supportive family network and loyal friends who they can grow up and grow older with. And I want them to be able to do and be in life whatever they want.

I have been hoping that the baby will look more like their dad than me. It's shallow to think of looks; after all, good health is the most we can and should wish for our children. But when I think of my own childhood, all goofy, gappy teeth, terrible eyesight and the years of self-loathing that came with it, I just want my baby to be a looker. To have a chance. I want them to have an easier life. A better life.

I want them to have my early childhood, filled with adventure and love. I want to be the best mum I can be in their

45

teenage years, to watch out for signs of unhappiness and to nip any nastiness in the bud. And if I learn that any teacher has stood by while my child was attacked by a child a foot taller than them, I'll rip the fucking teacher's throat out.

I don't want them to grow up to be judgemental like my sister did under my mother's tutelage, with words like 'slut' and 'little tart' always ready on her lips to describe women who my mum took against on the telly or in real life, and who my sister grew up to dislike too. Both saved their disapproval for women who enjoyed wearing revealing outfits and had multiple boyfriends, who didn't give a damn what other people thought of them. I didn't understand their perspective then, but now I think it stemmed from fear; that the woman who seems free will be more of a catch than the woman at home doing the dishes like a drudge.

Wherever it comes from, the result is the same and it's pure poison.

I will try my best to guide my child away from the hate and judgement and instil in them kindness and empathy instead.

And I will tell them the truth about where their father and I met. But I might leave out a few of the details of our sexcapades. After all, no kid wants to know about their parents' sex life.

What's a Nice Girl Like You Doing in a Place Like This?

This tedious phrase is most often used when a man is wiping the spunk off his body in a brothel or a dungeon. Ten minutes before, their mind will have been solely tuned to the frequency of 'tits!' and 'arse!' but, after the event, they can sometimes feel the need to impart some words of irritation, which they think of as wisdom, to their service provider. They say it while thinking they are terribly clever and original, a metaphorical pat on their own back before their face contorts into pity and they offer some career advice. Still. At least they are paying. They have a purpose. Unlike Jamie Dornan, who was so appalled by the research he undertook in a dungeon before he took on the role of Grey in *Fifty Shades of Shite* that he said he 'had to take a shower' before he touched his wife and baby. Which makes him, in my opinion, a total prick.

The idea that you have to be some kind of appalling woman to work in the sex industry has never made sense to me. I have met many nurses and carers in this profession and if the government don't start raising wages, I am sure I will meet many more in the years to come. And they make amazing sex workers. They offer the empathy and decency and respect that men generally require before they take their clothes off. Men need to feel some level of trust. If they feel that, they come back and become regulars. And it is having regulars that keeps the wolf from your door. How, if you are some man-hating Medusa who can't manage a conversation with a client about his stamp collection, are you going to get regs? You wouldn't last two minutes, either as a hooker or a domme. To do this job you have to be interested in people. You have to be nice. Even when they are irritating the hell out of you.

Loose Morals

It has always amazed me how two siblings who grow up in the same house can have completely different viewpoints on so many subjects. As a kid you don't give a hoot about politics or grown-up issues, I just knew that my sister irritated me on a fundamental level. It probably didn't help that she got the perfect vision and the perfect teeth and I had got the runt's lot. Then, in our teens, there were moments when we looked out for each other. I would come in late and pissed and she often waited up for me, my sister, to make sure I was OK. But as we got older, we drifted apart again. The more of life I experienced, the more our opinions were almost never in alignment.

When I began sex working at the age of twenty-one I told her, and instantly regretted it. But there was less judgement then, perhaps because her viewpoints were not yet completely set, despite Mum often talking of women's 'loose morals'. But over time my sister became more judgemental. She could never get her head around how a woman could have sex with a man she didn't fancy, for cash. Of course, she wasn't alone in that.

When I transitioned to domination, I thought my sister would be happy, as her revulsion for my work stemmed from what I was doing with the clients. I thought less physical contact with old dudes would lead her to relax somewhat. But it didn't. Instead, she would harp on about all my 'holidays', even though most people's idea of a holiday isn't controlling their diet so that they can urinate and defecate at appropriate times, of always being sparkling and amusing company and of never being able to scratch their arse in front of the man who is paying you to be his fantasy.

When I travelled to five gorgeous places in one year, she was able to reel the countries off in order, and finally I identified her behaviour as jealousy, pure and simple. Her words showed me that it was never what I was doing in the room with my client that troubled her, it was that I wasn't conforming to the stereotypical role that she and all the women she knew had so easily slotted into. I was never going to work on a till before finding a boring bastard with a BMW.

Where Did You Meet?

People are often surprised that a sex worker has a partner, as though we are in equal parts unlovable and soulless. Even some of my friends have been quick to make comments about why I, a sex worker, couldn't possibly find love. If a man ever bailed on a date, for example, the question was always, 'Does he know what you do?'

It's a comment intended to make me feel dirty and ashamed. I would say nothing at the time, but later I would think about it and feel waves of anger. If even my so-called friends thought that no man could love me, then that showed me exactly what they really thought of me. Yes, they might find my stories of sex work amusing and my company entertaining, but deep down they thought I was worthless. Those are friendships I have had to rethink. But the cruellest comments are always on social media. 'Must be a pimp' is a response I have seen thrown many times at sex workers who dare to admit they have a partner.

People find it hard to get their heads around how we are able to see other men for work while maintaining a personal relationship. A good, strong and loving personal relationship. I don't think it's a difficult concept and it comes down to this: our personal relationships are not transactional. Seeing clients is a job. I aim to keep the professional and the personal as separate as possible. I try not to talk to my clients about my partner because it's important to have a part of myself that is separate. But I have slipped up occasionally and said something about Adam that lets the cat out of the bag. One jealous client then asked what my partner and I do in the bedroom. I told him, as nicely as possible, that it was none of his business. Some clients will always want more than we are prepared to give. More of our time, our bodies, our souls, our truth. Those are not the clients we choose to spend our lives with. The ones who become our partners are the ones we can be ourselves with. No boundary pushing. No games. No bullshit. And that's what drew me to Adam; the simple honesty of what we have.

Less truthfully, however, I will tell people that Adam and I met in the pub. I don't like lying – it can sometimes bring on a bout of uncontrollable twitching – but occasionally it is necessary to protect myself or somebody else. Once you tell the truth that you work in the sex industry, you can't take it back, and people almost always think less of you when they know. I usually don't give a damn what strangers think of me, but when people I care about have a diminished opinion of me, that hurts. I'll always protect Adam. I'm also protecting the questioner from the full force of my bile, should they look at me with pity if I tell them the truth, that we met at work, that Adam was once a punter. After all, if men who visit sex workers are all abusers or rapists, as many people seem to believe, then my relationship with Adam makes me a victim, right? And that's the very last thing I am.

When I settled down with Adam, I stopped shagging clients. I was mostly domming by then anyway, but I had a few remaining clients from my escort days and I realized very quickly I couldn't do both. If I'm honest, I enjoyed the shagging part too much. If I didn't like the sex, then perhaps I could have carried on doing it. But that isn't healthy, is it? I could see that.

I remember an ex struggling to comprehend my whoring. I went out with him for years in my mid-twenties, between two stints of sex work. He asked me if I'd ever had an orgasm with a client. I said I had, of course I had, and the second it was out of my mouth I realized that it was not the answer he wanted to hear, but it couldn't be taken back. At the time I didn't understand why he would prefer me not to feel pleasure. Why would someone I loved, and who supposedly loved me, want me to be a victim? But people like to put others in boxes. Especially sex workers. We are either Jezebels and corrupters of men, or we are victims. Anything more nuanced is too complicated for people to understand.

Adam gets it and he gets me. He knows me. Meeting me at work comes with a huge advantage as he doesn't have to imagine anything. He knows what I was like when I was extracting cash from him, dressed in stockings, and telling him that he would have much more fun if he stayed for two hours. And he has also experienced me premenstrual, in joggers, bitching at him to empty the cat litter.

Adam worries about what our child will think of us, how we met, but I want to be honest and tell them that they were made from the love of two once-damaged people. Two people who managed to wade through a lot of shit and find each other.

Freaks Like Me

Along with my various jobs and the drama club, my life raft was a little group of friends I made towards the end of school. They were all freaks like me. Which is to say they were all in their own personal version of hell, but we were to each other a little ray of sunshine. One lad was disabled. Another had so many spots it was impossible to see his pale skin beneath the angry redness. Someone else's family was so poor that his tatty trousers were culottes, swinging around his skinny shins. And, like so many kids without cash and caring parents, he smelled of piss and BO. Then there was my very best mate, a girl who was so physically developed at twelve that she could have been twenty. She hated school even more than I did, which is hard to imagine, and truanted constantly. Still, when she was there, we had each other. We teased each other relentlessly, but there was no malice in our words. Just fun. And I badly needed some fun in my young life.

Around me, people were growing up fast; a friend of mine

was well on her way to getting pregnant at fifteen, while others were playing strip poker and fucking in the science labs. I was still so innocent. I particularly liked the boy with acne, who we called Gerbil. We would pull each other's ties and chase each other around, like little kids. There was something I just loved about him. Looking back, I probably wanted to fuck him – but I didn't yet know quite what that feeling was.

These little rays of sunshine couldn't keep me going. At fifteen I decided I'd had enough.

For a while I had been experimenting with cutting my arms, over-exercising until I collapsed with exhaustion, and not eating. All of which was an attempt to have some level of control over my life . . . but it didn't work. Nothing worked. I felt lost, and I knew I couldn't talk about it. Certainly not to my mum. I bottled it all up and didn't tell anyone about the pain. Or about the slow checking out of life that was going on in my head. Or about the thirty-three pills I took one afternoon in an attempt to end the pain.

I was very organized about it. I chose a day when I knew everyone in the family would be out for a few hours after I'd finished school. I had read in the paper that a schoolboy had killed himself with forty Paracetamols. I totted up that there weren't enough pills in the medicine cabinet to do the job, so I went to the local shop and bought a pack.

'Yeah, Mum's got another headache!' I smiled at the familiar face behind the counter.

It was as easy as that. I figured that thirty-three pills would be enough as I was a girl and younger and probably smaller than the boy I'd read about. I scribbled a long note of explanation and then ripped it up because it was wrong. I couldn't find the right words to explain how I felt. I replaced the aborted essay with a brief 'I'm sorry', then ripped that up as well. Just go, I thought. Stop fucking about. There was nothing that needed to be said. I gulped the pills down with water standing at the kitchen sink, and then went to lie on my bed.

I had an idea that I would drift gently away. I didn't. I don't know how much time passed, lying there waiting for something to happen, but suddenly, violently, I was met with brutal stomach pains and once I started to heave I knew it was all over. It hadn't worked. Up everything came. Somehow, for some reason, it wasn't my time to leave.

Because You're Gorgeous

A year after that, I left school. I went to college three days a week and got myself yet another job, this time at a theme park where, I realized, it was possible to have fun while making money. I was determined to save as much as possible. I wanted independence, and I wanted to enjoy myself. Of course, Mum decided it was time I paid rent and took from me what she called her fair share. It didn't matter. I was out of the house most of the time and away from the shitheads at school. And college was a fresh start. I had new friends in new locations and I felt I could start again. I had hope for my future, something I couldn't ever remember experiencing during the dark period at high school. I was happy.

The strangest thing happened at college. Boys looked at me.

Not just boys. Men. Men I would walk past in the street. Men who I would serve food to at the theme park. They looked at me. I didn't understand it. I thought I was ugly. If enough people call you a freak for long enough you believe it.

So why were men now staring at me? I wondered.

Initially, I'd feel their eyes on me and would wait for them to call me something horrible, something that would hurt. But 'Hey, freak!' seemed to have been replaced with 'Hey, gorgeous!' I would go to nightclubs with my new friends from college or work, and I would be chatted up all the time. I just couldn't work it out. I kept asking myself, Is this a big joke that everyone is in on? I eventually had to reason that the entire human race couldn't possibly be interested in taking the piss out of me, not on this *Truman Show* scale. The real reason for the attention eventually became apparent. Men found me attractive. More than that. They wanted me. They wanted to touch me, to be close to me. To kiss me. To fuck me.

I lost my virginity to a long-haired musician when I was sixteen, an underwhelming event. What was the big deal? I wondered, as he desperately tried and failed to make me come from oral. I was so ill informed I didn't even know that women could have orgasms; I thought it was something only men could do, and that it was their orgasm that made the baby. With me not feeling it, not understanding that an orgasm was something women could have and like and want, the musician and I didn't last long. In any case, I preferred my freedom.

It would be another two years before I found my clit.

Self-Control

I came alive at college. I adored it. I was studying drama and I felt as though I was living my dream, the dream of the small child who'd always wanted to be an actress. I was going to be an actress, I told myself; I could see that future laid out for me. School felt like a long time ago. I was more confident now. Things were going to be OK, I told myself.

Where I felt most confident, always, was on a club dance floor when I was drunk and playing men like the proverbial fiddle. How easy they were! How weak! I would have competitions with my female friends to see how many men I could kiss in one night. I almost always won the challenge, typically striking up a tally of eight even on a slow night. I would pretend I liked these men, that I would go further than a kiss with them . . . and then I would skip away and move on to one of their friends. They meant nothing to me. It was all just a game.

Sometimes I would go too far. Drink too much. Lead some man or other on too far. And then I did let them fuck me. Because if I were to use a different word now, if I were to describe what happened to me as rape or assault, I would become a victim. And I already knew, even then, that I would never give anyone the power to make me their victim. And so sometimes I had sex, when all I really wanted to do was snog anything with a dick, move on quickly to the next encounter and have as few feelings as possible. I learned how to wear my promiscuity like a suit of armour.

Despite these moments when I felt good about myself, whenever I got on stage I couldn't completely shed my shackles of shame and self-loathing. The doubt crept back in. I questioned myself. It meant I could never totally let go and embody a part. The only parts I excelled at were the angry ones. I had spent so long pretending I was OK – hiding behind a force field of attitude – that when a part required vulnerability, I just couldn't do it. I couldn't become small. I couldn't cry. I couldn't access that part of myself.

The Red Mist

All the women in my family are on medication for some condition or other. It has always been a lottery as to what you would get in our family – depression, addiction or just being a nasty cunt. Go back a couple of generations and our women were having electric shock treatment. I am the only one who has escaped being medicated, but that doesn't mean I feel totally sane. I feel scarred and, as I get older, I find the whole act of always pretending I am OK becomes more difficult. It's as though different pieces of me are scattered like a jigsaw and won't come together to make a whole. My temper worries me. The so-called red mist. A part of me knows that, given the right provocation, I could kill.

Most people could though, right?

The Test

I need to take a DNA test to see if my baby is OK. I am now forty and, in medical jargon, a 'geriatric mother', so there are risks. Down syndrome and Edwards and Patau, for example, which are caused, I am told, by my eggs being 'compromised'. When I first found out I was pregnant I thought that if any major issues arose, and the baby wasn't completely well, I would simply abort. I didn't want to bring a child into this world who was predestined to suffer. There's already enough suffering, even for those of us who appear to be healthy and who have parents who love us. But now, as I see my belly getting bigger, what seemed to be an easy decision is not so simple. When I see my dating scan, I see so much more than a cluster of cells. Nothing is simple any more.

I wait anxiously for the test results. I read stories written by mothers who have decided, no matter what, to have their child and they make me cry. Hormones. I worry about who would look after our disabled child when Adam and I are gone. Who'll be there to continue the lifelong support they need? Perhaps if we had money to ensure their future I wouldn't worry so much, but children with additional needs aren't always guaranteed love beyond their parents' unconditional kindness. And many don't even get that.

My mind races until I get the results back.

All clear.

Drama

In my last term of college, my drama teacher advised me not to audition for drama school. He said I needed more life experience. Apparently, I was young and naive with no understanding of life. What with my mum's manic moods, the bullying and the self-harming, the suicide attempt and working all hours to support myself financially, I felt as though I had experienced quite a lot of life and particularly how hard it could be. But I believed my teacher and didn't audition for drama school.

It can wait, I thought. There'll be time, I thought.

I decided to make my part-time theme park job full time. And I fell in love. Which was when my troubles really started.

How Can Sex Work be a Job?

The question 'How can sex work be a job?' has, at some point, been asked by every radical feminist and Neanderthal man. It's endlessly interesting to me how those two sides can despise each other so much but agree on this one thing. I've discovered there's no point debating it with them; there's no educating some people. They are so tied to their position that they will never hear you and never challenge themselves to think again. You're screaming into the void.

But there is a very simple answer to the question.

We use the phrase 'sex work' because what we do is work and we are in the business of sex – even if we don't always offer a full service, by which I mean penetrative sex. In broad terms, if your job is to turn a man or woman on . . . you are a sex worker. I've been a domme for longer than I was a hooker, and I know that some dommes get sniffy about being called sex workers, but they need to get a fucking grip. It may be true that your slaves think you are a goddess among whores, but you are still polishing knobs like the rest of us, honey. It's bad enough when the rest of society think we are damaged goods, but when women in our own industry think the same, we have a problem. My sex-work friends are all grounded and not at all elitist or hierarchical, but many of the women I've met who have come straight into domme work can carry a chip on their shoulder about being lumped in with other sex workers. Some think they are better than the rest of us. They're not. Maybe they'll learn that as the years roll by. And maybe they won't. Again, you can rarely educate the deluded and stupid. But, if I'm feeling a little kinder, perhaps it's only by creating this distinction that they're able to get out of bed in the morning and get through their day.

This is what we call the whorearchy, a minority of women who work within the sex industry and look down on other workers. The more physical contact with a man, the more morally bankrupt, the more socially unacceptable, the more corrupt you are deemed to be. So some strippers and dommes look down on hookers. Meanwhile, many of the hookers are judging each other for what services they provide, what they charge, and how they market themselves. And woe betide them if they offer bareback. They then have the 'She's a proper whore, that one!' line thrown at her.

As an independent dominatrix, let me tell you the work is relentless, but perhaps not in the way you'd imagine. There's a desk job element to sex work which might surprise you. Emails and marketing take up most of my time. There are a lot of time-wasters who get something – maybe it's a sense of control, and perhaps that's all the thrill they need – out of keeping a preliminary conversation going for as long as possible, whether that's on the phone or by email. But I can't be dealing with timewasters. I need to close the deal and get on with things. I save such men in my phone under TW Andrew or TW Arthur. With email it's different; it's so easy to set up new accounts, it means that as soon as you have marked someone as spam the guy can just pop up again under another account name and here we go again. In the early days I was patient and would go back and forth with them for what felt like for ever, trying to pin our meeting down, but now I give them a four-email limit. If they haven't paid a deposit by then they are ignored. I don't have the time or the patience. And I wish to fuck I had arrived at this strategy sooner.

I've got a job to be getting on with.

The Business of Sex Work

The truth is sex work isn't just a job. It's a business. It's entrepreneurial, it's competitive and – as we've already seen – requires a lot of hustling. If you're working in a brothel, someone else is doing the admin for you. But if you're an independent, then you're an entrepreneur with a business to run, and it's both a challenge and a chore.

To promote themselves, some sex workers post ten times a day on Twitter, usually something sexy that boosts their brand. It might be along the lines of: 'Which slave dare worship under my sexy heel? #stockings #stilettos #adoremistress.' Around seven years ago, my posts were like that too. Now I mainly post pictures of my cat, and wonder why my follower count is in decline.

As an independent sex worker you have to run yourself like a business because you are a business. Success requires you to answer the phone with a purr, not a snarl, no matter how you're feeling, and then to continue to purr sexily throughout the call, even when the potential client asks you if you have a boyfriend, a child, how long you have done this for, how long you are going to do it for, when you are going to get a real job, and does your family know what you do for a living. Bat it away, and keep purring.

I became a little lazy with the self-promotion around five years into domming, once I'd established a regular client base and moved away from London and the extortionate rent I had being paying. At that point, I dropped some of my regular clients, the ones who pissed me off. There were plenty of those. I had the newfound luxury of only doing sessions I would enjoy – yes, enjoy – with men that I genuinely liked. But even the best clients get ill, move away, die. You can't gain more clients without sometimes tooting the self-promotion horn, even when you're feeling too bloody old to be finding the perfect cleavage shot and the perfect light to make your legs look longer.

Even at the best of times, photographers have a job with me as my bored facial expression – my natural resting face – permeates right through my body and extends along my limbs. I switch it on for the game but otherwise I have to dig deep to find the requisite excitement. And, just to make it even more difficult to market myself, I never reveal my face, although some sex workers urge newbies to do so. The newbies can be so fucking naive. It's true that you might adore this job in your twenties, and be feeling loud and proud, but should you want a different career one day you will be completely screwed if your new employer decides to use facial-recognition software to probe into your background. And why wouldn't they want to do a thorough check on who they're taking on?

Many of us do sex work part time and also work in a broad range of other jobs; I even met a parole officer once. The women who value keeping their job have the sense to keep their faces hidden, unless they're in New Zealand and New South Wales, where they have decriminalized sex work and therefore the women have more rights and deal with less stigma. They're allowed to get on with their business. But there are a lot of young ones who haven't thought about where they might be in ten years' time. Your future husband or wife could find you. Or your neighbours. Your children. You have to think hard about whether you want that.

'To work on your brand, you have to be the face of it!' the crowing know-alls on social media say. 'Be proud of who you are!'

Oh, fuck off. Stop telling other women how to run their businesses.

We are as careful as we can be, but I have still been caught out a few times. I used to accept deposits via PayPal and the punter would only see the email address that I had given him. But PayPal changed their policy and began revealing our legal names and it was only because a guy called me by my real name rather than the name I'd given him that I found out what was happening. Goodness knows how long that had been going on for and how many men had got access to the real me.

Many of us work hard to keep ourselves as concealed as possible. It's a constant effort both to be out there hustling for work, and to make sure that it's only your business persona that is seen. We use virtual private networks, hosted in a country that won't throw us off their platform under the excuse of 'trafficking'. We never post the same pictures across our business and personal social media accounts. That's a huge no-no. I have heard of clients who have tried to friend their domme or escort on Facebook. How would the client like it if I rocked up at his house and introduced myself to his grandma? An intrusion into our personal lives is exactly the same thing.

Thanks to social media accounts and websites that advertise our services, sex workers keep getting turned away at the US border because our information is either being leaked or, less likely, because the US government has time to use facial-recognition technology to investigate every woman who enters the country. Even if they are just going on holiday with their family. Many have begun wiping their accounts from their phones before they travel but these border thugs still seem to know which women have sucked a cock for money. As always, it comes down to how important the cock is you are sucking. You suck a future president's cock and you get a chat show or maybe get to be called First Lady. You suck an estate agent's and you get chucked out of the US.

Details, Details

So, once we independents – whether that's dommes or hookers – have been as careful as we can be with our face, our name and our address, the next bit of work begins. Blogging, posting, pictures, social media. Networking and advertising. Website building and upkeep and, arguably the biggest task of them all, finding the best websites to advertise on so that we don't waste our money. And all this work happens before the client even makes contact. When they do, the job becomes about understanding what they want. Johns just need a discreet room with a bed. Subs are more tricky. Do they want a domestic setting? That means booking a hotel room or an Airbnb flat. Or do they want a more atmospheric dungeon setting? Dungeons, you may be surprised to hear, are incredibly easy to book. There are plenty of websites advertising kinky spaces, some with whips and chains thrown in.

Then you need to make travel arrangements. Simple enough. But getting all the kit you need – which in a dungeon space might additionally be a St Andrew's cross, which is an upright X-frame, a whipping bench, a bondage bench, a bondage chair, a cage, perhaps some stocks and a wheel, and many other wonderful items of furniture that you won't see for sale in your local Ikea – is less so. The next piece of the jigsaw, getting it all ready in the workspace, takes time and effort. Believe me, pegging – otherwise known as putting a strap-on penis into a man's arsehole – is much easier when you're using a strap-on bench rather than a bed that might be too high or too low, so you need to have got it right. I prefer working from dungeons precisely because you can have everything you need for a good time right there but, coming in at between sixty and seventy pounds an hour to rent, and with my typical session being two to three hours, they are a lot more expensive than booking a day-use hotel, even in London. Plus you typically have only a few minutes ahead of the booking to set up in a dungeon and are then thrown out on the dot at the end of the booking, a rush that's not very conducive to a relaxing session for the domme or the slave.

For hotels I have to be more imaginative. Does the room have a separate interior door that I can use for my bondage straps? After all, I can hardly fix my bondage straps to the hotel room door as the hotel staff would soon be suspicious of two metal poles protruding on the corridor side. Usually, the only option is the bathroom door. Is there something to lean on or hold on to above the bed, so that I can safely stand over my naked sub and make him worship my heels? Is the shower big enough for water sports? And, of course, there are two really important things to remember. Does the lift require a card to access the room? You do not want to have to collect your submissive from the foyer dressed in PVC. And the second thing is to lock the door. In my experience a 'do not disturb' sign does not always suffice. I once had a slave on his knees, dressed in a frilly pink frock with my knickers on his head while he frantically sucked a dildo, when the maid walked in.

Then, finally, putting on make-up, doing your hair and nails, shaving your arse crack, getting dressed – and *voilà*! You open the door to the client sexy and ready to go. As though it was effortless.

Charging £200 an hour sounds like a lot of money, but as an independent it can take nearly a whole day to be ready for a one-hour session – and then it needs to be good. Great, even. You need to make sure they come back for more.

Sometimes, I despair over my stagnant follow count but the truth is I'm tired of selling myself. I'm tired of this huge performance and of putting myself out there.

I'm just tired.

Exposed

It's not just sex workers who are vulnerable to exposure. Our partners' jobs could be in danger too if it's known they are married to a sex worker. Adam has turned down jobs that have required full vetting – at that point he has had to walk away. He would have no fucking chance with me lurking in his background. He says he doesn't mind because whatever job he does he dislikes anyway. He works with numbers and I've never met a man who worked with numbers who's happy. That's why they are our biggest customer base.

Then there are the clients who don't want to be exposed, but, unlike us, don't do enough to keep their play emails (as I like to call them) and their work emails separate. When I joined LinkedIn, seven men who I had shagged in the arse immediately popped up on my screen.

'You may know these individuals,' LinkedIn told me.

'Add them to your network,' it suggested.

I left immediately.

Sex workers have two phones with two numbers and two email addresses kept separately so that Aunty Karen doesn't get connected with Fisting Stephen on LinkedIn or Facebook. I always try to be careful and think, *What if. . .?* I even go so far as to ask friends not to post pictures of me on their Facebook pages. They might know about my job but many don't know about my criminal record. They look at me as if to say, 'Why is she being so fuckin' weird?' But they haven't been done by the police. I have. It means I'm now on red alert. Head down. Flying beneath the radar.

Even so, I've been caught out through no fault of my own, just a bit of a technology issue, when my Mac crashed. As anyone would, I took it to an Apple store to get it sorted. I watched anxiously as it was rebooted by a nice young man working on the shop floor as I knew that on it there were numerous pictures of me wearing dildos. Luckily no photos appeared as the computer came back to life. Instead, the calendar from my iPhone synced with the laptop and my next appointment popped up.

'Hugo 7 p.m. Fisting. Poppers. Huge strap-on.'

The Apple worker did nothing more than raise an eyebrow as I thanked him, grabbed the computer and dashed away, my face the same shade as Hugo's anus following a good seeing to.

Creature Man

Another submissive – let's call him Chris – was due to see me. The arrangement was that he would meet me at 11 a.m. at the hotel room. He was very clear that he would be bringing one of his inventions. OK, I said. As I opened the door to him I was surprised by the size of the box he was carrying. I eyed it up. It was long and thin; around four foot in length. Shotgun or Samurai sword sized. He was carrying a bag as well. Large enough for body parts, I noted. My hands became a little clammy.

As clients go, he had always been one of my odder customers. For fun, I called him Creature Man because that was a common theme in our sessions. He would stand in the corner of the room with a handkerchief over his twitching penis and hang his head in shame. I would mock him and tell him how pathetic he was, a sculpture of what a man would be . . . if that man was the exact opposite of David. Sometimes I would invite other women to the session to mock him too, a double whammy of humiliation that Creature Man had to pay for. I had inherited him from a retiring domme who I sometimes used to double with. It's a great way to get new clients as you are already familiar with the man and you already know whether or not you click with them. Creature Man and I definitely clicked.

And so, I would play with it, the thing, the creature, teasing him with my words, my hands, ignoring him, then ridiculing him. I'd make him turn his nose to the wall as I gave myself pleasure, make him watch while I kissed my friends, a physical intimacy he was excited to be denied. I put him in stress positions, made him take cold showers, made him wank in front of me, but then made him stop when he got close to coming. It's called heavy humiliation, but it was all fun because I liked him. It wouldn't work if I didn't.

The foreboding box and roomy bag turned out to be nothing

sinister. I could relax. It was a homemade milking machine, capable of milking and making him orgasm time and time again. He had synced the machine with an iPad and there were so many different functions I found myself playing with it for three hours – trying this, then that. Edging him until he moaned for release. And the best fun was that Creature Man couldn't stop me because he was tied to the hotel bed and gagged, as I knew he would get loud.

I made him come four times during that session and he was a quivering wreck by the end. But that didn't stop him from skipping out of the hotel with the biggest smile I have ever seen plastered across his face. His invention – a pleasure-giving machine that wouldn't tire – was utter genius.

Men can and will do anything when they've got the horn.

Love, Actually

Do you know it only takes around ten seconds to pass out when you're being strangled? I learned the hard way. The last conscious thought I had was that it was curious how everything around me was turning grey and grainy, like an untuned TV that can't pin down a signal and delivers only static. I also remember being surprised that the man strangling me was so strong, that he could so easily lift me off my feet, as though I was nothing more than a tiny rag doll.

The sex-worker narrative would suggest it was a client who did this to me, but that assumption would be incorrect. This particular man was my first long-term relationship. I know

many women who have been in domestically violent relationships. There is a stereotype that exists around the kind of
women who end up in that situation, but that – along with the
sex-worker narrative – is also bollocks. The reality is that any
woman, often the most unlikely woman, when vulnerable and
lonely can find herself sucked in by a predator.

I was seventeen when I met my abuser. Let's call him Tom. He
wanted to be a doctor, and at the time was volunteering at a local
hospice. He was beautiful, delicate-featured with fiery red hair, a
surfer who enjoyed reading about the Dalai Lama. We fell in love
in the cold room of a restaurant, where he was plating up cakes
and I was putting away dishes. I thought he behaved like an
angel, looked like an angel and that I had met a genuinely nice
guy. I thought, *Here's a young man who my parents will like too*.
Everyone told me how lucky I was to be with him, and I agreed.
After all, I was relentlessly gobby, was rat arsed four nights out of
seven and had kissed a lot of frogs. Tom, by contrast, was beloved
by pensioners and had a bright future in medicine.

When Tom's behaviour towards me changed I couldn't tell
anyone because I didn't think anyone would believe me. I
couldn't believe it myself. How could someone who wanted to
be a doctor refuse to drive me to the hospital when my dad was
rushed to A&E, saying he was 'too busy', even though he was
clearly doing nothing at the time? How could a man who medi-
tated and spoke so often about being zen and at one with nature
scream and shout and punch the steering wheel as he drove
at speed around a roundabout, leaving a wake of tooting and
petrified faces that mirrored mine? How could such a lovely,
upstanding member of society put his hands around my neck

and strangle me until I lost consciousness because I forgot to buy his cereal? Perhaps there were other signs along the way, but as a seventeen-year-old I didn't know what to look for. I didn't know that domestic abuse was a real thing.

What I've since learned is that it starts small.

'You don't need make-up.' As he handed me a wipe.

'I think you would look nicer in this.' With a pointed stare.

Then it gets a little worse.

'You could do with losing some weight.'

'I don't like your friends.'

If Tom had been violent from the outset I would have left him as I would have known that his behaviour wasn't acceptable. But his manipulation and control grew slowly, like a cancer that I couldn't see. Two years into the relationship, we moved away from my hometown to a strange new city. I stopped going out. Three years in and I would wake up to find him on top of me, having sex with me. I would lie still and wait for it to be over and he would go back to sleep without saying a word. The next day he would pretend it had never happened. We didn't talk about it. My mind was screaming, 'No, not like this. Love isn't like this.' But I couldn't find the words to say out loud.

I very quickly felt used and worthless. I was still a teenager, living away from home with no friends left to speak of; I'd dropped them one by one, without noticing, until one day I felt the need to pick up the phone and call one of them and realized with dazzling clarity that there was nobody I could call. Besides, even if someone had answered, who would believe me? I was the fuck-up, wasn't I? I was the one who was lucky to be with him. I'd tell myself, 'He's just having a bad day,' and that tomorrow would be better. Somehow, I'd blame myself. We always blame ourselves.

A year into our relationship Tom was offered a place to study medicine at a university a couple of hours away from where we were living in our hometown. I took a history A Level in one year, which was enough to get into a polytechnic university near his. I wanted to fit my life around him because I couldn't imagine being without him. We found a flat two hours away from home and then it was just the two of us. Perhaps there were happy times – there must have been – but what I mostly remember is feeling more and more isolated as time went on.

I loved studying, though. At least at first. It felt amazing to be somewhere where learning was encouraged rather than mocked. But I was finding it harder and harder to complete assignments. When your partner is constantly telling you that you're fat, and you think you're going mad even though it's him who's slapping and punching himself in the face, and it's him being loving and tender one moment and the next he's kicking the door so hard it buckles and you're both trapped in the house, it's difficult to concentrate on the Industrial Revolution and to think that it matters.

I so vividly remember standing in front of the mirror in that pokey flat, the face of a horrified gargoyle staring back at me. My mind was a mess, I couldn't concentrate and, however much I tried, I couldn't make sense of anything. Unrecognizable to myself, I could only wonder how it had come to this, how I could possibly keep going, how I could ever again feel safe. After I'd left school I had been determined never to be a victim again but now this was far worse than anything that had happened to me before. At school I could leave the bullies behind every day but now there was no escape. The bully was in my home.

I thought I was shit. I thought that I deserved it. All I could feel was a darkness enveloping me. My knuckles were white with fear and tension and my breath smelled of vomit because, no matter how many times I exercised on the bike that he insisted we get but which I had had to pay for, I never lost enough weight for him. I tried everything I could to make him happy, but nothing was ever enough. I didn't realize that it could never be enough.

Tom had friends who all thought the sun shone out of his arse. I had nobody left apart from my family. I needed to see them, I needed to feel their love. But I couldn't leave him. He'd threatened to kill himself if I wasn't there to look after him. He'd scream, 'Look what you make me do!' as he banged his own head with his fists. I know now that men who use these tactics to control a woman are never going to kill themselves. They are too narcissistic to take their own lives.

They are far more likely to kill you.

No Glow

My first trimester can only be described as dreadful.

No food cravings, instead an aversion to almost everything even vaguely edible. My tastebuds have completely deserted me so I don't understand why I feel nauseous every time I eat. At the same time, I have the sense of smell of a superhero with special powers. I can smell a fart from the next train carriage. And there are no pleasurable smells. It doesn't matter if it's a decomposing dog or an expensive perfume – for me the effect is exactly the same. Dry heaving and retching. My poor kitten has been banished from our bed and consigned to the floor as even he makes me want to barf, and he's adorable.

Then there's the tiredness. Friends are complaining that I'm not getting back to their texts, and I don't even have the energy to explain why the effort of picking up my phone and typing out a message sometimes leaves me so exhausted that I simply can't do it.

I am working when I feel up to it, which isn't often. The clients I've been seeing know that I am pregnant but don't mind. Some of them are happy for me. But I can't fit into my heels any more. I'm getting bigger, which means that trampling is out. A domme should never put her full bodyweight on the submissive while wearing heels, in any case, but now I worry I will lose my balance and slip a stiletto through a spine. Even though I've had some really sick-fuck requests over the years, no one has ever asked for that. And forget not being able to tie shoelaces or cut toenails; for me the issue is that before long it's going to be difficult to see the strap-on cock I'm supposed to stick into my client's arse.

Meanwhile I read articles about pregnant women who say the first trimester is wonderful. 'Smooth sailing!' says one. And the glow! Everyone keeps banging on about their glow. I look in the mirror and see blotchy, bloated skin. Dark shadows under my eyes.

Fuck those glowing women.

Prick and Privilege

I'm missing the trips I would normally take to Scotland to see a client, an elderly man who I've known since my early dungeon days. Let's call him Matthew. I had got to know him well over the years, so well that we'd argue from time to time, like an old married couple, and almost always about money. He's one of those men who doesn't like to pay cash, saying that the transaction makes him feel uncomfortable. Tough, I always told him, I'm running a business here. If you don't want to pay a domme or an escort in cash, then you should go and find yourself a wife who will take the Chanel gifts and take the diamonds and then take you for millions in the divorce settlement. Sex work is transactional. Pay me.

But despite being completely upfront with Matthew there were always heated arguments when he'd insist on taking me shoe shopping, and then think I should waive my session fee as he had 'paid in lieu'. A ridiculous idea. I can't pay my bills with a pair of shoes. It's not as though I ever ask for extra. I'm not one of those sex workers whose grandma always needs an eye operation. Pay me.

The shoe-shopping argument once happened just after Matthew had paid £7,000 to have a rug repaired. He had the money, clearly, but he just didn't want to give it to me. After a row he would sulk and see other dommes, but a few months later he would always come back to me with his tail and his twitching cock between his legs. And this was how we operated for years. We would regularly fall out over money, his politics, his privileged upbringing and his miserly aversion to tipping waiters generously despite being outrageously rude in restaurants – an attitude he'd adopt particularly with young, pretty waitresses. The strangest thing is that I actually liked him despite all the red flags. He made me laugh and was interested in me, my life and, importantly, what I thought. I like to think that knowing me made him a little kinder in his old age when the world became less kind to him and he finally had a sense of what it might be like for other people.

For the trip up to see him, he would pay my train fare, first class on the sleeper. I'd pretend that I was a lady with money rather than what I was . . . a grafter who never stopped working. But while I enjoyed that little fantasy, and our extravagant time together, at the end of it all he would owe me £1,000 for the pleasure of my company and the sessions. Ask any domme and they will tell you it's madness to go all the way to Scotland for four days for such a piddling amount. But I saw Matthew a few times a month, he was a regular if not entirely reliable client; there was always a question mark over how and when I would get paid.

Once, on the day I was due to catch my train back home, he went to the cash machine and presented me with £400. 'I'll give you the rest when I see you next in London,' he said breezily. I knew Matthew had just bought a Rolls, £100,000 paid upfront, which he'd been proudly driving me around in. Showing me off. I was back to loathing him. But, however I was feeling about him, I absolutely loved Scotland. The wildness. The open air. I could breathe better up there. It certainly made a nice change from a dungeon.

Healthy and Happy

The baby feels like a parasite growing in my womb, something which is sucking all the goodness out of me, leaving me a hollow shell. For something so natural, pregnancy has felt completely unnatural. But then a man in the street gets too close with his maskless face and his cigarette smoke and instinctively I put a protective hand on my bump. And I realize that it really is a baby in there. My baby. And that I'm its mother. And so what if the little parasite takes all the goodness from me? They can have it. It is their turn to have a life and, as long as they are healthy, I am happy.

Coming and Going

While escort clients generally leave after they have orgasmed, a natural end to proceedings, domination clients don't. In fact, some of them don't even want an orgasm. There are a lot more things to do in a domination session than climax, so it isn't uncommon for me to have three-hour bookings, which then makes more sense of all the prep. While this means domination is more lucrative, it's a lot more draining mentally. You have to think much more before and during a session. It's not just a case of lubing yourself up and ta-dah! Come here, big boy!

You have a brief from your client to work to. You have a lot of sometimes potentially lethal tools at your disposal. And you have a set time to fill. There will be more complicated clothes (for you and for them), health concerns, boundaries. Knowing what their preferred mix of pain and pleasure is and what form the pain takes is paramount. You have to make sure that you don't seriously hurt your client – it's a fine line between titillation and mutilation – and make sure he is never bored. More important even than that, the golden rule is to make sure that *you* never look bored. You can hide a lot of things from a client, but your eyes glazing over is instantly noticeable and a complete no-no. You have to approach each backside as though it's your first. 'I've been thinking about fucking your arse all day!' is one of my favourite lines.

Some daft women become dommes because they think it's simply a case of being mean to men. They never last long. Then there are the fin-doms, financial dominatrices, who market themselves by saying 'I'm sexier than your wife. Give *me* money instead of her.' They call potential clients 'paypigs' and the extracting of their cash is called 'rinsing'. While on the whole I feel that women should butt out of other women's business, having a view on fin-doms is an exception. I think these women belong in the same category of worker as bailiffs and traffic wardens. I'm sure their marketing works occasionally as a minority of men are into it, but in the long run it's making the BDSM world nastier. Inexperienced subs might find a fin-dom instead of a professional dom and once rinsed they are less likely to pay a deposit next time around, citing bad experiences in the past. Blackmail is common. One of my new regulars was told by a fin-dom he had met online, 'I have your number and your full name and I have found your wife on Facebook.' After that it took him a while to pluck up the courage to approach me.

A lot of dommes quit at the four-year mark, which I passed a long time ago now. Perhaps because I see fewer men I haven't yet reached saturation point. While in my early days of domming I never glazed, now I do occasionally. But I still enjoy it, ten years later. There is a buzz that you get when you feel you're really good at something. It's not all the time and not with every client. But when the chemistry is right it really is like magic; a performance that appeals to my theatrical side and, like being on stage, every time is different. I've had accountants singing to musical numbers while I've kept time by bashing them in the balls. I have zapped estate agents until they cried while using a vibrator on myself, matching them moan for moan. And I have steered a man by his nipples as he rowed me around his lake. Every time he drifted the wrong way, I would tug on the rope attached to the nipple clamp that would guide him back on course. This stuff doesn't get old. Although one thing that bores me silly is a willy. A man produces his pecker, proud as a peacock and I'm … What? Supposed to be impressed? Hardly. But I always find that some electrics applied to a bloke's organ is a good way to put a gleam in my eye and bring a smile back to my face.

By the Pricking of Matthew's Bum . . .

Matthew's eldest son, who happens to be a millionaire trader, sent me a series of increasingly angry texts about the £1,000 monthly standing order I had eventually insisted on from his fee-dodging father. 'Paying for your time??' he messaged. And then, when I told him that his father and I were friends, he responded: 'Friends don't charge.' Before the multiple strokes that had recently affected Matthew's mobility and taken away so much of the person he used to be, the money had been for spanking, feminization – dressing him in women's clothes – dinners, going on holiday, as well as the simple pleasure two people can find from sitting side by side and having a chat. Our time together now mostly involved companionship, giggles and watching *Antiques Road Trip*. Things had become different, yes. But we still knew how to have a good time.

Matthew's housekeeper had rung me to let me know what had happened to him. She had found him helpless on his bedroom floor. A man who had been so strong and self-sufficient when I'd first met him seven years earlier – though he was in his seventies even then – was now completely debilitated. Strong. Stubborn. Infuriating. Funny. That is always how I remember Matthew.

Our first meeting had been in my dungeon. I had just tied him, spreadeagled, to my St Andrew's cross, when he'd asked if I had any cocaine with me. I'd laughed it off – how on earth a man of his age could do cocaine was beyond me – and he'd said he would bring some the next time, if that was OK with me. I knew I had a livewire on my hands. As I got to know him more I marvelled at his drinking and his cigar-smoking too. How could a man of his age do all of this and still be alive? I wondered.

The good living and decadence had finally caught up with him.

Since the stroke the son had taken over his dad's phone and was keen to tell me I couldn't see him any more. But Matthew was still well enough at that point to overrule him. And so, to the son's dismay I was allowed to visit, and Matthew even insisted I keep receiving my monthly £1,000, despite the changed landscape. I was pleased for him about that; he deserved some pleasure in his now much reduced life.

The housekeeper, a woman who I had always got on very well with, died unexpectedly not long after she'd called me. Matthew missed her. And I missed her. Even more so after having the pleasure of meeting the head carer.

I found myself in the horrible position of visiting Matthew while his new carers were there, and they knew full well who I was and what I did, and they didn't like it. With barely concealed disgust, they would shout, 'Knock, knock!' every time they wanted to enter his bedroom, as if expecting to find me up to my elbow in Matthew's arse. Instead, we'd be watching daytime TV. They refused to make eye contact with me as they whizzed round the room doing their job, unable to see that I was just doing mine. I wanted to tell them that I used to be a carer. That I wasn't some money-grabbing horny cunt – if I was, I wouldn't be spending three whole days in Matthew's house and paying for my own trains because his son had seized Matthew's bank cards. No. I was putting up with their shitty attitudes because I cared about him. Someone had to.

Alive and Kicking

I haven't felt the baby kick yet. My twenty-week scan looms, but until then I google constantly, wondering why I haven't felt it and when it'll happen. It's still early to feel movement, apparently, but

I still wonder – and worry – why I'm not feeling a thing. The knowledge that I have a little passenger onboard is making me look after myself more. Booze is gone. Decaf coffee only, if I have it at all. More water. More fruit and vegetables. More stretches. I hold my kitten in one hand and my belly in the other and, despite the nagging worries, I feel happier than I think I ever have.

The Madam and the Baron

While I'm waiting for some movement, I spend time trying to keep warm in my draughty house. And I think about warmer times. Lying on a sunlounger in the Caribbean while my client spent the afternoon shouting into the phone on a series of conference calls in between inhaling huge lines of coke. The sun was almost unbearably hot, and every thirty minutes or so I'd take a bikini-clad dip in our private pool to cool down, the star of my very own Jackie Collins novel.

A month earlier the client had called me. 'Would you like to go on a journey?' he'd asked.

Here we go, I thought. Another timewaster.

I was a baby domme, a bit wet behind the ears, so, largely thanks to how well spoken he was, I agreed to meet him in the downstairs restaurant at the Hilton Hotel in Green Park. Nowadays, a client like that wouldn't get past the first phone call; I would demand a deposit before we meet. But back then I was still a little trusting, still a bit of an idiot, excited by my burgeoning new business. Of course, you could argue that it all worked out. And it did. That time.

He had told me not to sit at the bar because the hotel staff were hot on evicting anyone they suspected of being a sex worker. And, of course, a woman alone at the bar has to be a hooker. Instead, he would wait for me at a table. He gave me his first name, but not his last. I dressed up in a demure dark purple dress, and caught a bus to the hotel.

As I entered the restaurant, my fear was that I was about to embarrass myself – I was thinking about those men who get off on escorts or dommes turning up at locations and then standing them up. There had not long ago been a man who was notorious amongst my network for sending women to the Sanderson Hotel in Fitzrovia and not turning up himself. A classic power play. Still, it is better to go to a hotel and find no man, than go to a hotel room and find five. But when I approached the restaurant hostess, she showed me quickly and quietly to the table where a man in his fifties was waiting for me. He had a kind face, I noticed immediately, smiley and welcoming. You can tell a lot about a man from his smile, and this was the smile of a man who enjoyed life.

I have always found most men attractive in some way. Most of them have at least one nice feature, whether it's their eyes, smile, a good voice or – the most attractive quality – a cracking personality. I always look for the positives. I think when I stop looking for the good bits, it will be time for me to pack my job in and retire.

He discreetly handed me a hefty envelope full of cash as soon as I introduced myself. 'We didn't discuss it, but I like to have it out of the way,' he said, without a shade of embarrassment.

I was stunned. This had never happened before. I liked it.

Many men force you to ask for the cash. It's another power play you get used to.

We shared a bottle and then went to his apartment. We talked about our journey into domination, about how long he had been visiting dommes and how I had got into the business – a sensational, sanitized version. Domestic violence, debt and a criminal record does not excite a sub.

We did a line of coke. I am a great believer in never becoming addicted to anything and I moderate everything. I like alcohol in moderation, I like gambling in small doses and, since I had begun mixing with the middle classes in London, I had discovered I liked a bit of cocaine. I haven't met many drinks I haven't liked but, having been schooled on Thunderbird and Diamond White, expensive bubbles are my favourite now. I don't feel the rush after the first couple of glasses, so I generally stop there. I can go to a casino with twenty pounds and, if I make more, great. If I lose the twenty, it's time to go home. And with cocaine I feel a buzz with the first two lines, so what's the point in continuing? Besides, I've seen the mess people can get into with drugs and alcohol.

We talked into the early hours. I was learning that not all sessions involve nakedness. Sometimes you really are just there to talk, to be good company. Of course, there are signs when the session is moving in a different direction. Someone's breathing changes, you can see their raised goose pimples, their posture becomes submissive, their pupils dilate as they become aroused. But this man wanted to hold off. He wanted to build trust. When a client is paying for your time, you go with it. If they just want to talk, then that's fine by me. I felt as though I was really getting to know him. So, it came as a shock when I saw an envelope on the table with another name – his real name this time – including his landed gentry title.

'Oh, you're a . . .'

'Yes,' he said. 'That isn't a problem, is it?'

I said it wasn't. But it felt as though a huge chasm had opened up between us. The problem wasn't that I was a domme; it was that I was working class. Maybe it was the way I had been brought up in a monarchy-worshipping household: to be subservient, to know my place, to understand that other people are born to better things. Maybe it was because, on a bigger scale, society indoctrinates the cap-doffing into us, from cradle to grave. Whatever the reason, I suddenly felt inferior. Julian Fellowes has got a lot to answer for. He writes about servants enjoying their place beneath the stairs, when the truth is much more complicated. Most working-class people feel as though they don't deserve more, and that's because we have been told for hundreds of years that our place is to work and that that work involves making the upper classes and the elite happier and wealthier. We are told that we will never have more, and that we should be grateful for the little we do have. In my opinion, Julian Fellowes is a bit of a tit.

Now the pious middle classes are doling out the same message to sex workers. Get back to cleaning our toilets and have some dignity, they shout from their comfortable lives in the shires. A middle-class woman patronizing a working-class woman when she believes you have left the sex-work trade and moved on to what she considers to be 'better things' will say, 'Good for you!' I hate the phrase, and those women. The last time it was said to me I had been spotted working as an usher in a theatre. A do-gooder, assuming I had left my sex-work job and had finally made good my life showing people to their seats, bounded over to congratulate me. I told her not to worry. I was still very much spanking men's bottoms for cash, Thursday through Saturday.

For a moment, in that lovely apartment, in his delightful company and with a glass of good fizz in my hand and exquisite coke up my nose, my mind spiralled into thinking about 'them' and 'us'. About how 'they' think the working classes are there to serve them and we think they ascended to their castles by sucking off kings of old. Why we can't be more like the French and guillotine the lot of 'em, I don't know.

But maybe because of my ambition to have more and to be more, this man and I had a few things in common. This was my hang-up, not the Baron's, I reasoned. My stumbling block. I regained my composure. Whatever test I'd been set, I passed. He asked me to go to the Caribbean with him. I had no work booked in for the following week, so I said yes.

Why not?

You Should be Paying Me!'

'You should be paying me!' is the most common and most irritating phrase a client can say to a sex worker. It's invariably used after the woman has given the performance of her life, reaching an impressively noisy and theatrical orgasm. The truth is I have often come with clients. My clit is so sensitive you just need to wave at it. But, orgasming, I wasn't thinking of the man between my legs. I was thinking of a guy from the gym, or Martin Clunes, or whoever happened to be my crush at the time. It was my pussy and my active imagination that deserved the credit, not the client. Yet that moment of leg-quivering ecstasy and peace with the world would often be interrupted by that irritating phrase. Looking up – or more often down – at their Cheshire Cat smile and the combover of hair on their otherwise shiny bald head would bring me back to the world with a thud.

At first the phrase didn't bother me. I'd laugh a little. Oh, you are funny. But when you've heard it a hundred times it starts to grate. Another hundred times and you feel the urge to plunge your stiletto into their neck. I understand that in this scenario – in which he's paying a woman to make him feel good – the man wants to feel all-powerful. And I understand that my job is all about pleasure, and he – arguably – is the source of that pleasure. Some of us do this job because we like sex and we like giving and/or receiving pleasure. But it is hard work and requires a spirit of steel to put up with some of the prats we meet.

Never Never Land

I always use the term 'submissive' or 'sub' when talking about my domination clients because that encompasses all of them. Some of mine don't like being known as 'slaves', they prefer 'client' or 'kinkster'. Others don't even like the term 'client' because it sounds too transactional. That word again. Some want to be called words which are too loaded or offensive to put into print. I don't like racial humiliation and in both domination sessions and brothel sessions I have been asked to call a person of colour a racial slur. It's another red line for me, but many sex workers have no problem with it; after all it's a fantasy and nothing like how the man wants to be spoken to in real life. Just as in real life men probably don't want a woman to say, before getting into bed, 'My, what a tiny todger you have! That won't even touch the sides!' Yet penis humiliation is often requested in session.

Fantasy fulfils a nagging urge and, in the way that a scratch that once itched might travel somewhere else, fantasies can change over time. I can only think of one client, who I have known for ten years, who always wants the exact same session. For most, their kinks and turn-ons change. Perhaps they want a little spanking to start with and then they increase their pain threshold over time. Or their humiliation threshold changes, so where once wearing a collar and lead was a hard limit, a few years down the line they are flashing their knickers and kissing your foot outside City Hall. Or perhaps it's a cuckolding fantasy which morphs into forced bi, where a man is 'forced' to suck a real cock or get shagged by a real cock. Of course, they aren't forced; it's all part of the fantasy to pretend that it is the most disgusting thing ever . . . as they greedily gobble away.

I have worked with dommes that offer forced bi, bringing in guys who may be other clients or male sex workers, and everyone's happy. Often the fantasy is never even acted on, it stays firmly in the imagination. Plenty of my subs want me to describe them being made to suck off another man, which I'm happy to do, but would never actually go through with it. And I don't offer it. One cock in the room is quite enough, thank you. We all have hard limits. That's one. And, for me, racial humiliation is another. Even though the men requesting it are often incredibly powerful and successful in their personal and professional lives, I don't want to do it, so I don't do it. Words have power and there are some words that I don't want to come out of my mouth. But defecating on any man who's up for it I have no problem with.

The Negotiator

As a sex worker you develop outstanding negotiation skills. We have to know how to deal with difficult clients, calmly talking them round or talking them down before a potentially tricky situation escalates. Even if you are lucky enough to be able to choose your clients, to cherry pick, you still need these negotiation skills in your toolkit along with the lube and the condoms as, rich or poor, young or old, working or upper class, most men will try it on in some way. We have to cope with boundary pushers who tell us, 'You don't know until you try it', no matter how many times they are told, politely but firmly, that we do not do a certain thing. We have to be able to gently persuade a client not to do it, before they attempt to jam their tongue into our mouths or their fingers in our cunts. A horny man is as predictable as Santa on Christmas night. They will keep persevering until they have emptied their sack. And, not unlike

Rudolph, we have to guide them so they empty it in the right place. Which, for me, is not on my face.

As Jeff Goldblum once said, 'The cock finds a way.' Or something along those lines.

Killer Heels

The easiest part of sex working is maintenance, but it's still fairly time-consuming. The client may have had a shower before gracing you with his presence, or he may not. But that is the most that's required of him. The working girl, however, has spent a good while prepping her body. Gym. Waxing. Hair. Make-up. Nails. While it's true that clients have a variety of tastes – women who are curvy, skinny, blonde, brunette, old, young, from different races and with different skin tones – the fact is they never pay a woman who looks like Waynetta Slob.

Independents need an attractive yet discreet outfit to visit a hotel, perhaps some flesh on show, but not too much. And killer heels, which cause so much pain that trainers and gel inserts are essential at the end of the session. I only started to introduce blindfolds because it meant I could slide my heels off mid-session and give my poor feet a break. Brothel work is much easier in that respect. Once you are in the flat, you are there until the end of the shift. There's no hobbling from hotel to hotel, trying to look sophisticated, like a woman who knows what she's doing, rather than someone who makes bad footwear choices.

Here I Glow

'Pregnancy is the happiest time of your life,' swoons one online mum, forcing me to close my laptop.

Is it? What is wrong with me? My whole body is unrecognizable now, like a blown-up Violet Beauregard, if she were a pale corpse with rosacea spots decorating her bloated cheeks. Where is my fucking glow? I look shit. I feel shit. My back aches. My feet haven't seen a pair of high heels in weeks. They also won't stop itching but I'm so huge I can't quite reach them to find some relief. My centre of gravity has shifted with the additional weight on my core, leaving me constantly unbalanced. I lumber around and breathe heavily, like a dying animal which some kind soul ought to put out of its misery. I notice the smug women's magazine articles don't write about all this.

Just when I need it most, the twenty-week scan finally comes around. I see my baby's face for the first time. The sonographer casually tells me I'm having a girl and my world lights up. She is beautiful. An angel.

Finally, I glow.

The Madam and the Baron, Continued

The Baron greeted me with genuine enthusiasm. 'Darling! Champagne? Cocktail? Cocaine?'

Unfortunately, the rather immediate after effects of a plate of bad airline food meant I wasn't feeling my best, so it took a momentous effort to paste a smile onto my pasty face and trill, 'Absolutely!' After all, he was paying good money for this. I was there to perform.

I loved my stay with the Baron. He would tell me stories about the people he had met and I would lap it up with oohs and aahs in all the right places. I was discovering that in this job you learn things you really shouldn't know about well-known people. Though you get rather quickly to a point where you're not always sure which client or which working girl has told you what story, or even when, I soon got to know which soap stars solicit services from sex workers, which world champion sportsman creates havoc among the girls in a knocking shop because he spends so much money they're literally falling over themselves to get to him, which presenter likes coprophilia over a glass table and which chef flies sex workers in from Eastern Europe.

I also learned rather quickly to keep quiet. As all good professionals do.

Some men aren't helping themselves, though. I learned that one man from the House of Lords was visiting a cheap Romanian brothel regularly and that they were recording everything he got up to. But as politicians throw out peerages for favours like a paedophile throws candy at kids, there is no shortage of rich nobs in the Lords and his story probably wouldn't make much of a headline.

Money, I was discovering, was very good at making problems go away. When, one afternoon, the Baron ran out of coke, we both strolled down to the jetty where a boat was waiting to supply him with more. It crossed my mind that Crewe had only just got Deliveroo.

One glorious evening we sat with a view of the sea, eating dinner. 'I can tell you're working class from the way you hold your knife,' he said.

I felt tempted to stab him with it. But then, when I tried holding it his way, I found that it was actually easier to cut my steak.

I spent my days living like Eliza Doolittle and my nights beating his buttocks.

The Sex Life of Miss Trunchbull

A few nosy clients have asked whether it's true that pregnancy increases the libido. I laugh it off, teasingly telling them that they will never know, before flogging them as usual. But, for me, the real answer is no, it fucking doesn't. I have tried sex a few times with Adam since being pregnant but each time I feel weird inside. Like my vagina is alien to me. It hurts, and when his cock is inside me it prods bits of me I didn't know I had – which is saying something, given how many times I've been prodded. Even adding generous amounts of lube doesn't seem to help. My orgasms are so weak now that I know I'd have more fun watching a YouTube video on how to put up a floating shelf. But I dig deep because I love him. I have had enough sexual escapades to last ten lifetimes, but I still can't help but worry that this is it for my sex life.

Just Doing My Job

During my first visit to Matthew after his first stroke I tried hard to make inane small talk with his carers, but I got nothing back. The silent treatment made me want to have it out with them in a proper screaming match. Where I'm from, this type of bitchiness would normally result in a headbutt, and I wasn't entirely sure how to handle it without resorting to violence of some sort. But as I was there to visit a dying friend, a long-standing client who had been good to me over many years, I was afraid that if I did lose it with them I wouldn't be allowed back. I managed to swallow my pride, smile and say nothing.

Thinking long and hard about it on the sleeper train home, I was left wondering why people are so appalling, why there's this constant need to shame others for leading different lives. What's wrong with different ways of doing things? Different perspectives? Different choices? And then there's the ridiculous value judgements we put on jobs. As I saw it, we were all just doing our jobs, taking care of different needs.

We know that in olden times – going right back to the 1400s – strong women who dared to deviate in any way from what was considered socially acceptable for their sex were labelled witches and burned at the stake or drowned in the lake. I think that sex workers are the new witches; the new strong women who don't live our lives according to the patriarchy's rules. Instead, we're making our own rules. Money gives women independence, the agency to quit, to say no, or maybe yes. The point is that we are able to make choices. I wonder sometimes if achieving that freedom is why the moralists hate us so much. We have defied what society tells us we should do, which boils down to getting trapped in a marriage with kids, completely dependent on a man. That, to me, amounts to domestic and sexual slavery, as no wife gets paid for the labour she does in the home. How many women can't leave because they rely on their partners to bring in the money? I love my partner but, if I wanted to, I could leave him. I have money in the bank; if I had stayed in a minimum-wage job I wouldn't have the option to leave ... particularly after the baby arrives. Do the moralists not want the secret out that there is an alternative life should you be strong enough to pursue it?

Sex workers are among the best businesswomen I know, successfully doing all our own marketing, website creation and maintenance, bookings, accounting and admin, as well as providing the actual service. Never losing a grip on our independence, holding firmly on to our agency. And what do we get for our efforts? We get arrested. Our bank accounts are closed. We endure constant hounding from feminist politicians, disrespect from doctors, suspicion from lawyers and either distaste or pity from every other professional occupation you can name, particularly the suit-wearing pen-pushers who mistakenly think they're better than us.

Come the revolution, I will happily wield an axe against the people I have met over the years who have tried to make me feel shit about my job. About myself. And for you, Mr Trader, the supposedly dutiful son, for you I will draw back the hood of my glorious black cape and look you square in the eye. And before

I lop off your head I'll remind you of your words, thrown at me as if my business is a joke and that, therefore, I am a joke. I will explain the work that has gone into building my brand. I will tell you that I take my business as seriously as you take your job and that I, quite probably, invest more into it.

Matthew's son, with his aggressive messages about me 'using' his father during a vulnerable time in his life, tried his very best to make me feel shit. I wanted to argue that I was doing more good in people's lives than he ever could – because what real purpose does a trader have? What does a trader actually do for anyone else but themselves? – but it was pointless to try. The reason his father had sought me out in the first place was because his family were not around for him. They didn't take him on holiday or do even the most mundane things with him, like invite him round for dinner or send over a Sainsbury's order to make sure he had a well-stocked fridge. I had done all those things. I had been on holidays with Matthew and had a lot of fun with him. He trusted me so much that he'd even given me keys to his London flat, to use as and when I liked when he wasn't there.

I was the family Matthew didn't have and desperately wanted. And that wasn't what his son would want to hear.

Baby Names

Adam suggests names for the baby and I veto most of them because they are either a) one of my hooker names or b) the names of women I can't stand. I have a theory about names. I think that a real name shapes a person's character, or lack of character. Adam says that it is called nominative determinism. Get him. He also says I am totally daft and that it isn't true. But think, for example, of all the Pauls you have ever known. Would you trust any of them? Another suspect name is Ben. Normally great looking, great in bed . . . but often massive piss artists with insecurity issues.

We keep thinking.

Cut Off. Cut Out

Back home, after what would turn out to be my final visit to Matthew, the tone of the son's texts changed, moving on from barely repressed disgust to outright aggression. It was difficult to respond civilly to such hostility, but I did my best for Matthew's sake. And then one day that was it. I was cut off, and cut out.

The head carer – a bitter-looking woman, I'd always thought – had form for getting rid of anything she saw as an inconvenience. She had tried to persuade Matthew to get rid of the housekeeper, who had then died so that problem had been solved. A few months earlier she had seen off Matthew's beloved dog, saying he had bitten her. He had been a gentle dog and I had never, in seven years, seen him display any kind of aggression. Perhaps, in this case, the dog was just a good judge of character. Now, to see me off, she'd told the family that I was asking for more money, that she had overheard a phone call where I was putting pressure on Matthew to give me more. The family believed it because they wanted to believe it, despite it making no sense, as I had been told on multiple occasions that the son now had complete control of Matthew's finances and bank cards. But they had the excuse they wanted.

I know the family will have lied to Matthew about why I don't visit him any more. I think about him often and wonder what he would make of the baby. It makes me sad to think that he will believe I've abandoned him. It makes me fume to think that that is his whimper of an end.

Ink and Incapability

I had a week of London sessions lined up in March 2020, just as Covid hit home. I normally only go to London for a few days a month, but that particular week I had a lot going on, which would add up to about £2,000 for a week's work. Pretty good. Then one man cancelled, and I had to cancel another because his age placed him in the vulnerable category and I wasn't prepared to take that risk. As I did so I realized that the pandemic was going to be a nightmare financially. Most of my clients are over sixty-five, and it was simply too risky to see them . . . however much they desperately wanted me to. I had to stop seeing clients, and then I couldn't even travel to see them anyway.

For the sake of my independence, I scrabbled around to bring in some cash. I went online. The smart thing would have been to set up an OnlyFans immediately, before everyone else got round to it. But, given my aversion to self-promotion, I couldn't bear the idea of having to give constant updates, uploading new pictures and videos every day captioned 'Look at my gorgeous food/feet/fanny!' So, I went the way that made no financial sense whatsoever – personalized stories for my kinksters. Sixty pounds for a thousand words. A bargain. I set up a Patreon account and pretty quickly the business started coming in through there or via specific requests to my email, such as 'Dear Mistress, I would like a story about a group of bare-breasted women kidnapping me and playing with my balls.' Once the money hit my account, off I went. It was a tiny fee compared with face-to-face sessions but I loved this work – so much so that I still do it now, despite being able to session again. I let my imagination run wild.

I also set tasks for my subs. Sixty pounds for five tasks. I have had my clients doing all manner of daft things for my shameless amusement and their unlikely pleasure. From going to drive-thrus wearing only panties and a buttplug, to singing 'Bohemian Rhapsody' down the phone to me, doing all the voices in different accents, to applying Deep Heat to their bollocks every time they pass a post box, to holding signs that say 'Task for Mistress', while wearing a maid's costume and trying to avoid dog walkers in a lonely wood.

Some dommes I know wonder why I bother. After all, sixty pounds is not very much money for quite a lot of effort. You're emailing all week, setting tasks that suit the sub, reading their reports and watching their videos to assess the finished product. But I get a lot out of it and, of course, in tough times any money is a help. I do it largely because it's all great fun and almost pays the bills. But I can do it partly because Adam has a good job, enough to support us comfortably, which I'm aware makes me very fortunate.

The bottom line is this: I refuse to be a kept woman.

It was eye opening to see which clients helped me out by sticking around during Covid and which ones simply disappeared, too wrapped up in their own lives to consider the effects of the pandemic on someone they used to buy a service from. I don't expect loyalty as such. How could I? Many of my clients are clearly not loyal even to their wives, but I have known most of them for at least five years and I like to think there is, if not loyalty, then at least some mutual respect in the relationship. And, in that time, I had been generous in my own way. I'm not one for clock-watching, and a perfect session for me would be two hours of whatever constitutes fun for them and me followed by a walk around a gallery, a theatre visit or a lovely meal. Many professionals would charge for their social time, but I don't. I always believed that by going about my business this way I would get good, regular clients as a result. I was mostly right.

Farewell to All That

I liked the Baron well enough, and the money he offered was alluring. When you have experienced having to scavenge people's small change from the floor of a nightclub in order to survive, and you then step into that life of wealth and privilege, you don't want to step back again. He liked me too, and was pleased – and pleasured – enough with how things had gone that a month later he asked me to return for part two. I got the sense that, for all his bravado, he was just lonely. I was filling more than just one hole in his life. But that second time he flew me out in economy; I should have heard the alarm bells.

'Darling! Champagne? Cocktail? Cocaine?' he greeted me again.

Again, I enjoyed it all. And again, in the days before Adam, I toyed with the idea of a life like that – of finding a man like the Baron, whose needs were actually very simple, and sticking by his side to ease my path in life. But I knew that that kind of existence would kill me. It wasn't just the idea of being someone's well-kept appendage that troubled me; it was also that I had done more coke in a week with the Baron than I had for the past few years. This was not a sustainable lifestyle. And so I left the sunshine and went back to my underground dungeon. The contrast couldn't have been starker. But it was my choice to make.

When the Baron asked me to join him in paradise once again, the dates he wanted from me clashed with other work I was doing. I turned him down.

He never asked again.

Not the Worst Way to Go

The day I forgot to buy Tom's cereal was the pivotal point in the relationship for both of us. He was so angry he grabbed me, pushed me down onto the bed and wrapped his hands around my throat. Being strangled is not, I discovered, the worst way to go. Sound fades away and your vision becomes grainy, but I don't remember any pain. Then, just as suddenly as he'd turned on me, he let go. I lay on the bed, frozen. The room slowly came back into focus, and I sucked panicked breath into my aching lungs. The uncertainty of not knowing what he might do next was almost worse than blacking out. But wrapped up in all my emotions, the confusing thoughts swirling around my foggy head, was a powerful sense of anger. I was absolutely seething. Strangely, inexplicably, I was angry that he hadn't been man enough to carry on. To see it through. Don't get halfway through killing me and leave me a shell of a woman, I thought. You fucking coward.

Inevitably and thankfully we split up soon after. We both knew that there was no coming back from that moment. It had to be the end. Five years of highs and then the crippling lows ended with a brief, tearful hug outside Marks and Spencer's.

Twenty-odd years on, and I still think about Tom. I should have had counselling after we broke up, but I thought I would be OK. That I would get over it. I was tough, wasn't I? But the truth is I haven't managed to process that abusive relationship even now. I still have dreams where I violently push him in front of a train or rip out his throat with my bare hands. I google him occasionally to see if he has died. I'm clearly still angry but, mostly, I'm resentful that he got to continue his life as if nothing had happened while I have been forever scarred. Tom's behaviour meant that, for years, I couldn't trust any man. That makes me a victim, and I hate being a victim.

Whenever I now read about a woman being killed by her partner, which is about seventy women every year in the UK, I always check to see if that partner is him. I am sure one day it will be his name in the news; I'll read it and I won't be surprised. But for now he is a GP. A family doctor. A man people look up to and respect while I, a sex worker, get spat on by society day in and day out. And I know that if I was killed, people would blame my work – that is, they would blame me, and spin the story to make it my fault, something that I was asking for. But the truth is that no man I have ever met in a session as a hooker or a domme is as dangerous as the good Doctor Tom.

Loyalty

For years I used to see Douglas one weekend a month at his main home in the country and occasionally at his city house in Chelsea. When we first met, he was grieving the loss of his partner of forty years. Some of my colleagues would have looked at this man and seen he was 'ripe for a plucking'. I saw a man who needed to heal, and I was glad that he had found me and not someone with fewer scruples.

In time, as we grew closer and the haunted look faded from his eyes, he asked to see me outside of my dungeon setting. He paid me £1,200 for the pleasure, although at first he'd objected to the transaction. 'Why should I pay you to stay in paradise?' he'd asked. Like Matthew, he'd disappear for a while to try his luck with the sugar babies, the young, skint women who put up with richer older men so that they can have the nicest possible life with the least possible effort. It's a dynamic in which the man gets to pretend he has a girlfriend and the woman gets to pretend she isn't a hooker. It isn't for everyone and, a few months later he'd be back, ready to agree to my terms. Although he didn't get physical intimacy with me, it hadn't taken Douglas long to realize that, quite simply, I was more genuine and more fun to be around. Plus, I was excellent with a flogger, which was what he craved most.

I mostly enjoyed his company, but he had a controlling streak that I loathed, and occasionally he made me so mad I wanted to flog him rather harder than was safe. Of course, a domme should never session when angry, so when he really made me cross I would resist the temptation by taking myself off to change my outfit or go for a soothing bath. 'Darling, I'll be right back.'

When it became impossible not to, I told Douglas about Adam.

'If you really loved him you wouldn't be here with me,' he said, a simple matter-of-fact statement that I received like a body blow.

I let him know that he had gone too far. I knew that Douglas could get ugly sometimes with his petulance, his controlling ways and pettiness, but until that point I hadn't realized that he was stupid as well. But some men are having such a fabulous time in our company with their nipple clamps pinching and their bottom stinging they forget that, although we may be enjoying it too, it is still a job to us. All that familiarity can breed contempt. We need that pesky thing called money, not just a good time.

It took a worldwide pandemic for me to see which of my clients were worth it – were worth having around, were worthy of me. Despite the discounted weekend sessions, despite the fact I would often stay an extra night or see him for lunch in London just because I wanted to – time I wouldn't charge for – when Covid forced us into our first lockdown, Douglas said he was stopping my monthly standing order, citing financial reasons. As a multimillionaire he must have been suffering terribly. In reality, he was pissed off because the last time we had spoken on the phone he had heard Adam, forced to work from home, chuntering around in the background. I think he had honestly thought that one day I would come to my senses and dump Adam and settle down with him instead.

'All this could be yours!' Douglas had once said to me as we boarded a plane to the Maldives.

Thanks, but no thanks. I was finding it hard to picture my life with a difficult seventy-year-old.

By comparison, I had clients I had only just met who insisted on paying me £200 a month for a phone call every week, and other clients putting money into my account without even asking me. How long I'd known them was inconsequential. But the unfortunate fact remains that most will drop you without a second thought when they can't get their cock up any more.

The Demon Drink

I hate my mother's drinking. I don't give a hoot what the neighbours and our distant relatives think of it, but I will never forget Adam's face when he saw her totally smashed for the first time.

Dad was ill and I couldn't trust her to look after him properly, so we decamped to their house to help out. I was on

Dad duty while Adam was looking after Mum. Having got Dad settled, I went back to the kitchen to find Mum propped up at the table, eyes glazed, shovelling in the food that Adam had cooked for her, presumably in an effort to sober her up. She told me Dad was fine – what was I fussing about? – and she knew him and I didn't. Then she stumbled off to bed.

Dad's condition deteriorated and in the middle of the night, while Mum was in an alcohol-induced sleep, we had to call an ambulance because his oxygen levels were so low and he was hallucinating, and the paramedics took him to hospital. We couldn't go with him because of Covid protocols, so Adam and I, exhausted, went to sleep in my childhood bedroom. The next morning there was a sheepish knock at my door. 'Where's your father?' asked Mum.

She knew she had gone too far, and for a while at least, wine was out and gin was in. That was the only compromise she could offer, which at least made her less nasty and critical. I prefer her when she drinks gin.

Help

I am finding it difficult to cope, something I find hard to admit. Things came to a head and I blew up today while Adam was on the phone to his mother.

There's a lot going on. We are moving soon, into a house that he has bought, and I am finding the move incredibly stressful. What's troubling me most is that I am not on the deeds or the mortgage as I already have a mortgage for a flat I'm trying to sell, so I am being asked to sign a document that says, should something happen to him, I will move out. Legally, I'm just a tenant. To resolve this we should get married, or at the very least he should make a will. I ask him, and then I nag him. He has always been terrified of commitment – a bit like Chandler from *Friends*, I would joke in our early days. But it isn't remotely funny now. Not unreasonably, I'm concerned about not only my security, but the baby's too. And then I give up. I know he's busy with work and with his bloody mother, but we are his family now: me and the little girl I am growing.

To add to my stress my body feels as though it's falling apart, and I am having to take more and more rests throughout the day in order to get less and less done. I'm only in the second trimester of my pregnancy, so I can't understand why my body hurts so much.

Meanwhile, Adam's mother is always on the phone, requesting his time. Can he do this for her? Can he do that for her? She knows about the pregnancy, but her crumbling mind only allows her to think about herself. She wants Adam's attention, and she will get it. Even if she has to call seventeen times on my birthday when she knows he has planned a day out for me. In complete contrast, my mum is making a point – although I'm not quite sure what point – of not answering the phone when I call. I want Mum to ask how I am. To ask how the baby is. It surprises me that I still need her.

When Adam's finally off the phone to his mother I rant about it all to him. Anger always used to give me strength and energy. It distracts. And, eventually, it soothes. But, as I get older I find that it just makes me tired. Adam finally seems to get how much I am struggling when I burst into tears mid-sentence, no longer able to get my words out. He's profoundly shocked, his confused face a picture, as I never cry. At least, never about my own problems.

It comes down to this, I realize: I am no good at asking for help. I have an act in which I'm tough and strong. I've always done it. I have my armour in place. I am invincible. But these last few months, as my belly grows, and the hustle to make money intensifies and the tiredness escalates, I have felt increasingly resentful that Adam hasn't noticed how much I am struggling. I've started to wonder if, as well as having no support from my family, I might be left to cope with the baby by myself too. A single mother. It's a hideous thought, as I'd always imagined that I would choose my baby's father carefully and well – having learned rather a lot about men over the years – and that he would be in their life for ever But men change; I saw it with Tom, and that has informed every relationship I have had since then. I have never completely trusted that the nice man I was with wouldn't suddenly turn into some kind of rabid beast. And so I have spent a great deal of my life being single. This pragmatic thinking about men was a major factor when I decided in my twenties and for much of my thirties that I didn't want a child.

Being with Adam is what changed my mind. After ten years he still makes me laugh. I still fancy him and I still love him. Until now, our relationship has made me think that fairy tales might sometimes come true. But now that I am pregnant his excuses and commitment issues have taken me by surprise. I have felt it's time to grow up now that I have a baby onboard and I can't understand why he doesn't feel the same. I'm now wondering whether we really will live happily ever after. And, romance aside, will he ever put me in his fucking will? My head spins as I try to work out what's going on.

Aftermath

Almost immediately after the breakup with Tom one of my colleagues from a shop I was working in offered me a place to stay. My landlord had been harassing me because he was worried I wouldn't be able to afford the rent on my own, and perhaps he was right. I had dropped out of university and even the extra job I'd picked up wouldn't be enough to cover the shortfall. In any case, I needed to get away from the terrible memories that were encased in each of those tiny rooms. The problem, of course, is that wherever you go you take your worst memories with you.

In my new place, I was sharing with two housemates, who were lovely and wholesome. Gentle and kind churchgoers, they did their best to cheer me up. But it was going to take more than that. Some scars run so deep through your body that they create chasms of misery which seem impossible to fill with something better, something positive.

About a month after the breakup, I held a kitchen knife to my stomach. The wave of not wanting to be here, not wanting to feel this emotionally wrecked had once again built up and come crashing down with an almighty force. I wanted out. Surely a knife would hurt less than pills? I had heard that when you are cut with a sharp enough knife you don't feel the pain immediately. It would also be quicker – I hadn't forgotten how long I'd waited for something to happen last time. So, I theorized like the pragmatist I was, if I cut quickly and deeply enough then perhaps it would be over fast.

Even as I analysed the destruction of my life I realized that I needed to talk to someone, that perhaps that was also an option. I needed someone who would understand. I went to a phone box nearby and called Tom's mother. Unlike everyone else, she had seen what he was really like and I knew he had confided in her about his temper. I had been with Tom for five years and for some of that time we had lived in her house. She had behaved more like a mother during that time than my own mum. I loved her and thought she loved me. She seemed like the obvious person to talk to, to calm me, to explain how a boy she had brought into the world and raised could do the things he had done to someone else's child.

I had no change on me so had to call the operator to place a reverse-charges call. I could hear Tom's mum being asked if she would accept the charges. She said no, she wouldn't. There was a bleeping in my ear and the line went dead. The sound of the dialling tone was replaced by the pounding of blood as my head began to roar.

I walked home blindly, stunned, and went straight to the kitchen and picked up the knife, pressed it to my belly . . . and then I heard my new housemates outside, chattering as they walked up the pathway to the front door. I put the knife down, put on a smile, put on the kettle. And like that, I got through another day.

It's Getting Better All the Time

After the tears, it's all change. Adam is now doing everything for me, for the house and for the baby. I get on with what I can, but I feel as though we've turned a corner and that a weight has been lifted. I'm not in this alone. This is a partnership. This is a family. I pack what remains of my belongings from the flat I'm attempting to sell, organize, sand and paint, erasing my presence, making way for someone else's life. I write my kinky stories to order and, from time to time, summon the strength for a phone chat and even the odd session.

The anger subsides. The tiredness is under control.

I am getting better at communicating my needs to Adam. If I want my swollen feet or my back rubbed I ask him, rather than resenting the fact that he hasn't offered and then stewing about it, perhaps for days. And guess what? He does it. He does as I ask, and he does it willingly. It turns out he's not a mind-reader, but he does love me.

The air has been cleared. The tension has gone.

More clearly than ever, I can see our future coming together.

Confusion

As I go through life, I spend a lot of time confused. Confused about how people behave, including my own partner and family. Confused by religion. Confused by how daytime TV is filled with tips about how to save money on our dental care, on our fuel, on our food, when what the presenters should be talking about is how to make the politicians accountable for all the price hiking that has taken place since Brexit and Covid. Confused that Alastair Campbell and Matt Hancock are allowed to reinvent themselves as celebrity personalities despite the blunders that cost people their lives. Confused that we can spend our evenings clapping for the NHS workers, but they still have to strike to get a pay rise. Confused that a council didn't go bankrupt sooner when they have nineteen members of staff raking in over £2.7 million between them, and yet none of the overpaid dafties realized that a bonus to men and not women might backfire. Confused by long words that I still struggle to say and certainly can't spell. Believe me, no one wants to sit and wait for me to get to the end of the word superfluous.

But what confuses me the most at the moment are the stories I keep reading in magazines about women who didn't know they were pregnant. Every week I read about a woman who has unexpectedly popped out a baby while she's on the bog. Perhaps her pregnancy symptoms were more subtle than mine and perhaps the baby has grown into her back so her tummy didn't get bigger. But don't these women ever look at their tits? My areolas are so huge they've swallowed up almost all of the white flesh of my breasts. There is no not noticing this development. And even if you somehow missed that physical development, there is no mistaking the long brown line – which I discover is called the linea nigra – that points, for many pregnant women, from your belly button, down towards your baby. My baby.

Fuck 'Em All

I didn't look at another man for six months after Tom and I broke up. I went to work, and I came home. The routine and monotony calmed me. Eat. Work. Sleep. Repeat. Eventually, one of my housemates began to encourage me to go clubbing with her, but for a long while I simply didn't want to rejoin the world. Until I suddenly did. A switch in my brain flipped. I wanted to be back out there.

Almost immediately I met a man who seemed to be the total opposite of Tom. Dark-haired and muscular, he was confident to the point of arrogance, and because he was so different to Tom I was able to think about a potential relationship with him very pragmatically. OK, then. Let it be him. We went on a couple of dates that went well enough before I decided to go back to his place.

He fucked me like an animal. No gentleness. No foreplay. I can't remember if I asked him to stop. Perhaps I did. Perhaps I didn't. Perhaps I urged him on so that it would be over quickly. It hurt so much that I bled for weeks afterwards. My inner thighs were bruised and tender. I do remember that that was when my mind snapped.

All men were like this, I realized. All men hurt women. Fuck them all, I thought. And so I began to. I now sought danger. I became promiscuous, taking chance after chance with strangers in nightclubs, going home with them without a second thought, without letting anyone know where I was. Sometimes I'd take them back to my room, tiptoeing into the house with the two lovely church girls whose morals I didn't want to offend already sound asleep. I was no longer just a kissing slut, but a full-on shagging slut. It was another game. The next level up. This time, it was a dangerous one, where it could all easily come crashing down.

Who cared, I thought? I certainly didn't.

Hooking

Having been brought up going to church every week and hearing about Hell from men in pulpits, thoughtless promiscuity was the ultimate way for me to self-harm. I was an angry, confused, uninhibited, couldn't care-less, headcase. How does a woman go from using men's dicks to self-harm to making sex completely transactional? How does she make the step from shagging men picked up with reckless abandon in a nightclub to accepting payment for sex?

I fully believed that what I was doing by having promiscuous sex was wrong. By the letter of Christianity almost everything feels wrong, of course, apart from, traditionally, criticizing other people, bloody crusades and fiddling with innocent little kids. It felt wrong because I thought – no, I believed – my soul would be forever stained. For me, that made sex work the ultimate self-sabotage.

It's a reason for turning to sex work that will make the happy sex workers out there absolutely furious, adding fuel to the radical feminist narrative that we are all damaged, lost souls. While the messed-up childhood storyline doesn't play out for me, I can't deny that I would never have initially gone into sex work if I wasn't hurting so much. The pain was brutal and the promiscuity was out of control, a combination which led me to call a knocking shop and ask for a job. It was as easy as that.

I had always been interested in sex work. In my hometown, the street sex workers would hang around just one street – and indeed they do now – and when I was a teenager my friends would laugh at them and call them 'dirty prossies', but I was less quick to abuse these women. I always thought being paid for sex made more sense than giving it away to a man who felt entitled to it just because he had bought you a pint of cider. I'd also see the glamorous women who sold sex for a living; the women portrayed on television and in film who would do their business at the best hotels, wear the best clothes and be head to toe in diamonds. The sex was essentially the same, of course, but everything in their world smelled of perfume and roses rather than car fumes and sweat. That seemed far more appealing.

Of course, I wasn't Julia Roberts and this wasn't *Pretty Woman*. I went along to the house for an interview and it wasn't quite as I imagined. But the madam was a glamorous blonde with a convertible parked outside. At thirty-six, she was an age I thought ancient. She sat me down on an old sofa that had seen better days and, I imagined, a fair amount of action, and talked to me frankly and fairly. I confessed to her this was all new to me and she gave me some advice as I side-eyed the muted big screen of graphic porn playing opposite us. She told me that a standard service was covered sex and covered oral – covered, I gathered, meaning the use of condoms – but the main thing was to give the men a good time while not letting them get away with any shit. 'But smile as you scold them, dear!' she said. 'They are all naughty schoolboys at heart.'

I remember I liked her.

She worked there too, so my first experience of a madam was a woman who understood the job because she did the job. Since then, of course, I have met madams who wouldn't dream of doing the actual work, but who love the money that their women make for them. I despise these women even more than I do the male pimps. Nobody should make money from this industry unless they know how it feels to be alone in a room with a man and charge money for access to your body. As hookers we face what we do head on and have to reconcile with it in some way. We deal with the headfuck while the bosses take our money. Bosses should know how that feels. How we feel. I would say the same should be the case in any industry. How can a boss ever be fair to their workforce, and understand their needs and wants, unless they have done the work themselves? But the hatred I have developed for female pimps stems from the fact that, having never got their hands dirty, they think they are better than us, yet are happy to make good money off our backs. At least male pimps don't have the option of working; women almost never pay for sex because we don't need to.

I went back for my first shift a few days later.

Crossed Lines

Mum calls me. It has been a while. But it's yet another conversation that ends with us screaming at each other. The entire back and forth lasts approximately twenty seconds. It goes like this.

Mum: How are you? How's the pregnancy? Everything OK? Have you seen *Line of Duty*?

Me: No, not this series. I'll watch it soon.

Mum: Well, let me just tell you this . . .

Me: Mum, stop, no. I don't want to know. I haven't watched it yet.

Mum: But I'm telling you something your father said about the . . .

Me: Mum, can you drop it, please?

Mum (to my dad, voice raised): You talk to your daughter. She's being unreasonable and I can't cope with this.

Afterwards, when Dad has calmed me down a bit, Mum comes back on the phone and asks me, again, how I am. The truth is the question now has a very different answer to when I first picked up the phone, when I was fine. I'm now stressed and angry. In fact, I'm so fuming that I can't even tell if my mum is drunk or if she is just being herself – a little bit leery, a little bit thoughtless. Too honest for my own good, perhaps, I tell her that, actually, I was relaxed and having a really nice day, but now I feel wound up because she does not – no, will not – listen to me. Then I put the phone down.

Adam, having wandered into the room at the sound of my raised voice, tells me I shouldn't get so upset because it isn't good for the baby. Sometimes I put Mum on speaker so that he can hear what she's saying; sometimes I just need him to tell me that I'm not the one who's mad. That it's her, not me. I do get cross too quickly, I know this. I am not shy about calling a cunt a cunt. I know this too. I just wish that Mum was not always so stubborn. So insensitive. So self-involved. So pissed.

And I know that it has to be me who apologizes. This time, too, like every other time, I will have to offer the olive branch. But I also know that the same thing will happen again in a couple of days, when she calls me or I call her, and we'll be back where we started. It's almost better when she's sulking with me and doesn't talk to me for months. Then I can call at night after ten, when I know that she will be passed out on her bed and I can talk to my dad without her taking the phone from him.

Despite all this, despite the tension between us, my mum wants to be with me in the delivery room. Can you fucking imagine?

New Girl

My first customer at the brothel was a lovely-looking man, a professional football player. I gave him a blowjob. It was easy. On my way home that night I had £150 in my pocket, and I felt good. Better than I'd ever done after a shift in a bar or a day on my feet in a shop.

The set-up was that there were two women working each day and one maid who answered the door. The maid in a brothel is almost always a retired sex worker, and the maid who worked on my days used to work on the streets, so she took no shit from any of the men, even though she was now in her seventies.

A man would come through the front door and meet the maid; he'd meet me and whoever was also working at the time.

I often got chosen and would be asked to give them a massage, which is universal brothel language for shag. Then away we would go to the room. I soon got the hang of it. I was new and I was young, and the other girls didn't like me as I quickly took the bulk of the business. One colleague in particular clearly despised me and there was nothing I could do about it, no amount of smiling, conversation starters or offering cups of tea. We saw eye to eye only once, when a man walked in and said he wanted a woman with no scars, no cellulite, no body hair: a list of absurd demands that seemed endless. The hard maid was, for once, silenced and the three of us could only stand side by side in solidarity, staring at the punter's hideous concave frame and spindly legs, the nest of unnaturally black thinning hair which sat uncomfortably on his head, and the misshapen beak that perched in front of beady eyes. We took it all in. It sounded as though he expected a supermodel from the Savoy, not a sex worker from Stockport who couldn't be bothered to shave her arse.

'You can 'ave him,' the other hooker said.

'No, you can have 'im. I've got Geoff at two,' I spat back.

'He won't last long.' She jerked her head in the man's direction. 'Done in five, seven maximum.'

'Oh, for fuck's sake.' To her, with a roll of my eyes.

'Come on, then.' To him, with a disappointed sigh.

The now not so confident man trailed after me.

She was right.

Done in five.

The Men You Remember

There were a few customers that I grew surprisingly fond of. One was another sportsman and, my God, he was fit in every sense of the word. People are always surprised when we say that some of our clients are beautiful, fit and young. The good-looking guys want an uncomplicated shag as much as Derek the drycleaner. Those sessions would always end in the same way. With a knock at the door.

'You've gone over,' the maid would yell. 'Finish him, cos you've got Brian waitin' for you.'

Then there was the man who I never have and never will forget. He told me he was an archaeologist. His fantasy was that I would come to his door with a problem with my car. He would invite me in and make me a nice cup of tea, and I would suddenly realize I fancied him something rotten and then we would have gentle sex. He was a nice-looking older bachelor with a devotion to his work. If he was lonely, I thought, what chance did the spindly-legged fucker with the bad attitude have?

Sacked

I got sacked a few months in. I gave my telephone number to a client so he could check with me when I was working. I was delighted that he wanted only me. But taking phone numbers was a sackable offence and I was overheard by one of the other women. It was quickly fed back to the madam and that was that.

A week later I got a phone call from the madam.

'Emma, you had to go,' she told me kindly. 'All my clients were seeing you instead of me. I've got you another job, though. An hour on the train.'

So off I went to Leeds.

Eve's Adventures in Whoreland

Back in the long ago days when 100 per cent mortgages were available, and all you needed to qualify was six months of payslips, my full-time job in retail had allowed me to buy a house – something to do up and make my own. As soon as I got the keys I quit the retail job. I told my manager why. I told her, in a completely matter-of-fact way, that I enjoyed whoring more than working in retail, that there was much more money on offer, and that I was done being nice to customers who treated me and the other staff like shit. She found it difficult to argue with that logic.

My sex work at the brothel in Leeds gave me far more time in the day to call my own. Far greater agency. And, surprisingly, a greater sense of self-worth. Slowly, my spirit began to return. I renovated the house while I worked full time in the brothel. By full time I mean I worked two days a week. I liked it there, but I didn't need to work more, and so I didn't.

While the first brothel had been a two-bedroomed house, this was a much bigger establishment, a commercial building on a busy road. From the entrance hallway there was an open area into a bar that led to a living room of sorts, where the women would gather and sit and watch TV or read or chat between clients. The stairs beyond led up to four themed bedrooms. I could never understand why our VIP room was the more expensive room. Clients paid an extra ten quid so they could shag on a waterbed which, if you have ever tried it, you will know is not as much fun as it sounds. The wrong kind of bouncing mid-thrust leads to as much laughter as if Ricky Gervais was in the room with you too.

I still remember most of the other women's names even now. As with any job, these are your colleagues. If you're in with a good crowd you become friendly, you start spending time together outside of work. Much as I was enjoying the work, the friendship the women offered was a big thing for me too. I'd become isolated during my relationship with Tom and it was good to feel a part of the world again. Female friendships often outlast romantic relationships and there is far less bullshit involved. No games. Particularly not with hookers. If they like you, you know it. If they don't like you, you really fucking know it. We're all straight talkers.

One of the women I was now working with used to be a cleaner but was sick of not seeing her baby during the sixty-hour week she had to take on in order to make enough money to live, so she'd made the jump to hooking. Let's call her Rose. Rose was so kind, I simply adored her. When a new woman was crying at work one day because her gran had died and she couldn't afford the flight to go to the funeral, without a fuss, Rose just gave her the money she had earned that day and told her to pay her back whenever. Maybe we should have seen it coming, but the crying woman took off and never came back.

I asked Rose if she regretted giving it away. She said no, that she wanted to believe the best in people and would keep on believing the best, even against the odds.

We should all be a little bit more like Rose.

The brothel boss was a man who had a very pretty younger wife. I innocently asked them where they had met, and the others exploded with laughter. I walked straight into that one. Another day I found some white powder loose on the toilet cistern and reported back to the other girls that the cleaner had done a poor job and had left something behind – some kind of cleaning agent that hadn't been rubbed in properly, or hadn't dissolved. Again, they laughed at me. I was twenty-one and, despite everything I'd been through, still so innocent in some ways.

I would read Jane Austen novels between clients. The other women thought I was posh for that, but good old Jane got me quite a bit of business as some men want a woman who they believe is educated and therefore more refined. I like to think I fooled 'em!

I saw a lot of life there, and I soaked it all up.

I remember one client moaning to me about his overweight wife, and although it brought back horrible memories of Tom body-shaming me, I diplomatically ignored his complaining until it transpired that she wasn't fat, she was pregnant. Then I gave him such a mouthful – and not the kind he was paying for. After that, he'd glare at me whenever he saw me in the waiting room and make a point of asking for someone else. I wouldn't have seen him again anyway. It might not be the worst thing a man can say, but it wasn't far off it.

Another client told me that he had a woman in Manchester who he paid £500 a week on a retainer and he wanted to replace her. Was I interested? His only stipulation was that I let all my body hair grow. All of it, everywhere. I didn't particularly mind the body hair. I couldn't be bothered to shave at the best of times. But to see just one man, like a caged trophy wife? Not on your nelly. Besides, the guy gave off a dangerous vibe. He was the sort of man who makes the hairs on the back of your neck stand up, but you can't quite put your finger on why. It isn't anything they've said. And it usually isn't how they're dressed either. They could be in joggers or in a sharp suit. The only external clue is in their eyes. Cold, emotionless eyes. You have to watch out for those ones.

The Red Pill

It dawned on me that, despite how well everything was going and how much better about myself I was feeling, for the first time in my life I was involved in criminality. Previously – very simplistically and naively, I admit – I had always thought police equalled good and criminals equalled bad, a completely binary take on the world. Now, it finally occurred to me that life, morality, and right and wrong weren't that simple. Rather than a clear divide, I could see a blurred line. Instead of black and white, I was discovering the world was a tangled mass of grey. And the more I thought about where I was and what I was doing, the more I realized it wasn't right for me. So, after a year, I stopped working in the Leeds brothel. I knew that although there was much about it I'd enjoyed, my head simply wasn't right. I wasn't sure this was what I should be doing, and I was no longer sure why I was doing it. So much about life was unclear and hazy, but it was crystal clear to me that no woman should ever go into the sex industry because a man has done her wrong.

I got a job in a profiteroles factory filling a different type of hole.

I'd stand on a line, turning profiteroles, then on another, opening eclairs. That was the job. It could not have been simpler. It could not have been more boring. And the hours were brutal. Twelve-hour shifts, four days on, four days off. I took all the overtime offered, so I worked my days off too and turned my twelve-hour shifts into eighteen-hour shifts. But it still wasn't enough money. At the brothel I could make that in less than an hour . . . without getting varicose veins. Food for thought. And as I turned and opened, turned and opened, I couldn't get the simple maths of it all out of my head. I was still renovating the house. I had a bill that was due for the double glazing, and another looming for the plastering, and I still had to eat and pay the mortgage.

One morning, with an eighteen-hour shift ahead of me, I couldn't get out of bed. It wasn't depression. I knew how that felt, and this was something else. I was just so exhausted that I couldn't stand up. I quit the factory and slept for a week. Then I called the brothel. They welcomed me back with open arms.

Healthy Body, Healthy Mind

Six months later, when the house was finished and on the market, set up to give me a nice return, I took a much-needed holiday with a friend to Devon. We walked into a pub right next to the shimmering turquoise sea and behind the bar was the most beautiful man.

'I'm moving here,' I said to my friend.

I wasn't joking. At the end of our holiday I went back up north with ideas brewing. I jotted down my plan in one of the notebooks I always had ready in my handbag, next to whichever book I was reading at the time.

At the brothel the women roared with laughter as they told me what I'd missed. A new punter had pulled up at the brothel one day, only to see his wife's car parked outside. 'He was pretty mad that his old lady was a working girl . . . but she was just as mad that he was wasting money on us! They had a massive slanging match in the car park. Boss told 'em both to sling their hook as it wasn't good for business.'

It was the kind of story that made working there a lot of fun, but I'd made my decision. I worked a couple of shifts while I said my goodbyes. I would miss the women and the place, in its own way. But I had my plan and wouldn't be deterred. I got organized, put all my stuff into storage, gave clear instructions to my estate agents and solicitors and six weeks later I was living by the sea.

I got a job at a little shop that sold pearls from oysters, which I would place in a ring or necklace setting and flog to tourists. I loved it, the beauty of the place stunned me every day, whatever the weather, and the job felt calming. I'd never known anything like it. There was so little to think about, very little to do, and absolutely no stress. When there were no customers I read Austen or one of the Brontës behind the counter and wrote poetry in a notebook, dark verse about my life and my feelings, but I felt as though the words and rhythms were healing me as they poured out. When my thoughts lingered on being told to lose weight, being strangled, or being raped, I would do my best to push the thoughts down. I went for long walks and gradually felt myself knitting back together, all the kinks and hurt being smoothed out and a new lifeform emerging.

I was good at selling. No surprises there. Each day I'd smash our target, shut up shop with a sense of satisfaction and go home to the hostel to drink with my new friends. I had of course pulled the beautiful man but even that encounter, a kiss and a grope, had been hollow somehow. I had had enough of hard cocks and neediness. I wanted to concentrate on getting my mind and body healthier. And that worked, for a while.

But one night at the bar, I saw a man who looked like Joseph Fiennes. A red rag to a bull. I started to chat to him and after a while his friend, a South African with long black hair, joined us. He was even better looking, which you'd hardly have thought possible. I hadn't had sex since I'd finished working at the brothel and about six months had passed down at the coast. Out of the blue I realized I was horny, so I simply asked them where we should go.

It was as easy as that.

It was the most grown-up sexual encounter I had ever had. From the moment I suggested it to the act itself, I was leading the dance. The two men, despite being older, were nervous and I orchestrated everything like a skilful conductor; naturally and just going with the flow. I started to undress first and they followed my lead, taking their clothes off too. As they weren't gay they were a little nervous about there being another cock in the bed, and a hard one at that, but as the woman it is quite easy to position yourself so that that becomes unimportant. If their focus is on me, then it's not on each other. The South African went down on me as the other kissed me. I fucked both of them in turn. After we were all satisfied, they walked me home to the hostel in the chilly predawn hours. Fiennes lent me his hoodie, gently wrapping it around my shoulders. We parted company like old friends.

If you are going to fall off the wagon, that is the way to do it.

I Want Money

As my pregnancy progresses I realize I only have a few months left to session with my subs and after that I don't know when I will earn any cash again. I've always relied on my body – one way or another – to make money and it scares me to think that it now has other things to do. Earning money is firmly attached to my sense of self-worth. I have been totally indoctrinated by the capitalist system since I started earning at thirteen and am a proper little working bee who never calls in sick, and who never quits until they have another job lined up. Without the ability to earn I don't know how I will feel. How will I not go to work every day? How will I be a housebound mum whose only purpose is to love a tiny human? I don't know if I am up to the task and I certainly don't know if I can accept all the bills being paid by Adam.

I know that I will have to lean on him for cash and that makes me feel frighteningly vulnerable. Covid wiped away some of my savings and I know that another year or two off work, while the baby becomes a more robust toddler, will take the rest of it. I own property and once I manage to sell my now empty flat I will be able to relax a little. The problem is that nobody wants it. It comes with too many problems. The aroma of dog shit and crack in the hallway. Freeholders who refuse to do fire alarm checks or any kind of maintenance. And drugged-up men sitting in the communal corridor who alternate between singing raucously and punching holes in the walls. I can see why it's still stuck on the market. To help move things along I sit at my screen, diligently educating myself about how to manage bad freeholders and bad landlords. I am a woman with too much time on her hands and, at the same time, there are not enough hours in the day to get ready for this baby.

Despite my worries, my blood pressure is stable, which I know because I check it every time I feel my cheek go numb, an issue which the doctors say is caused by stress. Being a geriatric mother means there are a lot of check-ups and scans, and I'm grateful for them even if all they reveal is what I already know. Of course I'm stressed. Every time my midwife listens for my baby's heartbeat I hold my breath, but when I hear it and know my amazing baby is OK the stress recedes. And I know she's alive because she is always kicking me, especially when I'm dealing with the bureaucratic arseholes of the property world. It's like she is angry for me. Or perhaps she is angry *like* me, which is a less appealing idea.

It's OK, baby, I say to her. Mummy will be done with her nervous breakdown before you come along. I'll have money in the bank soon and then I'll be able to relax and enjoy being your mum. I can't wait to be your mum.

Living the Fucking Dream

Once my head and heart felt at least partially healed down in Devon, the old dream of acting returned. Why not? I thought. Never one to procrastinate, I applied for a three-year course at drama school. I could see from the outset that cash was going to be a problem. I had £10,000 in the bank from the house sale, but when I looked at the cost of getting to auditions and back (wherever they happened to be), plus the course fees and the cost of living (and I was once again prepared to move), I knew that even with as much part-time work as I could handle it would still be a struggle.

I carried on, regardless. I auditioned for four drama schools and got into two by presenting one classical and one modern monologue. My choice, in some mythical ideal world, would have been the school that boasted Oscar-winners among its graduates, but it was overseas and I finally had to admit that I couldn't afford to put myself through the first year, let alone the next two. That left me with one that was four hours away. So I packed up my belongings and moved once again.

I don't have many regrets in life. I find them pointless; all that looking back and hand-wringing about what might have been. My view is that everything you do brings you to a moment, the here and now, and if you changed just one thing about your pathway you wouldn't have the people in your life that you love. And I so love my partner and my baby. But I do regret that drama school. That fucking school. There, for the first time in my life, I became aware not only of Britain's class system but also of what it meant for an ambitious working-class girl from the Midlands.

I met real snobs for the first time. 'You're from *Birmingham*?' they'd chuckle, saying the word as though it was hard to push out of their sneering lips. 'Well, you would have had to move away from there sooner or later, wouldn't you? Well done.' As though I had escaped from Hell itself.

Most of the other students owned their flats or their rented accommodation was paid for by a parent. None of them were working three nights a week in a nightclub and all weekend in a cafe, juggling their studies, struggling to have enough money, struggling to find time to sleep. They would moan about their tiny overdrafts as I lurched from loan to loan. The money I had made from my house sale disappeared in the first year. And perhaps I could have dealt with the financial struggle if I was doing well in class, but with each assessment, performing in front of the people who congratulated me on leaving my home town, I got the lowest grade. Every single time.

It didn't help that the school objected to my regional accent. They demanded I speak with received pronunciation, like the well-educated southerner I wasn't, for almost every part I took on, other than when I had a role as a prostitute. Then – surprise, surprise – I was encouraged to use my natural tongue. For that role, they even told me to play up my own accent.

I got a reputation for speaking my mind, which certainly didn't improve my marks or popularity, and which is how my classmates came to give me a nickname: ASBO. The anti-social behaviour order had recently been introduced by the government to combat behaviours like intimidation, and being threatening in any way. Well, I can't deny I was pretty outspoken and there was that time I grabbed another student by the neck and threw him against a wall after he felt me up. Even so. The nickname certainly didn't help to build relationships. I was tired all the time, I was pissed off with the privileged people around me. But the fact remained that despite the poor grades I was stupidly happy when I was on stage. So I ploughed on.

I was in my element in my classes. I loved movement, stage combat and voice lessons. I loved learning lines. I loved it all. All the shit about class and money fell away when I was on stage; all the petty rivalries and niggles faded. The feeling that the other actors had your back and you had theirs trumped everything else. The knowledge that when things inevitably went wrong we would cover for each other made me feel alive. Theatre should be alive and in the moment. It should propel the audience away from their reality and into the same magical world the actors are inhabiting. It was our job up there on stage to make the audience feel. I loved making people laugh and, even better, making them cry. I loved when the whole audience was silent, and all of their attention was focused on the stage. It was a beautiful sensation which made me feel truly joyful.

My destiny was this, I told myself. Not working in a minimum-wage job or blowing accountants. This was it.

Comedy Domme

Domination is like mini theatre, and perhaps that's why I was eventually drawn to it. You have your stage and set, a glamorous costume, a set time for your role-play and of course a captive audience hoping for an experience that takes them completely out of themselves. In the allotted time, you want to blow the sub's mind so that they remember you and come back for more – the equivalent of a standing ovation. With me, they often do come back, and I'm proud of that. But not always for the right reasons. I was a klutz on stage and I am a klutz in the dungeon. I have electrocuted my own nipples and set fire to my laptop. I have bent down for water sports and accidentally farted on a man's face and face planted on the floor while putting on a strap-on. It's not easy to recover from a fall and be sexy again. But I'm very good indeed at getting up, dusting myself off and getting on with it.

The Nursery

I want to paint the ceiling, in what will be our daughter's room, pink. A simple enough task if it wasn't for the fact that it's an Artex ceiling left over from an eighties design fad. But I have an idea mapped out in my mind of how the whole room will be and I won't be deterred, either by a bit of texture or by Adam pointing out that it will take ages and that I am pregnant. I laugh. I know, I say, looking down at my growing belly. And I tell him how the rest of our daughter's room will look: a moon in one corner that glows in the dark and, beneath that, a constellation of stars that depict her star sign. Then, animal wallpaper on all the rest of the walls. I gesture around the space with animated hands, a spark in my eyes. He leaves me to it after reminding me that the last time I wallpapered a room I hung the trees upside down thinking they were cascading ferns.

The No Showcase

The drama school had a tiny intake, and the idea – its USP – was that there would be less competition and more chances to be seen by agents. Three chances, to be precise. The Spotlight showcase, which is intended to find the most talented acting graduates from each school and connect them with agents, the Sam Wanamaker Festival at the Globe and the school's own showcase. In the end, I got just one chance: the school show-case, the grand end-of-year ta-dah. Unfortunately, no agents showed up to that. The date clashed with a much larger, more impressive school's showcase and all the agents pitched up there instead. There was no chance for me to shine. Three years of graft and debt for nothing. I spiralled.

How the hell was I going to pay all the bank loans back

without an agent, without a job? I'd always thought working hard would see me through – that absurd idea beloved of the working classes that you'll be rewarded for your effort. I had thought, believed, that my tenacity would get me where I wanted to be in the end. But I had overestimated myself and the school's ability to do right by its working-class students. I learned that I was the only one from my year who was never seen by an agent. One boy got the Globe. One boy got Spotlight. The other girl got them both. At the end of term I refused to pay my final terms fees. What, exactly, was I paying for? I fired off a legal letter as well and, if I'd had money, I would have sued the bastards. Refusing to pay was a small triumph, but my optimism about the future began to wane and the anger I had worked so hard to suppress began to rise.

It wasn't when I got throttled. Or when I became a sex worker. It was right there in the heart of London, at the school's showcase at the Soho Theatre that I began to feel real rage, a knot of resentment forming in my gut. I knew deep down that, whatever I tried next, I would end up having to go back to a brothel. I had worked so hard through the three years of drama school, not only at my acting but in all my two-bit jobs, and I felt like it had all been for nothing. I didn't want to go back to sucking cocks. I didn't want to do that. I didn't want to go back. Not because it was so terrible, but because my journey into prostitution was tied up with being a victim. It was full of memories of Tom and his hands around my throat and being raped as I slept. And now it felt as though I was a victim again, but a victim of poverty this time rather than domestic violence. I like my life when it seems that I am going somewhere, moving forwards, making progress. But this sense of inevitability about what was going to happen next was a cloud not just hanging over me but fully enveloping me. I was back where I'd been four years ago, before I had moved to Devon and found hope again.

I didn't completely understand the anger at the time. I focused on the failings of the drama school. But of course the bigger problem was how I was seen by others in the world, a middle-class world that simply wouldn't yield for me.

My mother had always said that my face didn't fit, and now I knew what she meant.

The Road to Nowhere

I don't have much call for a résumé these days. If I were to produce one it would be very busy, as long as *Les Misérables*, and more depressing. More quantity than quality. But when my letters and email applications to theatre companies finally paid off and I got my first acting job a few months after leaving drama school it eclipsed anything else I'd ever achieved. A paid acting job. I couldn't have been more thrilled if I had won an Olivier. So what if I was a late replacement for an ill performer and the company was really desperate? I was on my way! I had three days to learn a pantomime that had three performers and was going to tour factories and schools around the country. We all had backstage roles too and mine was to navigate as one of the other actors drove, so, armed with maps and a script I was still learning, off we went.

As I am a trained classical actress, darling, and not a singer, three shows a day six days a week eventually took my voice and I was reduced to croaking my way through each performance, which couldn't have been much fun for the audience. The other actress was lovely and we enjoyed our scenes together, apart from the one time we realized we had left the lamp in the car. Tricky to perform *Aladdin* without that. But even when we felt we had done well, the other actor felt the need to give us long notes on the drive home. Actors. One in three is bound to be a prick. Then it was on to the next job. But without an agent to represent me, I launched myself into student films and profit-share theatre productions, which always means no money. I took a profit-share Shakespeare production next, which was much more my bag. Sometimes we would even have more than five people in the audience. Sometimes.

I then got a theatre-in-education job, which I loved. We would act out scenes from Shakespeare and get the kids to talk about what they'd seen, and then they'd perform the scenes themselves. Many schools were in deprived areas of the country and it was great to introduce Shakespeare to students who might not otherwise have any idea what the fuss is all about. The kids were often hostile at first but by the end they were almost always enthusiastic. We had them playing out the comedy and the tragedy in their natural tongue, making the words accessible to them for the first time. It's no wonder so many children feel disconnected if they think that Shakespeare is 'posh' theatre and not for the likes of them. It felt like the most incredible achievement to be able to engage them; it's work I remain very proud of.

But I still had the urge to act in the theatre, to be on stage as part of a company bringing a story to life. Entertaining and thrilling an audience. Making them think. Weep. Laugh. I kept writing to theatre companies in the hope that something would happen for me. I was in my late twenties and I didn't yet know – at least not for sure, though it was beginning to dawn on me – that the theatre world was a private members' club that I would never gain access to.

I found myself among the type of arseholes who were happy to tell me what they thought of me and the working classes. Who made it very clear that I wasn't like them; I was beneath them. Who are keen to preserve social hierarchies and want us to feel our so-called inferiority every single day. And the more time I spent with these people, the more I wondered what I really wanted from my life. I was no longer completely sure that it was a creative life in theatre, if this was the company I'd be forced to keep. My love of theatre itself wasn't dissipating; it was still there, a hungry sensation in my gut that was close to the feeling you have when you really, really like someone. Butterflies, almost. I would read plays and *want* the parts so badly it was visceral. I could taste the words of the characters. I could feel what they felt. But how could I navigate the theatre world without mixing with those people who left a bad taste in my mouth and made me feel like shit?

Even as I was struggling with this mental load, my debt was growing. With mounting panic, I wrote to more and more agents and theatres, hoping I could get someone to come and see me, and eventually discovering that agents don't like to leave London.

So, I decided to move there.

London's Calling

I took a job touring old people's homes with a singing and dancing routine. It wasn't a case of 'Look what I can do!', though the performer in me was still alive and well, it was more about getting the old people to be a part of it. Breathing new life into their weary bones. Their relatives would gently weep as they joined in the singing too. Occasionally a resident was too ill to leave their room so we would go to them and sing for them at their bedside. As I sang 'You Make Me Feel So Young' to a wasted elderly man whose blue veins shone through his translucent skin, he smiled and held on to my hand with a vice-like grip, and afterwards he thanked me again and again.

Only after I'd left the room did I allow the tears to pour freely down my cheeks.

Champagne and Cunts

To make ends meet, or at least come a little closer together, I started working at a hostess bar in Mayfair. From the job description it seemed like a breeze. Dress up and sit with the other girls until a group of men arrived. Same as a brothel. Be paired up with whoever liked you. Same as a brothel. Sit down cosily with them and get them to order expensive champagne while you chat and flirt. I thought, as I approached my first night, that it sounded easier than brothel work. I was wrong.

First of all, the women were almost all bitches – and I don't use that word lightly – with none of the camaraderie that, as you spend time together, inevitably develops in a brothel. Stomping on my foot in their cheap stilettos. Offering a fake apology: 'So sorry, Natasha!' in a sing-song voice, then doing it again five minutes later. For a bit of extra cash one girl offered sex to punters and the rest of the women thought she was the Whore of Babylon and didn't hold back letting her know. I couldn't care less what other women were up to. I wanted to do the job, enjoy the job, get paid for the job, and go home again.

But the money was shit in the hostess bar, which, I quickly realized, helped to explain the women's behaviour. If we earn, we are happy. And that's probably true for most people in most jobs. We want to be busy and we want to be good at what we do. We derive pleasure and, yes, self-esteem from that. It keeps us motivated. It helps us to get out of bed in the morning. Unfortunately, as we would only have one or two chances to earn per night, as the ratio of men to women was skewed completely the wrong way, we mostly sat around getting more and more pissed off with each other, and with life.

Inevitably some of the hate would be focused on the new girl. I was the new girl. The first night I earned absolutely nothing. The second I earned about thirty pounds. The third, nothing again. And the fourth, almost £200. Which sounds like a win. But it was then that I quit.

Here's the scam. The man buys the woman champagne so that he can talk to her. The champagne ranges from £200 to £800 a bottle. The woman gets 20 per cent of the price of the overpriced bottle, but if you are working with a 'friend', and I use the inverted commas very pointedly, the 20 per cent is split between the two of you. So it makes more sense to win the custom by any means necessary and go it alone. Occasionally, instead of a bottle, the man will just buy the woman a champagne cocktail, which is presumably Aldi prosecco mixed discreetly with something sweet and processed behind the bar, away from prying eyes. Then we drink with the man, but if we get drunk we get fired. The scam – other than charging vast sums for cheap fizzy wine – is that we take a sip of our drink and then make our excuse to go to the staff bathroom. We take our glass with us as we sashay away, then pour the champagne down the plughole, replacing it with the non-alcoholic fizz kept in a bottle under the sink.

I love champagne, so pouring it away, even the cheap stuff, felt like a crime. But what I really hated was that the poor sap we were with would get more and more pissed on substandard fizz, which meant we could get him to spend lots of money. Maybe all his money; money he really couldn't afford to spend. He thought he was making a connection with us as we hung on his every word, but he was just a mark, instantly forgotten when the next punter came along and we pressed reset on the game.

The night I made £200 – which means the guy I was with spent close to £2,000 – I was out of there. Enough. As he was thrown out of the door at the end of the evening he said to me something along the lines of, 'I thought you liked me!' He sounded genuinely wounded. But in fact the pain was mine. For me, playing with people's emotions was no way to make money.

I told the boss about whoring being 'much better than this shit' and I was through the door with my head held high. I said it to piss them off, to shock them, and they needed to be told. They were crooks, robbing men by selling false hope of a romantic life and getting them drunk so they would spend too much money. There is no consent in that arrangement. If a guy has sex with a woman too drunk to consent it's rape, and I couldn't see that this was any different to theft. And yet these people – the bar owners and the women who work there – think that they are doing nothing wrong. None of the men will complain afterwards as they probably feel too humiliated by the experience, and so these clubs continue to operate very successfully.

How dare these women look down on whores? I realize that that makes me part of the whorearchy, that I am looking down on those women, even as they are doing their best to look down on me. But I see them as crooks who will do anything for money. Whores are honest about what we will and won't do; a guy knows exactly what he is getting, at least from me – an agreed price for an agreed service.

My principles meant I was at a crossroads again. Late twenties, sleeping on a sofa, but I still wasn't ready to go back to sex work, precisely because it was going back. I wasn't ready to re-enter a life that I had left; I'd thought at the time I'd left it for good. It would take being treated like shit in a few more low-paid, low-morality jobs and the eventual realization that I would never make enough to pay off my bank loans before I'd go back to a brothel. But even as I left the hostess bar that night, a part of me knew that I would. I had known it since the moment the agents failed to turn up for the drama school showcase. Maybe I'd known it even as I'd signed up for the course.

But there was a little part of me that was still a dreamer. Aren't we all?

Holiday

When I was a child, we'd take the occasional day trip to Morecambe, but pretty much all our family holidays were in Wales. I would pack all my Enid Blyton books in my case and settle down with them as soon as I could, paying no attention to the glorious countryside all around me, not noticing the dramatic mountains on the horizon until I had been there at least a few days. 'Look at the beautiful scenery,' my mum would say, pointing at the spectacular nature surrounding us, and I would glance up from my all-consuming Secret Seven adventure, murmur something vaguely positive in response, then stick my head back in my book. So here I am, almost thirty years later, going back as an adult. This time with my partner, the cats and my baby bump. I find myself wondering about that sweet little girl who found such innocent escape and such joy in simple words, and I wonder at the woman I have become, the mother I am about to be.

We meet up with some friends who have young children and we spend a leisurely day watching their little boys run around. High energy, high maintenance. They are lovely but I do hope a little girl will be less work, someone who, like me, just wants to sit down and read a good book. My pregnant body feels all the more exhausted just watching the kids dart about, but I know that, apart from having had the occasional restless night, the real sleep deprivation hasn't yet begun.

I'm in a reflective mood. The boys' mother, Adam's friend, is an optimist, I note. I wonder how she's able to retain that positivity past forty. Surely all people start off as optimists and then, after the shit of life hits the fan, time and again, they become realists, adopting that pragmatic 'It is what it is' philosophy of life. More than a few then jump on the pessimism track, the express train to a disgruntled old age. I don't normally envy people, but I look at her – stare at her, really – and wish I was more like her. I so rarely meet optimists now that, when I do, I am intrigued by their energy and their mindset and can only wish that, along the way, I hadn't become so jaded and bitter. Optimists are lit with a kind of dazzling inner glow. At this point in life, I am grey. Even with the joy of my tiny baby aboard, I can't help but wonder how long it will be before it all goes wrong.

After a restorative day at a spa, where I am massaged to the point where I can get my rings back on my swollen fingers and see my ankles again, my mood is light and cheery. This is the me I like; the one who enjoys chatting to strangers and is always ready with a smile. I welcome her with open arms.

The Gift of the Gab

I had one problem as an escort that cost me dearly.

'Your mistake,' I was told, 'is that you talk to them, Charlotte. Just suck and fuck quickly, then you can move on to the next one. You make more money then.'

This piece of advice came from a woman who made four times the amount of money I did. She would see twenty men in the time it would take me to see five. The problem was that, if I liked a man, I wanted to chat. The purely mechanical bonking was never my thing. I like to talk, as I actually like men. Most of the time. Yes, I think they are too easy, too desperate and far too many of them can be dogs but, here's the thing: I have always liked dogs. They're entertaining and just so grateful if you throw them a bone.

In the brothel I would be chatting to the men, sprawled around the sofas, while the other women were playing Candy Crush on their phones and talking about whatever mind-numbing reality show had captured their attention lately. The men liked me. They liked chatting with me. I was genuine and, although I could also play them in different ways if I chose, hustling to get more money out of them during our time together, I really wanted to know about them and their lives.

And then I'd get better acquainted with their dick.

Computer Says No

After our day at the spa, I get back to our holiday accommodation and open my emails.

Two are from clients. One, who is on an orgasm denial course, asks when I will be granting him a release. What grates is that he knows I'm on holiday, but the need for his willy to receive some attention is clearly greater than my need for a well-deserved rest.

The next is from a man who has being emailing me for years but has never yet met me. He has seen my blog about my approaching sabbatical from in-person sessions. After years of dithering, he now wants to see me for a session, perhaps in a few months. 'Is it too late?' he asks. Too fucking right it is. Some men always want something they can't have, and perhaps that's the appeal for him. To be denied what he wants is exactly what gets him off.

The third email is from my estate agent letting me know that the elusive buyer for my flat, who I thought was the answer to so many of my problems, has backed out.

The fourth is the worst of the lot. My sister. She has been sending me the occasional email since I became pregnant. I don't answer all of them as I'm not sure I want her in my life. But my parents, still hankering after an if not happy then at least happier family unit, even after all these years of friction, play the guilt trip with me. 'Can't you just let it go?' they ask me from time to time, and, 'I want you to make up before one of us dies.' That one really stings.

Why does whoever has been wronged have to 'be the better person' or 'forgive and forget'? And why, just because I'm pregnant, do my family think I am now a soft touch? The experience of carrying a new life is making me re-evaluate my own existence and relationships, that is true, but not in the way they think. Pregnancy isn't smoothing out the rough edges and making me feel sentimental; it's making me think very hard indeed about who I want in my life, and who doesn't deserve to be in my life. I handle people judging me because of my job and I'm good at either putting it to one side or coming out fighting, but the question now is whether I want anyone with poisonous views about me and the work that I have done, and still do, to be around my daughter.

Six years ago, when she split from her husband Patrick, my sister chose to date an ex-boyfriend of mine even though, when she let me know he'd asked her out, I told her very clearly that that wouldn't be cool with me. To make sure she'd completely understood my point, I said: 'You do know he cheated on me?'

She responded, 'He said he didn't.'

She went out with him regardless of my reservations, which was not the sisterly bond I was looking for.

Her disapproval of my job – the way she looked askance at me, disdain paining her expression, every time there was a hooker on TV; the way she feels able to say, 'Your job disgusts me,' in the middle of an argument about something else entirely; the way I have had to live with the constant refrain, 'Can't you get a normal job?' – makes our relationship untenable. Believing a prick that you've just started dating, who you barely know, rather than standing with your sister and her version of events is beyond the pale. Are there not enough other men in the world? I have probably fucked a thousand men but I have never fucked one of my sister's ex's. They're not difficult to avoid.

It broke us. And I'm not sure the pieces can be put together again. But as she now has a child with him and now that I'm pregnant, she wants to reconnect with me, so that we can – what? Sit around the table at Christmas and play happy fucking families? It's painfully funny how, as they go about their own day-to-day business, people can on the one hand be so laissez faire about their own morality – whether that means sleeping with your sister's ex or having affairs with married men – but on the other be so quick to accuse sex workers of lacking moral fibre.

It comes down to this: my sister is a woman who thinks that strippers, escorts and any other sex worker are subhuman. Do I want that in an aunt for my daughter?

Hell, no. I close my laptop with a decisive snap.

The Moral Maze

I like men. I like sex. But married men are off-limits for me. I deplore women who think it is OK to pursue a man who is attached.

When we got engaged Adam told me that some women were now looking at him more often, more closely, with more interest – and I think that's quite common. There are plenty of insecure twats out there who want to prove that they are better than another woman by fucking her man. The man is the same man as he was before he put a ring on his fiancée's finger and most women wouldn't have wanted him then. But I've found that because he is wanted by another woman, he becomes prey. It's all about validation. But while the insecure cow may be fucking the man literally, it's the man's partner who is actually being fucked. It's behaviour I find repugnant and completely unacceptable.

Of course, whether I am working as a hooker or a domme, most of my clients are married and, at first, I found that difficult to wrap my head around. I didn't like it. It didn't matter that it was them approaching me, I still struggled with the morals of it. But the financial transaction is the thing that makes the difference; it makes it a job. I am not asking these men when they are going to leave their wife. I am not sleeping with them as a romantic pursuit. I'm rarely sleeping with them at all, of course. I deliver the service, and we then go our separate ways. Generally, then, I've found that in sex work the married man is easier to manage. He doesn't get as emotionally invested. He doesn't ask why you won't go out with him. He doesn't suggest you leave your partner. He doesn't call you on Christmas Day.

The married man makes my life much easier.

Choices

After I left the Mayfair hostess bar, I tried all sorts of jobs in an attempt to avoid hooking again. Promotional jobs are the lifeline of actors, dancers and writers: ten pounds an hour to leaflet in the early morning and, after pounding the streets, you can sell a product at a trade show for the rest of the day. Then, because two minimum-wage jobs still isn't enough money, you can work in a bar at night. I've done it all. I have played a giant *Big* style piano with my feet, which is at the very least good exercise. I have sold expensive prams to rich Londoners. I have advertised waterproof socks while standing in a bucket full of cold water. I've sold weight-loss products for a company which claimed to have a special channel to God. I have sold shots while wearing orange hotpants and leg-warmers that marked me out as a target for all the arse-grabbing perves in the vicinity, and there was no shortage of those. I have worked through the foam parties, through the punch-ups, the sarcastic comments and the unwanted sexual attention. I have cleaned up reef vomit on the stairs, and picked up used tampons and damp tights from bathroom floors, discarded in a hurry so that horny women could get their meaningless shag right there and then. I have done jobs that have made me look back on my days in the Leeds brothel and wonder why I had been so desperate to leave. And I have worked alongside saleswomen who were colder and more calculating than any sex worker I have ever come across.

When I collected glasses in a club I had to wear a T-shirt that said 'Chlamydia testing here', with an arrow pointing down towards my vagina. As I worked my way around the various rooms, I saw many a finger, thumb and cock inserted into various holes in the dark corners. At least this club was trying to remind their pissed patrons to stay healthy while having fun. I had to approve of that. Every night at 3 a.m. I would be on the first of two miserable night buses on my way back to my studio in east London. I knew never to sit upstairs and never to listen to music. Even after a long and exhausting shift that left me dead on my feet, I needed to have my wits about me. My caution didn't stop one man squeezing in next to me one night and making obscene suggestions that would have made the average woman blush. He'd picked the wrong person. 'Fuck off, you prick!' I shouted in his ear, and he quickly moved away. Silence is the dangerous pervert's friend. Being loud doesn't mean that someone will step in and stand up for you – you can't count on that. But if you act deranged and psychotic enough, the solitary pervert will more often than not think better of choosing you as a victim. I repeat: I refuse to be a victim.

These jobs, grim as they were, helped to get me off someone else's sofa, where I'd been sleeping since arriving in London. These jobs enabled me to find a cheap, tiny studio to call home, a place where my sweet Turkish landlord was always popping by to check the shower, which we were both aware worked perfectly well. But I was getting tired. The human body can only do so many ridiculous shifts; an entire day filled from dawn to dusk with physical labour is hard.

Years later I wrote a play, a cathartic comedy featuring two struggling actresses doing some of the jobs that I had done to keep my head above water. A friend hosted the readthrough at his house and invited a few other creatives to give feedback. Ever the dreamer, I was excited to find out what other people made of my work. I was excited, apprehensive, but as the evening progressed I listened increasingly slack jawed with disbelief as two middle-class women concluded that the play was too unrealistic, that nobody would really do the jobs I'd described. They were exactly the type of women who don't understand why women turn to sex work. Exactly the type of women who don't realize it's a choice that women are making all the time. And when they do know that such choices are being made, they don't like it.

It's interesting how threatened the other classes are by working-class women earning a good wage, daring to buck the notorious narrative of the working classes spunking what little money we do have on booze, gambling, big TVs and package holidays, because – the mindset goes – who knows when we will have enough cash to enjoy life again? The government tells us to save, but what's the point if what we can afford to put aside is such a piddling amount that it will never accumulate to anything? Taxes and costs rise, while wages stagnate. At the same time, the state pension age is pushed up and up so that many of the working classes won't even reach it. We'll be dead long before then. And forget having a private pension when you're in minimum-wage work on a zero-hours contract. There are higher mortgage rates, loan rates, extortionate payday loans. There are payment schemes like Brighthouse, Klarna. It costs more to be poor. I have always worked hard, and then harder, trying desperately not to be poor.

Dreams

I was still singing in care homes but it was a tour a season, a few weeks at a time. And although it felt worthwhile, I yearned to be acting great roles on the stage. Playing Lady Macbeth or Kate, Joan of Arc or Medea: strong women who nobody could accuse of being victims. Deranged or evil, perhaps, but not victims. I was always drawn to roles where women seized what power they could, especially when the odds were stacked against them. In this man's world, they resolutely refused to let their gender humble them, and I loved them for it.

But I eventually had to conclude that I had been a fool; I should never have gone to drama school. What the fuck had I been thinking? How on earth was someone like me ever going to be able to make acting my life? Instead, at night, I now dreamed about my debt and how rising interest rates were pushing it up, beyond reach, every month. Every month I owed more and more, and I had no way of paying it off. I would wake up in a sweat, a pressure on my chest. Each day, I pounded London's pavements, going from one promo job to another, lugging the huge bag that contained the clothes I needed for each job; casual blacks for leafletting, a suit for trade shows and heels and clubwear for shot selling. As I finished each workday searching pub floors for coins that patrons had dropped, small amounts which were nonetheless vital to top up my wages, I kept thinking, *Could I? Could I do it again?*

The Sparkle

My old promo-work pal Stephen comes to visit me for lunch. I usually only see him once a year since we had first met over ten years ago and I adore him.

'You look amazing!' he exclaims, his eyes on my bump. But I can tell he's being economical with the truth. While his smile says one thing, the expression in his eyes says something very different, and it's obvious to me that he can see that my sparkle has gone and the tiredness of the pregnancy is at the tipping point. When I look at him I see myself through his eyes; the dull complexion, the extra weight, the lank hair and the smile that is not so ready any more.

He knows all about my domination job and I jokingly tell him that I am winding down my sessions because I can no longer see my stilettos, but he doesn't laugh with me. Instead, he suggests that I stop working in domination, period. He thinks that being a dominatrix is the reason I've lost my lust for life.

But there is a lot he doesn't know, things that I will never tell him about because they will break his heart. Same way as I don't ever talk about being in an abusive relationship. I will never say to anyone who questions my choices that being a domme has allowed me to earn enough money not to have to worry about whether I can afford a latte in Costa, which used to be a very real concern for me. That domination has pulled me out of the brothels where I was surrounded by drugs and the non-stop drama of the other girls' chaotic lives. That domination gave me a way back into acting, tenuous though it might be. That it has made me feel a little safer, more distanced from the police and from the most dangerous clients. The way I see it, being a dominatrix means that a man sucks my cock, not the other way around. I can prance around and perform as though I'm on a stage, with the 'audience' captive in the palm of my hand. I can spend an entire day without having to hear lines like 'Nice tits! Can I come on 'em?' I can insist on seeing solely submissive men in a dungeon, who are less likely to kill me.

So I say, 'I'm good. It's good.' And I am. It is. And as Stephen and I chat, time shifts a little. The years roll back. For a moment I feel as though the old me – sparkle and all – is just there. Just there on the periphery. Just out of sight. Almost close enough for me to touch.

Then she is gone again.

The Sissy

I have not been taking on new clients since I discovered I'm pregnant, but I have a 'last hurrah' moment when an email pops into my inbox and I suddenly think, *Why not?* I know that a new client can bring problems with them, that's why not. They can be too clingy, too difficult, too unpredictable. I feel safe with my current stable of slaves and I know what to expect of each of them. But I like how the email which arrives in my inbox is phrased, and the new session they're proposing sounds fun.

My prospective client is what we call a sissy, which is generally an easy session: dress them up, apply their make-up and add hair, followed by a little bit of pegging on my strap-on bench. They are normally so excited by that point that their instinct is to come quickly, so I have to ensure that doesn't happen. A little more tease and then, finally, after they have begged some more and their session is almost up, they are allowed to explode. I think I can handle that, even with my bump.

The new client is delighted that I accept him. He gives me a female name I should use, and from now on in he is she. She says she needs a high level of discretion because of her job. Absolutely fine, I reply. She pays a deposit so I know she isn't a timewaster. I patiently explain that I never take photos without permission, I never give any names away and that I never share either telephone numbers or email addresses. After I have put her mind at rest she asks if she can arrive dressed as a sissy and although that means I won't get to transform her myself, which I love doing, I say that's OK with me.

Finally, something to look forward to.

My present dungeon is in a shithole up north, a place that has been left to rot like many of our old industrial towns. Levelling up, my arse. The high street is littered with betting shops and charity shops and crime rates are high. It is not a pretty place, it lacks colour and life, ambition and hope, but it's home. And once you're in the dungeon it's easy to forget what's happening – or mostly not happening – in the world outside. Today I'm ready and waiting for my new client, the sissy, and even the very ordinariness of the exterior can't detract from the little frisson of excitement I'm feeling inside my special and rather extraordinary space.

As my client was so insistent on the need for discretion I assumed that she would turn up in conservative women's clothes. That's more than enough to get you noticed around here. So imagine my surprise when she turns up, all six foot seven of her, in bright pink heels, with a body The Rock would be proud of, wearing a tiny fluorescent pink mini dress and sheer stockings, all topped off with a white stole. She comes through my door accompanied by whooping and whistling from the builders next door. I try to be discreet – I don't need everyone knowing what goes on in my dungeon – but with her spectacular entrance I feel that I may as well have a red neon light above my door that says 'Strap-on service here!'

In her email she has gone into detail about the cuckolding fantasy she wants to play out with me, which, now that she is in the room, I realize is going to be a problem. 'Your girlfriend is at home getting fucked by a real man with a proper cock,' I dutifully say, as I stroke a bicep that's bigger than my thigh and ready my dildo that's dwarfed by her own massive penis.

Criminal

I like to keep up with what's written about the sex industry, and that's easier to do with time on my hands. I've long been aware that the radical feminists want to criminalize the buyer of sex, arguing that having sex with a man for money constitutes violence against women, that it's nothing short of rape. The rad fems argue that the women won't be punished with this legal model but the men will because it will be illegal for a man to purchase sex. Tell that to Eva Marree Kullander Smith, a sex worker in Sweden who lost custody of her children before being murdered by her ex-partner, whose track record of violence was still preferable to Smith's job, when it came to granting parental custody by the courts.

There are various names for this approach. End Demand. The Swedish model. The Nordic model. The EU voted for it in 2014 and since then Northern Ireland criminalized the buying of sex in 2015 and France did the same in 2016. I hate the viewpoint and I hate the legal shift. Clearly, it effects our livelihoods but, more than that, in the countries that have implemented it, the statistics show that violence against sex workers has gone up, with sex workers feeling more fearful, marginalized and stigmatized.

If you think about it, this isn't surprising. If you already have a conviction for violence against women then that is your way of being and this law won't deter you from booking and abusing a sex worker; that it's against the law is not going to be a deterrent. But it will deter little old Albert in his holey raincoat who wouldn't dream of harming us and just wants a bit of fun from time to time. Amnesty is with us on this, agreeing that the new laws would leave us open to harassment by the police, with compromised access to justice and equal protection and that the door would then be open to violent men who could pretty much get away with it. They released research in 2016 that infuriated all our opponents, including the actresses, led by Meryl Streep. I'm not sure we should heed the words of a woman who once called Harvey Weinstein God. While people who had never walked in our shoes were pontificating, academics were doing actual research on the impact on sex workers in Sweden, where the model began, recommending that a more nuanced understanding of commercial sex was required, and that, primarily, criminal penalties for sex workers should be removed.

The rad fems gloss over the negative effects of criminalizing legislations on us by focusing their argument on how the men should be punished. As I settle in, I read a piece in which they attempt to win their argument by presenting as evidence the vile comments about escorts that some men have posted on message boards. To be fair, it's hard not to want to punish these rancid little men as severely as possible when you read what some of them have written about us, while no doubt furiously twiddling with their tiny knobs. Morbidly curious, I wade into one punters' message board and click into a yawnathon thread about working girls: which ones now do bareback, which have saggy tits, which have got too many tattoos. And then, further down the rabbit hole, having googled my working name, I come across a post about me.

'I had sex with Eve when she was changing her service from sex to domination,' it says. 'She asked me not to tell anyone because it would affect her business. I gave her a wonderful orgasm.'

It is dated very recently, which means that the sad little twat has been thinking about the experience for almost ten years, since the end of my shagging days. Other than the lack of respect, the awful thing about these sites is that the reviews and posts can't be taken down. The negative comments are particularly harmful. The punter's attitude is: 'Tough. She should have left me with a smile on my face.' But negative reviews may get a girl sacked if she's working in a brothel and will probably force her to change her working name and start the hard work of building a new profile. There's no humanity here, no recognition that she's just trying to feed herself and quite possibly her family too. I shouldn't carry on looking but I am too deep into it now. I decide to read what other punters have written about other girls.

'Honey was good back in the day but she's had kids and trouble at home and has lost her spark now. Though she still gives great head!'

'Toothy bj was a real disappointment. No reverse oral or fingering allowed. Paid £65 for half an hour.'

'Neutral, because she tried to get dressed up after the first round thinking her job was done. Had to confirm that it's 2 rounds. In my head I thinking sorry honey, jobs not done, you have to work the full shift love!'

'Great pump and dump with this innocent Romanian. Very tight pussy. It's quite clear she's not enjoying it but I keep fucking anyway . . . Eventually she starts to tear up.'

As I stare at this last one with rage in my stomach I realize I can't bear to read any more. I want to rip their fucking heads off. I can see why someone would read that and want to punish all clients; for once I'm seeing eye to eye with the rad fems and can hardly believe it. If we could criminalize those poisonous sites and the lowlife men who post on them, then I would have no argument with the rad fems. In fact, I'd go further. I'm all for cutting off their little willies and putting them in a display worthy of the Turner Prize, for all to come and see.

I remind myself that most of my clients would never post on sites like this, but the minority are out there, typing away. The rapist's post gets a lot of abuse from other male posters, who are as angry as me, but the fact that it is there – with the woman's name for all to see, even now – shows what the owners of the website think of women. The posters are mostly the saddest of the brothel creepers; tragic little men who count going for a weekly shop to Sainsbury's as a day trip. But, at worst, they are rapists.

Much as I feel the need for retribution, it remains obvious to me that if you criminalize all clients you criminalize us as well. Criminalization is an attack on sex workers. Fewer clients doesn't mean fewer sex workers, it just means that we will be forced to see people we normally wouldn't – the ones who post reviews on these sites, the ones who make the hairs on the back of your neck stand up, the ones where you keep an eye on the corner of the room where the screwdriver is tucked away – and that we will have to become more competitive with our colleagues by offering all sorts of extras while charging less. It's simple supply-and-demand economics. The power balance will shift. If sex workers outnumber punters we will become more desperate, more willing to take risks. Street sex workers will be far more likely to come to harm as they will be forced to work in more isolated places, away from prying eyes. And there'll be no vetting, no real paper trail should they decide to rob us. Or murder us.

Toxic

To my surprise, I have forged new friendships with some other pregnant women and new mums. I had originally posted on Mumsnet but I didn't find much friendliness or support there. The attitude seemed to be, 'Well, you got pregnant. Did you really think it would be easy?' No, but I did expect to find some kind of sisterhood to help with the bad bits. In a world where pre-natal classes are not available and it is difficult to access advice that makes sense, these new women in my life are so important. I am lucky. One is an ex-theatre colleague who I always liked but we now have something more than just theatre in common. She is a few months ahead of me in her pregnancy and so knows what I'm going to need. I'm delighted when she sends me a mama pack for soothing sleep and moisturizing my tummy. She and the others offer support and tips, but what I like most are the stories of constipation and the other side effects of pregnancy that I had never considered before. Like waking up and finding a new bit of skin under your armpit. Like feet ballooning. Like teeth wobbling. And piles. These women make me laugh and it's a huge tonic to the pain that's constantly radiating across my back.

My two childless friends, who I've known for a long time, have been more elusive.

One, who I've known since I was twenty-one, hasn't called me since I told her I am having a baby. It has been months. But that friendship is special and I refuse to let it go. We all fuck up. We can all sometimes either say nothing when words are needed, or say the wrong thing. I know my news has knocked her sideways. We had said for decades that we weren't bothered about having children. That men weren't reliable. That we didn't have any maternal instincts. We'd bonded over it. She probably expects that I will abandon her as some of our other friends have done in the past, peeling off into their exclusive club and shutting the door firmly behind them. We have both been ghosted by new mothers who have cited reasons like, 'You don't know what busy is!' as they disappear with their sprat. But I'm not like them. I send my old friend a text to say that I am disappointed she hasn't been more supportive. She replies quite quickly with a simple apology, and we exchange a series of messages which make me feel as though we are back on track. I have never cared about having lots of fair-weather friends, just the ones that matter. The ones who really know you. The ones who accept you for who you are and love you regardless. Those friends I would give a kidney to.

When I'd called with my news, my other old friend had given me the third degree, almost as though she was trying to make me feel guilty for doing what I'd previously said I'd never do. People are allowed to change their minds, I told her. Circumstances change. All I could say to her was that one day, instead of thinking 'No,' I suddenly thought 'Yes.' Or at least 'I would like to try.' But that's a decision to be made by me and my partner, and no one else. In my view, my friend has crossed a line. Why would someone who claims to be a friend want to make you feel shit? How insecure must they be that they have to put you down? By peering at my life, has she been making herself feel better about her own all these years? And now that my life has taken a magical turn, she doesn't like it. It's not what she wants to see.

We haven't spoken for a while, so I pick up the phone. I launch into a spirited update as though three months haven't passed. I tell her my worries about moving house in the lead-up to giving birth and all the stress involved.

She says, 'At least you are not homeless.'

I change the subject to my pelvic pain.

She says, 'Just wait until you go through the menopause!'

She asks me whether I have bought anything for the baby yet and I tell her briefly that I am terrified that something will go wrong at the hospital. I confide in her that I am protecting my heart the best I can, in case the thing we can hardly speak about happens.

She says I am being negative and that I should go out and buy all the baby stuff now.

Suddenly the Mumsnet crowd don't seem so bad.

There and Back Again

I thought about going back to sex work as I put in the hours in this job and that job, day and night, and as I grew more and more tired. I thought about it as I searched for dropped coins to help pay the bills, and when I ate as much food as I could get away with at my food-sampling promotional job so that I wouldn't need to eat later. And I thought about it at the end of the evening as I clocked the ring of predators taking their positions around the dance floor, watching and waiting to approach the drunkest girls. All the do-gooders who say that strip clubs make men violent and should be closed down have obviously never been in a regular club, where sexual assaults and violence are a normal night out. Nobody is trying to close those places down, where the drunken young women, like lambs to the slaughter, are summarily abused and made to feel used while they're just trying to have a good time. Meanwhile, across town, the sober stripper is using her skills to entertain the drunk man who is paying for his pleasure and no one's getting raped.

I quit one of my club jobs when a barman, for no reason at all, decided to kick me on the arse. I complained to the bosses, and he was made to apologize. But there was no sacking, no suspension. Just a smirking apology. That's all that I was worth – and I received the message loud and clear. *What are you doing?* asked the voice in my head. I couldn't muster a coherent answer. If I had to choose between soul-destroying minimum-wage labour and sex work, then surely that was an easy choice to make.

One afternoon as I was waiting for a Tube to take me to yet another job I didn't want to do for peanuts and which wouldn't pay the bills, I looked hard at the tracks below me. I thought, just for a second, *If I step forward, I can finally sleep*. It made me wonder how many other jumpers are just tired people aching for a good night's rest, some time off work and maybe a holiday that they can't afford to take but desperately need. It was a moment of clarity for me. My body couldn't do this for much longer.

Finally, late one night, on the long bus ride home from work in the early hours, with my head spinning as it so often did with thoughts about money, or the lack of it, the lights of London no longer appeared so bright. Right there on the night bus I found myself taking gulping breaths of panic. What an idiot I had been. I was doing my very best but I was out of options. I was done with minimum-wage jobs that come with a branded T-shirt or a name badge and a white-knuckle night bus home.

The next morning I bought a copy of *Loot* – a weekly paper which had pages and pages of listings for buying and selling just about anything and everything, including sex – and flicked to the back section. Every part of London was looking for working girls, it seemed. I called a place in north London and got an interview. I was back on the game.

Work–Brothel Balance

And like that, I was no longer dreaming of debt. Thanks to my brothel wages I found some balance in my life. Yes, I was lying to almost everyone I knew about how I was living that life, but at least I was paying off my drama school debt and I could afford to eat.

To feed my soul I was still touring care homes, performing to the elderly, and that warmed my heart and made me happy. I was auditioning for theatre as and when, but still not getting anywhere. I loved performing, but I was tired of auditions, which came with a rollercoaster of emotions. The excitement of the invitation versus the realization of how much the train fare would set me back just to attend the audition. The excitement of preparing monologues versus the realization that the table of auditioners wanted me to work for free before deciding if I was good enough to work for pennies.

'Can you be sexy?' one director asked me. Me? Someone who worked as a hooker and a bloody good one at that. And the absurd thing was I couldn't. I now needed cash to be sexy. I couldn't turn it on without it. As I failed to get part after part, my attitude started to stink – I was angry and sulky – which meant I had no chance of landing a part. It was a vicious circle.

If they had been casting for a pit bull I might have been in.

How Low Can You Go?

Back in the sex industry I found things had changed enormously. Now, for brothel interviews in London, I had to strip off and show my body, which I had never had to do before. Rather than fees increasing as the years rolled on, the money had got worse. Seven years earlier up north it had been sixty pounds for half an hour. Now it was sometimes as low as fifty pounds for half an hour in London, and the madam or pimp took 50 per cent of that. You were now expected to offer extras, whereas before if you so much as kissed a john you were laughed at by the other women. The john would be sure to tell the other women what each of us got up to in the privacy of the room, in the hope that it might encourage someone else to do the same or take it even further. In any case, you had to offer extras to make any real money. That's how it was now.

The place in Archway certainly wasn't the greatest brothel in town, but it was a start. From there I could make money and think about finding somewhere better to work. Most places are essentially the same, but each has its own particular set-up, its own vibe. Some will have microphones in the rooms so that the boss can listen in to make sure we are not robbing them in some way. In others there will often be a menu, so you can really feel like a made-to-order piece of shit. In some you have to watch your stuff constantly because the other women will nick anything that isn't nailed down. In Archway, most of the clients were OK and that made a huge difference to getting out of bed each day and going to work. They were working-class men who understood the need to make money. To them, we were all in the same leaking boat. They unblocked clogged drains for a living, I emptied balls.

For all the good things that the return to sex work now brought me – and bought me – I was quickly reminded that brothel life is exhausting too. I would finish each day mentally drained from all the acting – all the high-energy fakery of it.

And of course you also feel physically knackered from all the fucking. And that's whether you work in day places or night places. Archway offered both. The drunk punters and the unsociable hours made the choice between the day and night shift a no-brainer. But as I had twenty grand to find and as they would often be short of girls I would regularly do a day shift and then go straight into a night shift. Man after man, with few breaks, for eighteen hours.

You quickly get smart about how to handle the fucking fatigue, and how to conserve energy. I remembered what I used to do when I was up north. I would start a man on his front and give him a massage. Ten minutes in he was aroused and ready to go. Then, missionary and doggy, which didn't require too much effort from me. Maybe some riding if I could be arsed. Then they're out the door and you're onto the next. Anyone who says sex work isn't work has never delivered ten blowjobs in a day. My jaw still clicks.

Take *That*

Today I very deliberately hit a teenager with my shoulder bag and it gives me enormous pleasure. 'Take that, you little bastard,' I mutter under my breath.

I am now much bigger in my pregnancy and, while I don't expect the world to stop for yet another pregnant woman, I do expect younger people to move out of my way on the pavement. I have spent weeks apologetically manoeuvring my growing belly around them and finally I've had enough.

'Jesus!' Adam says, as the teen goes flying.

'Fuck him,' I say.

And then to re-emphasize my point, I say '*Fuck him!*' very loudly over my shoulder to the retreating boy and his family. The teen looks back, surprised, but keeps on walking.

It's good that Adam isn't aggressive like me, but I do think he is a little too soft sometimes. Occasionally I want him to be a toxic masculine male and stand up for me, the little – or not so little – woman. The problem is that neither of us is cut out to play those stereotypical roles. I stand up for myself. I always have. I assume I always will. But, sometimes, I want him to speak up for me and defend me. It's confusing for men, I know. We say we don't need looking after and we don't want to be treated like weak women, but occasionally, God damn it, I feel like a weak woman. Now more than ever, I'm feeling vulnerable.

Brothel Life

Day places are generally just two women working with a maid, so in the Archway brothel there were just two rather plain, magnolia bedrooms. The customer would be buzzed in by the maid, and the other woman and I would be expected to be ready and waiting for them, each of us standing in our bedrooms looking all sexy and pouty, hoping the man would choose us.

One maid thought I was wearing too much clothing in what was really quite a cold room so, as the potential punter looked on, she pulled my cardigan from my shoulders, exposing a bit more flesh as though she was displaying a prize hog at the market. I didn't like that. Most maids are lovely. Some are cunts.

If I didn't like the look of the man in my doorway sizing me up, I would find ways of putting him off, hoping he wouldn't choose me. I already had enough experience to tell whether a man was going to be vile, so I would scratch my vagina or hack up some phlegm as he watched me. He'd choose the other girl.

If there was an issue with a client, I didn't take any shit. I once got into a row with a drunk man who was being belligerent to an Eastern European woman in the brothel, mocking her accent and her lack of English. At 'Turn around and let me see what you've got,' I stepped in. My maid told me afterwards that the guy had married into one of the biggest criminal families in London and that I should be careful. Did I give a fuck? What I'd said needed to be said. Weeks later the bloke came back sober and contrite this time, and apologized to me. From then on, we got on like a house on fire.

The men I really couldn't stand were the upper middle-class students who could afford to go somewhere better, but had somehow ended up with us. They always wanted to try and make us feel shit, probably as a distraction from their daddy issues or their suffocating mothers who had instilled in them a sense of entitlement that they could have anything they wanted and would achieve anything they set their pampered little minds to. The weight of expectation cast on poor Dominic or Edwin must be a terrible burden. So they'd visit a brothel to make themselves feel better about their lives. One puny student put his hands around my neck, which was a mistake. I don't like to be strangled. I threw him off the bed and shouted for the maid, a huge woman, who came bursting in. He argued with her, saying he wanted his money back and how 'disappointed' he was. She threw him sideways down the stairs and into the street. No refunds for abusers. I loved her for that. This is why we need maids there with us – to offer some protection.

Since 2012, when police raids in brothels increased because of a 'cleaning up the streets' initiative in time for the London Olympics and the thousands of expected tourists, for whom the streets needed to be paved with gold, many brothels have been shut down. The upshot of which is that the maid will often now work from her own home, taking bookings and answering calls while the working girls have to let their customers in themselves and deal with anything that happens on the premises. It means maids won't get arrested if the police do come, as they are never in the building, and that's good for them. But of course that makes the sex workers on the ground much more vulnerable. A john might think a maid is just a slightly jaded middle-aged woman with a sharp tongue, but maids know how to handle themselves with the average brothel creeper.

Tony

When I was told I had an investment banker waiting for me – let's call him Tony – I expected him to be like the students: arrogant and ignorant, though perhaps with a more refined repertoire of insults to fire at me. Everyone hates a banker. When I entered the room I was surprised to find him with another girl up to her elbow in his arse. He had a bottle of poppers in one hand, a bottle of champagne in the other and I could see several chunky lines of coke racked up on the small table next to the bed. Jumbo lines usually indicate that the coke is bad quality, or the cocaine user has built up a tolerance. In this case, taking it all in, I decided it was the latter.

The hooker, from her position up Tony's arse, glared at me, so I started to back out with an apology. But then Tony smiled a huge smile and said, 'Come on in! Gloria's beginning to get wrist ache, aren't you, love?'

It was an odd start to what has been an enduring friendship and I have come to love Tony dearly. In so many ways he's a total one-off. And yet I've never met a banker who didn't like something up his arse.

Men Behaving Badly

In Archway, I spent a few lovely hours with a nice Irish guy. It was his first time in London and he was about to start a new job, which he was excited and a little nervous about. He did poppers as we chatted and then we finally got down to it. Off he went, completely satisfied, and I thought nothing more of it. Then, later that week, at the promotional job I was still doing regularly, we were all asked to gather together to meet our new boss. He was a nice Irish guy who was new in London . . .

I managed to keep the surprise off my face and behaved with him as I would any new colleague, especially one who was the boss. I had no intention of telling anyone at the promotional job about our previous fun encounter but, in an unexpected twist, he told my supervisor about it and she told some of the other women. And just like that I went from being popular with my colleagues to being the shit on the bottom of their stilettos. I had no real choice but to quit. Needless to say, the nice Irish guy kept his job.

Not long after that shabby experience, I got fired from the brothel. Our male boss wanted to ramp up our marketing and had sent us all to a photographer. I agreed to be featured on the website as long as my face was obscured. The boss agreed.

Then, there it was. My face on the internet for the world to see. He had completely ignored my request. I kicked off, and they fired me. Fuck them, I thought. I had been about to quit anyway; this wasn't the place for me. And now that I was back in the game I knew that there was plenty more work out there for me. Horny men are my bread and butter. And they were in no short supply in London.

Lucky

Strangers don't normally have the power to upset me. Piss me off, yes. I've met too many strangers to allow them to get to me. But today, perhaps because I'm hugely pregnant and hormonal, I am upset.

As I heave myself into the back seat of a taxi and settle down for the short trip the driver asks me if I have been swimming. I have not. A shake of the head.

'Really? Your hair looks wet,' he ploughs on.

It is stupidly hot. I spent six hours in a car yesterday. Today

I have been painting the flat, a last-ditch effort to secure a new buyer. And I am seven months pregnant. Sue me if I haven't washed and blow-dried my hair.

A deep breath. A short answer. 'I'm pregnant.'

Adam, sensing I'm not in the mood for this conversation, picks it up when the driver changes tack and asks what we're having – a boy or a girl? On and on he goes about having children. We shouldn't stop at one, he tells us. And then he reveals that he has fifteen of them dotted around the country.

I bite my lip. It is on the tip of my tongue to say what a fantastic achievement that is, for a man to empty his ball sack, hang the consequences, and then move on to another woman. I want to tell him what an amazing specimen of a man he is. How proud he must be. But I'm so upset I find I can't speak.

I look up from my phone's screen saver, which is a shot of me, my bump and Adam, and take a moment to look at my partner. Properly look at him. How lucky I am that this is my man, not the irresponsible prick at the wheel.

Take Two

Fired from Archway, I was once again looking for another brothel in which to ply my trade. I called Tony. Since that first unexpected encounter we'd become pretty friendly. I had been to his house and had been introduced as a hooker to his banker colleagues. And that was all OK; I didn't judge them for their career choice either. My chess game was getting better as he was a good player and forced me to think ahead more. And of course, I regularly played hide my fist with him. He told me about another place that he sometimes visited where I might find work, this time in north London. Always keen to help, he called the boss, gave me a glowing recommendation, and that was it. I was in.

Walking in for the first time, I couldn't help but think, *What a shithole*. A few old brown leather sofas were scattered around the shabby upstairs room and, through a doorway, I could see a tired and slightly mucky kitchenette. The toilet had no door and past that lay a back door with an unloved patio, all sprouting weeds and mossy paving stones. The bedrooms all lay down some stairs, in a slightly damp basement. It was solely a night place, and was dark and gloomy, which was also the mood of the Romanian women I found myself working with.

In the time I'd been away from the industry, another change in the sex workers' landscape was that brothels had gone from being all English girls with perhaps one Thai girl in the mix, to me now being the only English girl in the entire place. Why was that? I wondered. I realized that a lot of desperate girls from outside the UK needing jobs was the main reason that extras had now become standard. As with other jobs where demand for work outstripped vacancies, the wages had also gone down. The bosses were rubbing their hands together, delighted that there were more workers than positions. But the change in the demographics also meant that the police could raid places, citing trafficking offences – using it as an excuse to turn a place over and, in the case of the migrant women, threaten them with deportation if they didn't hand over their money willingly. The result was that life had become more uncertain than ever for marginalized and vulnerable workers. It made the brothel a frightening environment in which to work, and London a difficult place to live. Of course, these women were moody.

I was put through the normal routine bestowed on new girls, the usual 'You can't sit there, that seat's taken' nonsense. But I was polite, took a seat somewhere that didn't appear to offend anyone, and waited for the boss to arrive. He was not what I expected. He spoke with a posh drawl and was wearing a shabby raincoat that had probably been an expensive look twenty years ago. If he hadn't been so stoned and grumpy, he might have been nice looking. Let's call him Max.

'You're the new girl. Angel?' Max asked. He jabbed a finger at each of the women. 'Don't let any of these bitches scare you. They're nice when you get to know them.'

Here we go, I thought. He's one to watch out for. But I was wrong. No audition. No talk of menus. No looking at my naked body and evaluating every scar, every stretch mark, every dimple. I very quickly found Max to be hilarious and mad and hugely endearing, and he was the main reason I worked at the north London brothel for two years. And he was right. I also made friends with the 'bitches' over time and they were more generous and kinder than many of the English women I'd ever worked with. Once the women in a brothel know you, they start to share their food, their clients, their lives. Even in these dark and unloved, criminalized and marginalized spaces, friendships are forged that can last a lifetime.

A Good Time

Max was very impressed that I sometimes performed in care homes and taught theatre-in-education in schools, but the other girls couldn't understand why I did it.

'How much do you get for that?' they'd ask, and when I told them that in either job I earned in a week what we earned in the brothel in an hour they would fall about laughing.

At around £200, it's an amount that, in his memoir, Michael Ball complains about earning each week after he had just come out of drama school in the mid 1980s. Imagine, almost thirty years later and drama school graduates are still earning the same or even less. Is it any wonder that the acting world is now saturated with poshos who come from independent wealth?

'Why do you do it?' would be the next question.

'Because she is a good person, you fucking imbeciles!' my boss would roar.

On the nights when there was a good crowd in, it was an amazing job, and I really did love it. The music was loud, all Pink Floyd and Jimi Hendrix, The Doors and the Rolling Stones, and we would chat and dance and smoke and drink. A regular party. The men would arrive and wonder what unlikely paradise they had stumbled into, as there was no line-up of girls giving them the hard sell, no pressure to take us downstairs. The focus was on fun. There were TV producers and West End stars, jazz musicians and artists. I always preferred the nights when the creatives were in. They knew how to have a good time.

But, often, nights in the brothel were quiet for hours at a

stretch. The Salvation Army would rock up every Thursday and sit drinking our tea in their M&S cardis as they told us that God loved us. The lulls meant we had time to watch TV series like *Fanny and Alexander* and *Bleak House*. Max wanted to educate the Romanian girls and he thought introducing them to Bergman and Dickens would teach them something. And it did. How to feel less horny. It's hard to get in the mood when you've spent five hours watching an uncut bleak Swedish drama about grief and child abuse. It was possibly the worst thing a pimp has ever subjected me to. But then we'd hear 'ding dong' – a punter at the door – and a shout would go out from Max: 'Get ready, girls!'

Woe betide any man who called us on a slow night. Max would be stoned by the time the phone rang and he could and regularly would say anything. He was a brilliant advert for why not to do drugs. He was always buggering up the figures and customer times so we would have to fill in the book ourselves, keeping our own record of who had been downstairs with a client, for how long and when. In the early days I wondered how he could manage the business by himself, but I found out there was another, very silent partner behind the scenes. My boss also had a boss, and we knew better than to ask too many questions about him.

While most clients were absolutely fine to work for, there were also the wannabe gangsters and the rude lawyers. It's surprising how much those two types have in common. But the type of man I disliked most in this gaff turned out not to be the student, but, very specifically, the Old Etonian. They would march in as though they owned the place. They would talk about us as though we weren't there. And if they did deign to speak to us you could find yourself on the receiving end of a comment like, 'Didn't you bother to get an education?' We would try to take any other customer than the Old Etonians. I'd rather put my hand up for eighty-six-year-old Frank and his colostomy bag, a lovely but somewhat smelly man. Or Ernest the rapist, who would take the condom off when he was behind you and you couldn't see what he was doing. Both were preferable to the Etonians. They didn't understand our aversion. They really thought they were the dog's bollocks. Until one night I threatened to redecorate the walls with 'hint of posh twat'. They left me alone after that.

Nightmares

Sometimes there were nights when I was so angry I couldn't breathe. When men from countries I wouldn't be able to place on a map would come to the brothel door and tell us they had a girl they wanted to sell to us. I would tell them to fuck off, and Max would tell me to be quiet. That underbelly of society, where men look to make money from vulnerable women and think that brothels are the venue to take them, is dark. It's not a place that many people see, but when you have seen it you don't forget it. I wonder how the police – the proper police, not the cowboy police who like robbing hookers – ever get over seeing the things that they have seen. The evil that men, because it is usually men, do. It must leave a mark.

She Died with Her Stilettos On

Before Covid, I had a play commissioned and it is supposed to be workshopped but the lockdowns have put paid to that. As things begin to open up again, a tortuous wait, it's eventually given another date. For a while we have actors and a director lined up to see if the play is good enough to go on the stage. But, right on the eve of it coming together, the director comes down with Covid. I am six months pregnant so I realize the chance of it all being rearranged before the baby comes looks unlikely. It's a huge disappointment.

In turn, I cancel the client who I have arranged to see specifically so that I can cover my expenses for the workshop. He says he understands. And then tells me, 'My cock will just have to cope.' I fume. Why does he think his pathetic cock should take priority over my life? He says he will carry on paying me for phone calls until we can meet again, after the baby's born, and I thank him, as a good and grateful whore should, and I wonder why more sex workers haven't killed their clients.

I know the longer my play doesn't get workshopped the less chance I have that the theatre will ever put it on – and it feels like my last chance to step away from sex work and into the creative world. Otherwise, I have a feeling I will still be wearing stilettos and stockings until I die. And that is a genuine fear – that I will be a sex worker until the bitter end. The alternative, it seems to me, is to become a Stepford wife who does nothing more than look after her husband, her child and her home, her self-esteem eroded and her body falling apart, until her partner leaves her for a perky-titted secretary. As I envisage this alternative future I think that perhaps dying in stilettos and stockings isn't the worst way to go, after all. Suddenly, I want to drink and sing and dance and forget and fuck and wake up with a bad head. But instead, I do the dishes, put the washing on and clean out the cat litter.

Don't Give up the Night Job

After a year and a half of whoring in the north London brothel, I was bored with the nights and exhausted by the nights in equal measure. Some of my Romanian friends had moved on and there were new, less friendly women establishing themselves. I had had enough of working alongside them. There was a lot of booze and cocaine knocking around, which made the clients and the girls behave in ways they wouldn't normally. The last straw was when I had to take a knife off an Estonian hooker who was intent on stabbing one of the other women after a petty row about nothing very much. I still had some debts to pay off, and I was still doing tours and taking on the odd promotional job and those two things felt like a constant in my life, two things I could always count on. But I needed something to change.

Rather than leave, I asked if I could start working during the day. Max was reluctant, warning me that I wouldn't make money. We were a shopfront brothel with neon lights; there was no mistaking what it was. And that's OK for most men under cover of darkness, who slip in and out unobserved. But day johns want to be more discreet and so prefer to visit flats, as though they're visiting a friend. It's a different kind of man who's happy to pop into a brothel during daylight. But I convinced Max to let me have a go by saying I would also be available to work on the nights he was short of girls. It was in his interests to try it, I argued, as he wouldn't have to do anything and he would still get the door money from the customers. That reassured him, but he said that I would need another girl to work with, for safety, and he left it with me to choose who I wanted alongside me. The girls who I liked and had known for a while knew that daytime work was probably a lost cause, so I asked a couple of girls who had previously come to the place looking for work but hadn't been taken on.

That was how I dipped my toe into managing.

Now it was me who answered the phone, taking the door money, making notes of times, and the perk was that I didn't have to give 20 per cent of my room money to the boss.

However, it was soon clear that three clients was the most that we could expect during the day and, split between two women, the pay was abysmal. The other women quickly abandoned me; I persevered alone for a few more weeks filling my time with a short Open University creative writing course, jotting down storylines in my notebook. Finally accepting defeat, recognizing that less manic daytime work just wasn't viable, I went back to nights.

My pride had taken a knock, but it wasn't really about me. The truth is that no night brothel looks appealing to a punter during the day. Those tired old sofas have a certain charm in the evening, like going into your favourite dive bar, and the general dimness hides a multitude of sins, all of which are exposed by day. I should have known I couldn't make it work. It was a mistake that would cost me dearly.

An Honest Profession

I made a new friend at the brothel called Tara. She was English, which was rare, a pisshead, which was less rare, and as chaotic as she was hilarious. We got on immediately. We would tag team, and the clients loved having two English girls working together. We had become an exotic rarity. If I say so myself, we put on a spectacular show, which mainly consisted of her shielding my pussy from view with her head while licking my inner thigh as I moaned, writhed and pretended to come. The men would leer, jeer, call us wild and, most importantly, book us for another hour.

Tara lived in Exeter, so I only saw her when she could be arsed to get the train up to London and had a babysitter lined up. So the next time I went on a tour of care homes around the south-west – singing old-fashioned songs and wearing an Easter bonnet instead of stockings for a pleasant change – we met up.

Home for Tara was a council flat she shared with her son, who at just six years old had learned to look after her when she was too drunk to remember to eat. Her flat was small and filthy: cigarette packets, empty vodka bottles and discarded takeaway cartons everywhere. I had never seen squalor like it. Until I met Tara's best friend. She lived down the road with her three children and two huge dogs and the mess was on a much larger scale: ripped and stained carpets and the smell of dog shit heavy in the air.

Tara and her friend talked openly about criminality in front of their children; which benefits they were claiming that they shouldn't and how to get more. They knew the system back to front, and how to exploit it. It was like being in an episode of *Shameless*. It made me uncomfortable, but what could I do? They had welcomed me into their homes and shared their vodka and their pizza. So, I did the sensible thing and kept my mouth and nostrils shut. I made sure my eyes didn't widen with disapproval when they talked about claiming disability benefits for their able-bodied children. I nodded and smiled in all the right places.

In the British class system these two women would be placed alongside me. Working class. But how are you working class when you have never legitimately worked? When she wasn't hooking, Tara was shoplifting, and it's the taxpayers who cover that. Unlike me, she had never paid tax, and she would certainly never take on a minimum-wage job to make ends meet; she'd see it as beneath her. Now, not paying tax when you are a sex worker I understand – after all, we have no workers' rights. But Tara and her friend looked down on anyone who was, as my dad would say, earning an honest crust. They were intent on playing the system until they got caught or died. There's not a lot of love in this society for benefit frauds, but they're probably less frowned upon than sex workers. I wondered how the system could so utterly fail the people who desperately needed help, people like my dad, and at the same time enable others who made more money from their non-disability than I was making from my numerous non-sex-work jobs, all taxpaying and completely above board.

Of course, benefit fraud is not the biggest expense to our country. That odious honour belongs to the tax-dodging billionaires and their cronies who get rich from their shares while little old dears can't afford to turn their heating on. But seeing it all in action at Tara's, that look behind the scenes of how some people lived, was another of life's lessons. And what I took away from it all was knowing for sure how I preferred to get my money, however low paid, however demonized.

Memories

Trying to find sleep has become more of a challenge. I lie on my back. I try my side. I try the other side. Obviously my front is off-limits. The baby kicks, restless too. I put a hand on my stomach as if to say, *Shh. Sleep now*. I toss and turn, and the bed creaks with every lumbering move, but somehow Adam manages to keep on snoring beside me. The snoring is like a drill through my brain. I finally drift off. But even when I'm asleep, snatching moments of rest, my mind is whirring. I dream about people I haven't thought about in decades and remember times when things felt easier.

My mind surfaces on a sunny day, back when I was around seven, and how uncomplicated, light and wonderful life felt. Sitting on the back step of our house with my dog's head resting on my knee. Mum hanging out the washing while Dad waters the plants, and Mum gently scolding him for getting her washing wet. Laughing about it, they give each other a quick hug. Reading my favourite book, *Matilda*, still the only friend I have who likes books as much as me.

I'm comforted by the idea that nobody can take away your good days. They are yours to keep.

A Shift to Remember

I caught up with Tara in the loo one night as I was packing up my things at around 5 a.m. She gave me a hug and offered me a line. Both were very welcome. 'Now, how do you fancy making some serious money?' she asked. She had just spent an hour with a man who was loaded and wanted her to come back to his house to carry on the party. 'But I said I'm not going without you. You up for it?'

I was exhausted after a long session, but another grand on top of the one I'd already made would make it the best night I had ever worked. Hell, it would make it the best week I had ever worked. A few hours' sleep versus the most money I'd ever made in one night was no contest. I nodded and, minutes later, the client transferred the money into my bank account.

I settled up with Max for my previous customer. Anywhere else, if two hookers left the brothel with a client the boss would expect a cut from that job too. But Max never wanted money from our outcalls. That was another reason I liked him so much and adored working there.

Tara and I climbed into a taxi with the client, armed with booze and coke.

I hadn't asked where we were going but the drive felt endless and I nodded off for a while – a welcome power nap and energy boost for what lay ahead – waking up just as we arrived, the taxi pulling up next to some enormous iron gates. I worked out that we were somewhere near Heathrow, the early morning planes low overhead. The client entered a code, the gates swung open, and we found ourselves inside the grounds of a house that almost rivalled Highgrove in its size and splendour. I was fully awake now.

But while it was a beautiful house, the client was a large, odious man with a manner that was already getting on my tits. He rang the doorbell and we waited. And waited. Why, I wondered, was he ringing his own doorbell? Perhaps this wasn't even his house. These vague thoughts that perhaps something wasn't quite right were interrupted by the sound of broken glass. A smashed window.

'That will wake the lazy bastard up,' the client muttered, as an alarm sounded from within the house.

The door opened moments later and there stood a skinny man, black hair, light brown skin, barefoot and wearing nothing more than what looked like a tea-towel around his waist. My friend and I glanced at each other, eyebrows raised. We didn't like it. Somewhere in the back of my mind a little alarm of my own was going off. This scrawny man didn't act like staff or even a servant in the traditional sense – not by the way he was dressed or by his excessively subservient manner. His exaggerated humble body language, and the way he wouldn't – couldn't? – look the client in the eye made him seem more like a slave. But even as the alarm bell in my head continued to jangle, we stepped past him and followed the client into the vast marbled foyer.

He proudly showed us around the basement sauna and enormous swimming pool; we peered out at the tennis courts and into the high-ceilinged, grand rooms that were currently empty and under renovation, clearly with no expense being spared. It was his mother's house. She had some official role in a foreign government, incredibly high powered, out of the country a lot, which meant that she blah blah blah. I was no longer listening, wondering how we were going to extricate ourselves from what was a deteriorating situation. Our client was physically manhandling his servant and telling him in English that he was now going to watch a real man make two women very happy. That he, the servant, was nothing. That he was a piece of shit. And the skinny man, in response, bowed and cowered and whined like a dog.

My face was smiling, and I was pretending to have a great time as he pulled our clothes from our bodies, but I felt very sober. As the client tucked into more and more coke, and became increasingly excitable, I recognized that Tara and I were in a situation that could get out of control very quickly. Normally we had the safety of our brothel and Max. We'd be surrounded by other men and women. But in this mansion, set on its own vast plot of land, it was just us, our mad client and his abused slave. And as well as instilling the feeling of horniness, cocaine makes the cock limp. Which can make a man angry with the woman, who is trying, and failing, to bring the prick to life.

Tara felt it too. She whispered to me to go to the loo and put my clothes back on, which I did, as she distracted the client. A minute or two later she joined me, shouting to the client as she retreated as calmly as possible up the hallway: 'I'll just find her. Back soon, you sexy man!'

She dressed quickly. Then we ran, shoes in hand. Down the stairs, through the front door and along the endless gravel drive to the gates. They were locked. Luckily the wall was only about five feet high with a low tree beside it, giving us a leg-up. We threw our bags over, jumped down the other side, and raced down the empty road, giddy with fear and excitement. Eventually we slowed to a rapid walk and kept going until we stumbled on a train station and, twenty minutes later, caught a train back to London, alongside the freshly showered suits off to do a day's work in the city.

When I told the story to Tony – odious little man, heaps of coke, middle of nowhere, doing a runner, a slave of all things – I thought he would laugh. But I had never seen him angrier. He berated me for not realizing sooner that we could have ended up missing or dead, with no one knowing where to look for us.

'I thought you were smarter,' he told me.

I felt embarrassed. I knew he was right. I had been daft, all for an extra £1,000. I had thought we were safe because there were two of us. I had allowed myself to be led. By Tara. By the money. I wouldn't take such a risk again.

Bloody good story, though.

The Raid

Sometimes I wondered why I was still working in minimum-wage promotions. Hobbling around on heels all day, promoting an average alcoholic drink to suits in Canary Wharf, could make me look forward to getting stuck into my second shift of the day with men keen to take off those suits. But I knew that if I only did sex work, if £200 an hour was routinely what I earned, I would become lazy, complacent and bored. Many of the working girls I knew spent all their time shopping in designer stores and I refused to let that happen to me. The ethos of hard work and honest grind was too ingrained. Promoting kept me grounded and it meant that I never took money for granted. I fully understood its value. Of course, in an ideal world I would be solely acting. But that required money and contacts that I didn't have and I was slowly admitting to myself that I never would.

I was content enough. I had worked out a good routine. I had long since given up my tiny studio with my helpful Turkish landlord and rented a flat in the Midlands where I would live Saturday to Wednesday, spending my time doing promotional work, visiting the gym and writing and reading, and then I would travel to London and work at the brothel Wednesday night through till Friday night. I had rented a beautiful apartment in central London because I was planning, before too long, to market myself as independent. Despite the element of fun, I had become tired of the drama that the girls in the night place brought with them, tired of having to jump out of my shower to break up drunken fights in the predawn hours. There I'd be, starkers, wrestling with two tiny Eastern Europeans while the clients whooped and jeered as though it was all part of the entertainment. Recently, one English girl had brought in some heroin and had smoked it with Max. It was too much. I was in a permanent grump that standards were slipping; it wasn't the same place it had once been. Or perhaps it was, but I was awake for the first time and seeing it more clear-sightedly.

Although I had had to give up on the idea of working days from the brothel, I thought taking on the London flat was worth a punt. I could offer a discreet service. I knew that some of my regulars would be happy to see me there, even during the day, and I would pick up a few new clients too as I had just posted a profile on an advertising site. For two years I had slept at the brothel between shifts and I wanted to have somewhere nice to stay that didn't resemble all nine of Dante's circles of Hell.

I was feeling settled and confident. I should have remembered that life has a way of knocking you down when things are going well. Of all the lessons I'd learned by then, given my experience so far, I should have known that.

And things were much better with my sister. Having suffered her remorseless criticism for so long, I'd told her that I was out of it, spending my working life doing promo and odd bits of acting and that was how I wanted it to stay. She had organized a rare family lunch and I was determined to go, so after another day standing around holding a tray of drinks in some faceless corporate outfit, I went back to my flat to pick up my stuff for the journey home to the Midlands that I would make the following morning, straight from the brothel.

I had worked the last two nights and had around £1,000 in cash, my laptop and my usual array of notebooks that I used to write everything down – from shopping lists to short stories to business ideas. I was loaded up like a pack horse, red-faced and huffing by the time I arrived at the brothel, around 9 p.m.

The girls didn't look happy to see me. Firstly, more girls means more competition. They had been there since 7 p.m., although the place only really got busy after 10 p.m., and here I was swanning in in the nick of time with my baggage and my apologies.

'Angel. How nice of you to join us,' Max sneered through a marijuana haze.

I ducked into an empty room to get ready. I took a restorative shower and enjoyed a moment of peace as the hot water cascaded down my weary body. I patted myself dry, wrapped a towel around me and wandered back up the stairs to join the others.

My first thought on seeing the policeman standing at the top of the stairs was that he was a stripper. We had plenty of policeman clients, of course, but they didn't tend to turn up in full uniform. He saw me on the staircase and beckoned for me to join the group assembled in the communal space. I saw then that the place was swarming with the fuckers. Plain clothed and uniformed, men and women, all visibly buzzed to be there. I perched on a chair next to one of my ashen-faced colleagues and quietly asked her where Max had got to.

'They took him away after he said he was the manager,' she whispered.

We were on our own.

I watched as the police searched the place, eyes and hands everywhere. I watched with interest, but not with too much anxiety. I was a bit concerned about Max. I was fond of him. Though, as a man who had been in prisons all over the world, I knew that he would be OK, that somehow or other he'd weather the storm. I thought we girls were safe, and that only pimps got done in a raid like this. HMRC says that being an escort is a profession and even that we can expense things like condoms and lubrication. But the law says that two escorts working together is a brothel. The police were searching for anything that pointed to the space being a brothel, rather than somewhere men and women, consenting adults, simply gathered to hang out, have drinks and have fun. A customer in the corner of the room was giving his details and, understandably, looked terrified about what this would mean for him.

They were out of luck when it came to porn, finding only a large illustrated book called *The Book of Pussy*, which they put in an evidence bag. I bet they'll enjoy looking through that later, I thought. One female PC was told to count the condoms that were stored in a box under the reception desk, the possession of condoms being used as evidence. You don't have to be Albert Einstein to realize that the police criminalizing condoms is a bad idea.

She kept making excited comments as the tally soared.

'Two hundred and forty-two,' she said. 'This is *definitely* a brothel.'

What was your first clue, you dumb fuck? I thought. Hadn't she noticed the women hanging around in underwear and the shagging, so rudely interrupted, that had been going on downstairs? But I stayed silent, taking it all in.

I clocked that some of the women were dressed too frumpily and typically middle class to be coppers – those M&S cardis again. We were told that they were from an anti-trafficking organization and that they were there to help us. I looked at them. We don't need to be helped, thank you very much, I didn't say.

'Is anyone here even English?' an older plod roared into the silence.

'I am,' I replied. I matched his tone with defiance gleaming in my eyes.

I had had enough of this. The other women were terrified, I could see, but I felt unrepentant. Their efforts to shame us and make us feel like victims were not going to work on me. I was a sole trader. I had an accountant. I paid tax. What could they do to me?

I was told to dress and, as I made my way to the bathroom to put on some clothes, a female plod followed me, saying that she had to watch, that she couldn't let me out of her sight. By this time the police were opening Max's vast collection of CD cases searching for God knows what and the other women were being led downstairs one at a time into a bedroom to be questioned by another female plod and one of the anti-trafficking women.

I was taken last and was asked a series of questions that I answered mostly truthfully. I had never been coached by anyone on what to say and what not to say in a situation like this, so when asked I said that we paid 20 per cent of our earnings to Max, our boss, and that we did whatever we liked in the room. He had no knowledge of what we did in there. That was a little fib as, sometimes, when he got really stoned, Max would burst in on us like a naughty teenager in search of fun. Once he'd jumped into my room as I was doing ballet poses for one of our quirkier clients. 'Fuck off!' I had shouted at him, laughing as I fell out of my pirouette. How could these narrow-minded government servants ever have the imagination to comprehend the full spectrum of what went on here?

The second I said I was happy to be there and that we were all consenting adults, the plod's face changed. Her eyes narrowed and her lips became a hard line. It wasn't what she wanted to hear. She quizzed me on who the drugs belonged to, forgetting that I had joined the party late, so had no idea what drugs she was referring to. I looked back at her, blank. Perhaps it was coke, as the client who'd got caught liked a line or two and we all knew the woman he was with was a coke fiend. But I couldn't – or wouldn't – say. Then there was the grass that Max smoked all day, every day. They'd found it tucked away on the reception desk. Asked again, I replied that I didn't know what she was talking about. She then said that she was going to search my bag. I handed it over. No drugs, of course, but she couldn't help but show her glee as she unearthed the cash that I'd packed to take home with me.

'One thousand pounds in cash,' she exclaimed. 'That's *a lot* of money.' And for the first time I got a cold feeling in my gut. Pure terror.

Some Assembly Required

Between us, Adam and I have a wealth of experience. Street smarts, of course, but academic smarts too. Adam has had the best education that his fine brain could get him; four years at Oxbridge studying physics. Then there's me. A quick learner and streetwise, with a side of strong muscle that comes from beating men in arm wrestles for drinks since I was twenty, and then later for cash. And never underestimate how strong you have to be to get past two sphincters. So, I often think that with both brains and brawn we can achieve quite a lot together. That we're quite the team.

Four hours of consultation and cussing, sweating and swearing, and we still haven't been able to assemble the fucking cot.

Final Destination

I was arrested for assisting in the management of the brothel.

'Time for a different career, love,' said one of the anti-trafficking women as she patted me twice on the shoulder on her way out. She was lucky I was in shock, otherwise I would have broken her fingers.

The police gathered my bags and escorted me to a waiting car. Our neighbours who ran the newspaper shop were outside, gawping and grinning at the spectacle. People always like to watch car crashes, don't they? They had had no problem taking our money for years when we'd popped in for odds and sods, but now we were getting nicked, it was pure entertainment. They couldn't get enough of it.

In the car my arresting officer, Kate, asked if I was all right. I snapped at her that I was fine. But I wasn't fine, and neither did she care either way. As we entered the police station, we passed one of her colleagues, who was just back from another raid.

'I've got one, how many have you got?' she asked Kate.

Kate inclined her head towards me and smiled a tight, smug smile that made me want to rip her head off. Was this really how the police were supposed to act? So excited and self-righteous and casual about the damage they were doing to people's lives?

At the custody desk I was introduced to a man who took all of my belongings: my laptop, three phones, notebooks, Oyster card and all my money, down to the small change rolling around at the bottom of my bag. Kate went through my wallet and was delighted to find a Young Person's Railcard.

'You are clearly not a young person, so I am arresting you for fraud.'

Arrested for being a madam and for fraud all in one day? My only previous visit to the cop shop had been after I'd retrieved a mewling kitten from a tree. If she'd bothered to ask, I'd have let Kate know that I had been studying when I'd been issued the Railcard, and that mature students are entitled to discount too. But there was no point saying anything. I couldn't let her see that it was getting to me.

'Right,' said Kate. 'I need to strip-search you.' As I had been naked when the police unexpectedly arrived and they had watched me dress, I didn't think that was necessary but as I wasn't some virgin milkmaid, unused to people gazing on my naked flesh, I stripped off and bent over so she could look right up my arse.

I bit back the urge to say, 'Kiss me, Kate.'

Part of the Process

Then came fingerprints and mugshots. As they took my pictures, both in profile and straight on, I thought of the various times bosses had tried to make me use my image to sell their business. Surely those images would confirm my innocence, that I was a hooker not a madam? All the photographs were on the computer they'd taken from me. The pornographic pictures sat next to the headshots I used for acting work, serious poses that confirmed that I would be great for whichever Shakespearean tragedy I was auditioning for. What madam would have those in her possession? I winced as the police captured my image.

At the fingerprinting table I looked at the wet ink and the stamp on the page that would forever be associated with me. I didn't like it, this record of who I supposedly was.

And then I was taken to a cell.

Despite it being summer, with a wonderful warmth in the air outside, there was a deep chill in that tiny room. The mattress on my concrete bed was a thin and worn blue pad. There was a sparkling clean metal toilet without a lid in the corner. They slammed the door behind me and I was alone with my scrambled thoughts.

Seventeen hours is a long time to be locked up, particularly when you're on your own. Goodness knows how people in prison cope with the isolation and the boredom. They brought me potatoes and beans and a coffee so weak and tasteless that it could have been tea. A policeman, a brick of a man, occasionally checked in on me. I asked him if I could have a shower, but he told me there were no female officers around in the station to facilitate my request. He then said that they might search my flat up north, but it probably wouldn't be necessary. That hadn't even crossed my mind. Another thing to stew about. They seemed to have got into their heads that I was a powerful madam from a Martina Cole plot, not a woman who sang songs to the elderly while wearing an Easter bonnet.

I cried after he left, which surprised me as I almost never cry for myself. But this felt different. It felt so unjust. I knew that it would blow a hole through my family, which we would never recover from. Thinking about them, and how my dad would look at me, made me put my head in my hands and weep. Then I pulled myself together and did some press-ups in an attempt to get warm – it seemed like a good idea at the time and the kind of thing people did in cells. It certainly helped to pass the time, and the light was so blinding there was no chance of sleep.

Finally, out of boredom, I masturbated. I thought it might relax me. It didn't.

Years later, when I was watching a true-crime police show, I realized that there was probably a camera in my cell. Roll up, roll up! Free show in cell seven!

After many more hours of staring at the scuffed wall the brick came back and feigned surprise that my cell was so bright. He said he would get the light turned down a few notches. I could have blown him for that.

As Tight as a Gnat's Twat

At eight months pregnant, I am now permanently tense and grumpy, even more so after I attempt an orgasm and it goes by with me barely noticing. I have never before realized how orgasms have always helped me to stay sane. Fuck meditation, I say, when you can have the pleasure of an orgasm at your fingertips. But if that pleasure, and release, has gone – what now?

I give Adam some tingle lube and a couple of porno magazines and tell him that my vagina is closed for business.

'Get used to wanking.'

He laughs as though it's a joke. It's not.

I wonder, briefly, if he will be tempted to start seeing hookers again. I hope not.

And now I get it. No wonder men are more likely to cheat when their partners are pregnant. I used to think it was because of the change in appearance, that they had an aversion to their partner's new life-carrying shape, and it would make me fume. But, really, I think it's because the changes our bodies go through are so significant it's like we're a new person completely. Our focus is on keeping our little passenger safe and, for me at least, sex is the last thing on my mind.

Interview

My duty solicitor was a small woman with mousy brown hair, wearing a cheap navy suit. As I sat down opposite her in an interview room I told her I felt as though my life had been destroyed, and she raised an eyebrow in a way that suggested I was being over dramatic. I hoped she was right about that. She told me to tell the truth. She said I couldn't be done for selling sex as I had no keys to the premises, my name hadn't been found on any documents, like utility bills and rental agreements, that I was clearly only there a few nights a week and as I took months off at a stretch to act and tour, how could they possibly build a case against me? Her words gave me some comfort. I felt a little easier within myself as we waited in silence for the police to join us for my formal interview.

The brick was one of two men who arrived to do the job. Smiling, he took a seat opposite me, while the other, an older brick, took his seat with a stern look on his face. Even before they began, I started to shake. I did as I'd been instructed and told them the truth. Everything they asked, I gave them a straight answer.

Now I know that I should have said 'no comment' to the whole interview. Fucking duty solicitors. Never trust them to know the difference between their arse and their elbow. The only thing I wouldn't answer was a question about drugs – I had no comment to make about that. I knew the dealers, and it was rumoured that one of them was a killer who worked for a notorious London crime family, so on that point I thought it better to keep my mouth shut. I also thought it best not to mention the new flat I'd taken on in London so that I could start seeing my own clients as I didn't want to be chucked out before I started. A hooker tenant is one thing. A hooker tenant with the police sniffing around is another. I thought my honesty would keep me safe, but the police were convinced that Max, being drunken and permanently stoned, couldn't possibly be the brains behind the place. They weren't wrong – of course there was someone else pulling the strings – but I was saying nothing. They wouldn't have believed me if I had told them who the real boss was.

We took a break in which they brought me water, which I gulped down. Then the grilling continued, pressing and pressing about my phones, wanting to know why I had three. I explained that one was for my brothel clients, one was my personal phone and the last was for my new profile on Adult Work, a website on which escorts can advertise. They didn't believe anything I said. But I was convinced that if they just looked at my phone contacts, they would see I was telling the truth. Sex workers save their clients using descriptions. We have to. Do you have any idea how many johns called John we meet? We'd be lost without giving them a defining characteristic: 'nice John', 'tight John', 'fisting John', and so on. They were all there in my phone. What kind of madam would have a contacts list like that?

After what felt like a couple of hours, I was taken back to the custody desk, where I was issued my bail conditions. No contact with Max. No going within a hundred feet of the brothel. They would hold on to my phones and laptop, as they were key pieces of evidence. I was presented with my empty wallet – they had taken all my cash and all my cards save for just one debit card – and was told I could go home.

The original brick walked me to the door. He asked if, for a financial incentive, I would be a confidential informant. I said yes, as I thought at the time it was the best answer to give. I wanted my things back and I wanted out of there. I wanted to be free. Outside, I could see the big boss, talking on the phone. He must have come to collect Max, who, I realized, would have been put through the same ordeal as me.

'Do you know that person?' the policeman asked, following my glance.

'No,' I answered.

He told me that they had raided my flat up north and taken away my safe and some pills. I was confused about the pills because the only ones I had were in my vitamin drawer, clearly branded Holland and Barrett. But if they wanted to waste time and money checking them in a lab, then fuck 'em. He asked me for the code for the safe, which I gave him, and then I was turfed out into the bright late afternoon sun.

I had missed the family lunch, and I knew they would all be frantic as they'd had no word from me since the day before. What the hell was I going to tell them?

Going Home

Dazed, I walked to Euston station, and managed to get myself on a northbound train, where I fretted for three hours. I walked the two miles from the station to my flat, only to find a huge piece of plywood nailed across the gap where my front door had once been. I walked another mile to the nearest police station to inquire how I was supposed to get into my home. That was my problem, apparently. The woman on the desk pointed to a pay phone. I tried my best mate, who didn't answer, so I was left with only one option.

Through gritted teeth I asked if my sister and her husband, Patrick, could come and get me, and I asked them to bring a crowbar and whatever other tools they thought might help me to break into my own home. They arrived at the police station within the hour, full of questions. I apologized about missing the family lunch and told them I was in a bit of trouble. Quite possibly a lot of trouble. I had been arrested for fraud and assisting in the management of a brothel. Not something one hears every day. 'Well, at least it's not drugs,' Patrick said, and then they drove me to my flat. With a bit of effort, he removed the makeshift plywood as I busied myself dismissing the nosy neighbours who had come to gawp. Nothing to see here, I informed them. Then we were in.

The flat was a complete disaster. Body oil had been knocked onto the carpet, creating a sprawling, sticky stain, and everything had been moved out of position. Manhandled. Pictures askew, furniture facing the wrong way, and my otherwise pristine bed sheets in disarray. I felt more violated than when a client tried to stick his finger in my cunt without permission.

This was my space. My sanctuary. And it was ruined.

The Pram

Now that the cot is finally up, I begin scouring Gumtree and eBay for prams. I wanted a Silver Cross as they are beautiful, and I find one for sale at a good price, just twenty miles away.

Adam is concerned that we won't be able to fit the pram in our three-door car, even after he has taken the seats down, but my optimism is at peak fantasist level, so he knows it best not to argue with me.

The car ride is not easy. With my large bump it is impossible for me to get comfortable. But it will be worth it. My daughter is about to get a lovely pram.

When we arrive, we are shown into a living room by a woman and her husband. And there is the pram, standing by the window and absolutely perfect, just like its picture.

'My daughter has outgrown it now and it's just taking up space,' the woman explains.

'Lovely,' I say. Followed by 'May I?'

I push it slowly around the room, getting a feel for it. There is no doubt that this pram will fit in our car.

I am not sure when the penny drops. Perhaps it is when I become aware of the curious silence that descends as the three adults survey me, or perhaps it's when I have a thought that, surely, my baby will outgrow it quite soon. Or perhaps it's when Adam says, 'It's a bit small . . .' – a helpful hint and quite an understatement – that I realize that I am pushing a child's toy around the room.

Money, Money, Money

I had a wallet stashed away that the police hadn't found, with £200 cash in it. But, of course, my safe was gone. It had held over £6,000 in cash, money I'd gradually transfer to the bank to clear away my debt. I'd grown up with a nanna who'd kept a shoebox of cash tucked away under her bed and, like her, I enjoyed seeing what I was earning. Money in a bank never feels real. Cold hard cash does. And now it was gone.

The money the police had taken was all I had, apart from £400 in my bank account and the £200 in the wallet. With no job, due to my bail conditions, and rent to pay on two flats, plus loan repayments approaching, I didn't know what the fuck I was going to do. I just couldn't understand how they could simply take my money – ask me for the code to my safe, and take my money. I didn't know – and they hadn't told me – about something called the Proceeds of Crime Act, or POCA, where anybody under suspicion of making money through unlawful means who is found with more than £1,000 can have their money and assets seized. Although many sex workers pay tax on their earnings, that doesn't matter to the police.

The act was brought into law in 2002 to take money away from drug dealers, but the police had found it far more lucrative and far less trouble to take money away from sex workers. Why fight a hard, armed bastard of a man when you can steal from a little woman in her underwear? In carefully planned manoeuvres, the police raid brothels on a Friday – as they did with us – when they know the maximum amount of money will be on the premises. The police keep 25 per cent of the money they take and the rest is handed over to the Home Office. They have the power to freeze bank accounts and will take any property that a sex worker has acquired, even if she lives there with her family. In my case it was lucky that I was renting, that since I'd sold my house to pay drama school fees I no longer had a home I owned.

The second reason our money and assets can be seized, and this is a more difficult reason to argue against, is if the money is going to be used for illegal purposes in the future. It's very hard for the average person to prove what they are going to spend their money on. All of which means it is very easy for the police to get away with the theft because it is a civil matter and, therefore, we can't get legal aid to fight it.

If we sell sex and someone takes a cut, they are a pimp. It's also difficult to argue against that.

Fighting Plan

In case I ever lost my phone I had written down some key telephone numbers – of friends and clients – so went off to Tesco to buy a pay-as-you-go. I texted a select number of people to tell them what had happened. Tony called me immediately. Bless him.

'Are you all right?'

'No,' I told him. 'I just don't know what will happen now. I have no job and no money. They took it all.'

'Christ.'

He sounded as devastated as I was.

We talked for some time, me reliving everything in a stream of consciousness and him listening, and calming me down with his soothing words, and the next day he called again.

'There's an article in *The Guardian*. A woman was

interviewed who runs an NHS outreach programme for sex workers. I have her number.'

A brief moment of light. A sense of hope.

I called her and she said she knew of an organization that could help me, a charity called the English Collective of Prostitutes, or ECP, who had contacts with proper lawyers who really knew their stuff and could offer me legal support. I didn't much care for the organization's name, but I was in no position to protest. The following day I went back to London – the train fare another dent in my diminishing funds. The woman I'd spoken to, Natalie, a willowy, no-nonsense type, met me at the station and together we made our way to north London and to the English Collective's office space.

Almost in one breathless outpouring, I told them everything I possibly could about what had happened. Their first sugges-tion was to sack my duty solicitor as her 'advice' had cost me dearly. It turned out that I was the only woman in the brothel who had admitted I sold sex, so I had effectively been arrested for assisting myself. Then they arranged an appointment with the solicitor they used in cases like mine. And there were plenty of cases like mine.

That night, as I walked into my beautiful W1 flat, I thought to myself that I had just under a month to make a shit ton of cash to pay the rent and to rebuild my life while my new solici-tor and I built my case. But how on earth could I start doing that with no job, no smart phone and no laptop?

It sounded pretty hopeless, but I knew I would come up with a plan. I always did. I just had to think of it as a game of chess.

I'd fucked up the opening so now I had to consider everything that could happen in all future moves. Keep thinking. Keep going. Keep fighting.

Locked Up Again

Every week I don't work I nip into town to check my dungeon windows haven't been smashed, the kind of mindless vandalism which is a common occurrence in my town. And while I'm there I see one of my regulars for a session. I have already packed up all my stilettos – they don't fit my swollen feet, in any case – but money is money, and this CBT client is easy. I can do cock-and-ball torture while sitting down, culminating in a painful wank of Deep Heat, chillies and nettles.

Arriving, I am relieved to see the windows are intact. I unlock my door and push. It's stiff and I have to put my shoulder against it and give a good nudge. My additional heft comes in handy. Inside, I text my client to tell him to give me an extra five minutes to get ready.

I cover my belly with a low cut, black tent dress. My breasts are enormous and I know the male gaze rarely travels south of the tits, so as long as they're visible I should be OK. Of course, he knows I'm pregnant as I have told him already by email, to avoid any difficult surprises, but subs rarely like to think that their mistresses have sex. Unless they are into cuckolding, the idea of us shagging other men makes their cock go limp. And we don't want that. They like to think of us as goddesses, untouched by mere mortals like them.

There's a knock at the door. I put my game face on and turn the handle, but nothing happens. 'You're going to have to push!' I say through the door, and obediently – of course he is going to be obedient – he does. The door gives.

He enters and I shut the door behind him, but it closes too quickly, with a bang, and rattles in its frame. 'The spindle has gone, Mistress,' my carpenter client says from his knees on the floor. It's his usual position after entering my domain but he's not usually engaging in a bit of DIY.

'If I hadn't been on the other side, you would never have been able to open the door,' he says, as he inspects the problem.

Trapped in my own dungeon.

After a bit, he shuffles around, still on his knees, and kisses my feet.

'I'll sort it out later,' he says.

Political Awakening

I started to become politically aware after my arrest. Even though I had worked in the sex industry since I was twenty-one, I had no idea about the laws that affected us. I had honestly thought only bosses and street sex workers could be arrested, which was terribly naive, and my new friends at the ECP quickly educated me on the law. I met sex activists for the first time, women who had worked in the industry, or still did, and who fought every day to make their voices heard. They were desperate but exciting times as my eyes and mind were opened.

I formed an immediate bond with Maggie. As a sex-work activist Maggie would go into universities and speak openly about whoring. I went to support her a few times, surprised by the vile comments, the bile, the judgement that was levelled against her. Not from the students, who were always curious and polite. But each debate had a radical feminist along for 'nuance' and without fail they would sneer at my friend, who they believed too old, too fat, too not-what-they-expected, to work as a hooker. It showed me how little they knew of men, that they would assume that one size fits all. I didn't understand why there needed to be another side to the argument, why the event was framed as a debate at all. Imagine any other industry in which the workers were advocating for more safety for themselves, and now imagine that there was another side arguing against it. 'No need to send down the canary! We'll soon find out if there are harmful gases in the mine when the men start dropping!'

I discovered that the rad fems wanted to combat prostitution by killing as many of us as possible. It is worth repeating that in every country that has criminalized the purchase of sex, violence against sex workers has risen. The more criminalized we are, the more disposable we are perceived to be by society. In America, where prostitution is totally illegal (save in Nevada), sex workers additionally have been nailed by the FOSTA-SESTA bill, which became law in 2018. While it was put in place under the guise of preventing sex trafficking, in reality it has meant that sex workers can't advertise online. That, in turn, has led to more sex workers being exposed to violence as it drives previously independent sex workers back to pimps and/or to the street. Donald Trump, a man obviously pissed off with hookers after our pal Stormy fucked him, signed off on that law.

The problem is that radical feminists have a voice, and we don't. And when we object to being silenced, or at least not being heard, they tell us that they know best. If we argue too articulately, we are called privileged and dismissed as a tiny minority who can string a sentence together. If we argue too aggressively, they accuse us of being mentally ill and claim that they've proved their point, that we are vulnerable, no longer having any idea who we really are and need protecting.

I realized very quickly once I started to educate myself that we would never win the battle with the rad fems, but that the important thing was to keep fighting, like Maggie, and to keep trying to educate people about sex work and sex workers. When a sex worker is killed, it's important that as many people as possible understand that the killer is just like the gangs of police that rob the brothels. It's a man who knows he will get away with it. It's important for as many people as possible to know that the laws in this country are there to protect him, not us.

Protection Plan

During the ongoing shitshow my brothel colleagues hadn't bothered to reach out and I couldn't understand why. Well, one had been in touch, having got my new number from Tony. Alice. To tell me that Max wanted to kill me for talking. Apparently, he had told all the women that I had been singing like a canary about all of them: the bosses, the drugs, everything. I hadn't talked. But it was a clear threat in case I was thinking about it.

I remembered Alice once saying, 'In my country you can have someone killed for five hundred pounds', so I took her seriously. She was an unpleasant individual, occasionally bringing to work unhappy-looking women who she claimed were her cousins. I'd told Max what I thought of her, but he was loyal to her. After all, she had worked there since the brothel opened ten years before and I was a relative newcomer, someone who came and went quite happily, more or less on their own terms. Less happily now.

While I was confident that no one knew where my London flat was, it was easy enough to find my northern home as it was on documents sent to Max's solicitor – as we'd been arrested at the same raid our criminal cases were connected. After that, whenever I was up north, I carried a weapon. Just in case.

Scan

As a geriatric mother I get more scans than usual to check that my baby is growing as she should be. So, each month I drink plenty of water and then present myself at the hospital, my full bladder enabling the team to get a clear scan. This excessive intake of water to the point of a bursting bladder is one of the torture tactics I have used many times to humiliate my submissives. And now it is being visited on me. As the doctor presses down on my abdomen I wonder why on earth a man would pay to be tortured in this way. I beg to be allowed to wee, whining like a child: 'Just a little bit. I promise I'll leave some wee inside me.'

The doctor and the nurse laugh and say that's impossible. That once I go, I won't be able to stop the flow. But of course, I can. I am a trained dominatrix. Weeing on a man in short bursts throughout a session is as easy for me as them taking my blood pressure. I wee a flood of water in the bathroom down the corridor, and then hop back on the bed with a bladder half full. They express amazement and I bite back the urge to tell them that one slave once called me the Queen of Watersports, an accolade that made me ridiculously proud.

Work Plan

My first night back in London Tony came to the flat with booze, cocaine and a computer.

'It's my spare so you can have it,' he said, as I threw my arms around him.

The next morning, I tracked down my password for Adult Work and finished setting up my independent account. I got a couple of clients quickly from that, but not as many as I was hoping for. I was charging the same as I had at the brothel, I thought that was only fair. But men looking online, sober and during the day, maybe sitting at their desk or wearing a suit and feeling reasonably sensible, were unwilling to pay so much, even if they were going to be visiting me in the salubrious surroundings of W1. So, on Gumtree (you really can find anything on Gumtree) I found a couple of brothels that were looking for staff. I also applied to escort agencies, and I looked for promotional work. Anything to make cash. My W1 rent alone was £2,600 a month – and it was due in just under three weeks.

I decided to tell the W1 landlord my situation. He knew I was a working girl as he was one of my clients. He said I should let him know as soon as possible if I couldn't afford to stay; there were going to be no concessions. I knew that there wasn't a hope in hell of me getting the money together, but I was still occasionally an optimist, believing in myself, in my resilience. And I genuinely thought the case would get dropped and that I would get my money back. I just needed to hang on. Ever hopeful, then, I started to walk the brothels of London looking for work. I started with the sauna that was just down the road from my old place in north London. It was more than 100 feet away, so I wasn't breaking my bail conditions. I knew this place charged the same rates as the brothel, that much was familiar, but I realized as soon as I walked in that they wouldn't take me. All the women were like Hugh Hefner dolls. False lips, false boobs. Barbie lookalikes. Not a northern gobshite like me among them. I spun on my Primark canvas shoes and left. But there was work out there. The question was whether or not I could do it.

Vaccine

I'm trying to stay away from reading the news, but can't help looking when I see a story about a pregnant woman. A few have ended up in comas due to catching Covid late in their pregnancy. Fortunately, the NHS has done enough research to recommend that pregnant women should get vaccinated. However, they also insist that we should not get the Astra-Zeneca jab but go for Moderna or Pfizer. And so, when I get a text to tell me to ring and book an appointment, I duly do so.

The woman on the phone books me a slot at my local centre. I thank her, then say, 'Just to check, that won't be AstraZeneca?' Immediately her tone changes. She huffily tells me that she doesn't have access to that information, but it will either be that or Moderna. I tell her that if it's AstraZeneca then I can't have it due to being pregnant. She thinks I am being difficult. Perhaps a conspiracy nut.

She tells me I can't make any requests. If they don't have the jab I want I can walk away.

'So, just to be clear,' I can't help but say, 'the plan is for me to take my enormous bump to the local vaccine centre that is ten miles away, stand in a long queue, then just before the needle is plunged into my arm I have to check which med it is? And waddle away if it's the wrong one? Brilliant.'

I'd say it's the last straw, but I know that there are so many last straws yet to come.

In the Shit

I found work but couldn't stick at a place for long. Each brothel was just a bit shitter than the last. Thanks to the crack-down, there were no shopfront brothels left for me to try, so I was back to menus and being spoken to by managers and maids alike as though I was the dirt on their shoe. Worst of all was that the men in these places were much pushier about us doing extras, and the bosses insisted on us offering them if we wanted to keep working there. I was back to working while on my period as well, which I only used to do when I was really skint, in the days before Max's brothel. This meant a sponge stuck deep up in my vagina so the dick doesn't come into contact and then struggling to get the slimy fucker out at the end of shift.

My ideal day client was a typical brothel creeper, middle-aged or older with a few strands of hair covering a bald patch. A small pot belly. I really didn't mind too much what they looked like, I just wanted them to be quiet, polite and malleable. These men were our bread and butter. We welcomed them. Unfortunately, in the cheaper brothels what I got was a lot of boundary pushers, the men who say, 'I have paid an extra tenner for kissing so I want tongue!' Of course, there are ways to manipulate them. A compliment to their cock always distracts their tiny brains. But I fucking hated the boundary pushers.

And it wasn't just that so many men were trying it on physically. It was the way they tried to get in our heads too. 'What would your boyfriend think if he knew I was fucking you?' asked one creep. I didn't have a boyfriend and, by Christ, this man was lucky I didn't have a gun either.

Sex workers say time and time again that brothels where the workers have no choice but to do extras, are more dangerous to our health. But the police still insist on raiding the shopfront brothels, the ones where we can earn more and can say no. The most I was making in one day was £300 and that just wasn't enough to justify the awful conditions. It wasn't enough, period. It barely scratched the surface of the money I needed to find.

One brothel was run by a short, physically unappealing Romanian husband and his wife, a brassy woman with a baying voice. Occasionally the wife took a trick but generally she was out shopping. They had a fourteen-year-old and an eleven-year-old who lived in the flat above. The day I saw the fourteen-year-old girl answering calls at the desk from horny punters I left and never went back. Why were the police not raiding places like that? I wondered. Was it because it required just a tiny bit more work to find them, a google on the internet rather than seeing a neon sign that says 'sauna' on the street? Or is it not worth their bother as the takings are smaller due to the shockingly low rates? Of the ten or so places I worked after my arrest, none had been raided, despite the clean-up that was happening across London. But every sauna I knew of had gone.

At another brothel, run out of a flat in the City of London, I was asked to strip at my 'interview'. It's an indicator of just how much I needed the job that I obediently removed my clothes. The maid looked at my naked body critically and eventually said, 'You'll do.' Christ, what was she hoping for in a place that charged £120 an hour and the boss keeps half? Claudia fucking Schiffer?

Then there was another place in north London. That location was risky for me as the same police force could come crashing through our door at any time, and I was constantly on red alert now. If I got arrested again I would be in so much more trouble. No matter if it was my first day there, if me and one other hooker were doing business, then according to the law we were assisting each other. But because of the cheap prices for punters, I reckoned I was safe from grasping police hands. And surely even I wasn't so unlucky as to get done twice within one month?

The man who ran it hadn't a clue about discretion. He kept all the phone numbers of the punters in a little database and one day sent texts to all of them advertising 'thirty-minute full service £50!' and for the rest of that day the other hooker and I were taking calls from crying wives who couldn't believe this was happening to them. I left for good that night, telling the other girl I wouldn't be back. I couldn't face it.

I got a phone call a few hours later. 'I was going to let you run the place, you ungrateful bitch!' the boss ranted. One impending conviction for pimping was more than enough for me, ta very much, so that was an easy no.

Supporters of the End Demand model say that we go somewhere else in our heads when we are shagging clients, a coping strategy to help us deal with being – as they would put it – 'raped'. And the former is true, but not in the way that they think. Even with the men I hated I was able to rationalize that they were all serving a purpose, and I was counting cash in my head 90 per cent of the time. I used to do the same when I was working in factories but the numbers had been so piffling I'd given up.

The least welcome knocks on these doors were from groups of young men. Some brothels simply won't let the groups in, which you would think would be easy, but they don't present as a group. One of them gets the door open while the others hide out of view of the camera. Then they barge in. Suddenly you've got a fired-up pack on your hands, which takes some managing. If they are horny and there are enough girls on, then they can be controlled. I have worked at brothels where they wouldn't allow black men in. Full stop. But that didn't sit well with me as bad behaviour can come from anywhere, and a gang of volatile young men is as easily white as black. Scum is scum and the colour of someone's skin is irrelevant.

The gangs are the very worst and often they wouldn't be there for pussy. Gaining access to a brothel means easy money as they know that brothels won't report a robbery. And even if they do, the police won't bother turning up. Why would they when they are too busy robbing the brothels themselves and getting an easy conviction as the cherry on top? I learned from a very reliable source that that's what happened to a woman in Sussex whose place got raided by a gang, with her maid and working girl beaten up. The gang had come in with guns and there's no arguing with guns. The manager, an ex-working girl, wasn't just scared for her life, she was livid that this could happen. She went to the cops, who patiently took down all the information, then immediately arrested her. Her life was ruined. They went after the house she lived in with her family, including her partner's money, and what she got instead of support was a criminal record. The police didn't bother themselves with the gang. They couldn't be less arsed.

I found all this out via a girl who had worked for the poor woman as she had also lost her dependable brothel and was, like me, lurching from place to place and chatting to a whole load of people along the way about their experiences. This was now my world – with no sense of security or safety, no idea of what might happen from day to day. Each new brothel had bitchy hookers to negotiate and none were happy when I turned up, a Brit with good legs and good boobs with an ever-ready smile that might or might not be genuine.

A Diamond

The element of surprise wasn't always bad. In one flat during this uncertain time I met an older man who was absolutely lovely. I can still see his golf socks, which he had kept on and which I had to tell him to take off because, let's face it, even Brad Pitt would look ridiculous in just his socks. He became a client for years and, more than that, he became a friend. He was unhappy and lonely and I was able to fill a gap in his life. His wife hadn't allowed him to touch her for the thirty years since she had had their children. He should have left her, I always thought, but many middle-class men don't leave, they stay because they enjoy the family set-up and the security and respectability that brings and instead will have affairs or see hookers in order to satisfy their needs. And perhaps the wife is OK with that; maybe it's an arrangement that works for everyone. Sometimes putting your head in the sand also does the trick. Meanwhile there's someone like me who can make that man less unhappy and less lonely. I sometimes accidentally blur the line between business and friendship if I like someone, and I did really like this man.

Two years into our relationship – and it was a relationship, albeit transactional – I took him out for his birthday and bought him a curry. The next day I got a text. 'Check your account.'

He had put £30,000 into my bank.

That money allowed me to get back on the housing ladder. It was an act of generosity and kindness that completely changed my life. He insisted it was a gift, but I have always seen it as a loan. I want to pay him back. I say 'want' because now, ten years later, I have only paid him back £7,000. But if I ever have a windfall, he will get the remainder of it. And another curry.

Silly Plod

When I told my W1 landlord that I couldn't stay, that I wouldn't be able to make the rent, he said I could stay on for another month, but that he would keep my deposit. He was never going to give me back my deposit anyway, so I accepted the deal. At least I could work for another month from London and gather together some more cash before working out what to do next.

Meanwhile, Fred, the policeman in charge of the Proceeds of Crime Act investigation, had sent my solicitor an email demanding he inform me that if I didn't give them the real combination number for my safe they were going to hire a safe cracker. 'This significant expense will be billed to Miss —' the email said. It was an expense I could ill afford.

Of course, I had already given the safe code to the policeman who'd escorted me out of the police station after my arrest and they, in turn, had given the code to the police from my hometown. The safe had been taken from my house, but the northern police hadn't been able to open it. So Fred and the copper in charge of my criminal investigation, Bill, drove up north to pick up the safe, drive it back to London and have a go at getting into it. That's how much they wanted my money. But Bill and Fred couldn't get into it either. This made them angry, so they sent another threat to me via my solicitor about safe crackers and costs if I didn't yield the correct code. Again, I gave the code to my solicitor. This went on for a while, with each letter from Fred to my solicitor becoming increasingly irate until, eventually, I decided to go and open the safe for them.

I went back to the London police station, where they were waiting for me in a side room. Bill was just a plonker but Fred was a man any hooker would be wary of in a brothel. He had a smile that didn't reach his eyes and the look of a classic misogynist, Nietzsche-eyed and rubber lips that curled in contempt. He looked at me as though I was scum, but at the same time I could see how much he enjoyed dominating me. This, I could see, was how he got his kicks.

Fred turned the safe towards me and I turned it back, so that the numbers faced them.

'No,' I said carefully. 'This is so that you can see that I gave you the right code. Every. Single. Time.'

I was enjoying this too.

And I pressed the numbers that the northern and London

police hadn't been able to get their heads around. 123456 followed by star.

'Star . . .' Bill muttered as the safe pinged open.

Definition of Madness

Adam is having a nightmare at work and when he comes off one particularly argumentative Zoom that I have overheard, he is very quiet. I tell him he needs to talk about it, which makes his mood worse. I should have given him a minute to cool off before wading in. But I am saved from his shouting by his mother.

'What?' he roars as he answers his phone.

She is calling to let him know that her eighty-year-old neighbour is stealing an oak tree from her garden and that Adam should come immediately as there is also poisonous gas coming from her light fittings.

As if we don't have enough on our plates.

Workin' 9 till 7

Alongside my various new brothels I managed to pick up one month's promotional work. It was only £100 a day, but it was guaranteed money and, frankly, I was sick of the awful day brothels I kept finding myself in. Max's place seemed like a total dream now, the music and the great customers, doing what we wanted in the room with the clients we wanted to see. I remembered with something like misty eyes the Japanese man who had given me and a Hungarian hooker £500 each to give him a wank that lasted all of three minutes. I remembered the young, attractive man who had inherited a lot of money and paid me and another girl £200 each so that he could wrap us in bondage tape, fashioning two strapless dresses from the stuff, and then had us strut a make-believe catwalk for him. The men we got at Max's were like no others. Wonderfully bonkers. But that was in the past. Now I had to get used to my new normal.

I had signed up with a few agencies and thought I could do promo in the day and escorting at night. It didn't quite work out like that. I got a call one day from an agency telling me that I had a job at three that afternoon.

'I'm sorry, I'm already working.'

The man swore at me and said he was taking my profile down. This is the nature of agency work. If you sign on with one agency, there are no guarantees that there will be enough work, or enough money, from them. If you sign on with more than one, there may be clashes, and they don't like that. Somehow, you have to be available to all of them at all times. It wasn't really working for anyone.

The month-long job I'd signed up for was at the Stratford Centre in east London and was a huge campaign aimed at directing the extra footfall that the Olympics was bringing in through the shopping centre. The irony wasn't lost on me that I'd lost my brothel job because of the Olympics and yet, here I was, working a job that existed purely because of the Olympics. The month passed in a blur. I wanted my arresting coppers to see me working ten-hour shifts and realize that they had made a terrible mistake. I was not a madam. I was a grafter. And a good one at that because, very quickly, I was asked by my boss to fill in a few days as an assistant manager. My smile for the punters, coupled with my reliability and the fact that I looked good and took no shit, made me a perfect fit. Extraordinary what life skills you can learn from whoring.

'I'm Sure It Will Fit'

As I was shagging more and providing extras to help ends meet, I went for more sexual health appointments than I normally would. I really hadn't needed to in the brothel of cocaine, Jimi Hendrix and not much sex. But my circumstances were very different now. I was also more worried about getting pregnant. I always used condoms for sex but, after a long day of shagging, it didn't matter how much lube I put on, my cunt was drier than the Sahara. And condoms would occasionally break. I had the implant, which protected me up to a point, but I decided that I wanted a diaphragm as well. Triple check. At home for a few days for a family do – as I was getting on unusually well with my sister since she'd helped me in my hour of need, and my parents were still blissfully unaware of what I was going through – and with an afternoon to spare, I decided to use a fake name and go to a local walk-in GUM clinic.

I should have known better.

Before it was shut down due to essential cuts, there had been a marvellous clinic called CLASH in central London, which only catered for sex-worker clients. The staff were sensitive and never patronizing and they always had time to ask us how we were. They did outreach, and so would visit brothels and give us condoms. Good bosses like Max welcomed them, at most with a shout of 'Hide that coke!' as he opened the door. Of course, some brothel bosses would never let the health professionals through the front door as they had a lot more to hide. But after the 2012 directive, with the police using condoms to prove a place was a brothel, CLASH was turned away by more and more of the good brothels as handing out hundreds of condoms to ensure the safety of the working girls was no longer an option.

We all visited their clinic for our health checks, where they provided soft drinks and sandwiches. I never accepted them – I never needed to – but they meant a girl who worked on the streets could sustain herself for another day.

Things were very different elsewhere.

My doctor was a middle-aged Pakistani man and a young, white, trainee female doctor was also present. The consultation began. And, as always, I was truthful. That was a mistake. When I said I was a sex worker the man looked at me with a look of contempt.

'How long have you been a prostitute?'

'I have been a sex worker for a few years.'

As the questions continued, I noticed that the disgust on his face was mirrored on his colleague's.

Did I have anal? Did I do oral without? How many men had I had sex with this week? Last week? Today? How many men had I had sex with altogether? And so on – each question more probing and dehumanizing than the last.

Eventually the doctor gave me what I had initially asked for.

A diaphragm. He threw the box in my general direction and it skidded to a halt on the chair next to me. While he turned back to his notes I looked inside and saw that the diaphragm was big. Much bigger than the ones I had seen in the past that belonged to my friends.

'Don't they come in different sizes?'

'I'm sure it will fit,' he said.

And with that I was dismissed.

'Do You Need to See a Counsellor?'

I visit my midwife. 'Does stress affect the baby?' I ask her as I come through the door.

When I lift my dress so that she can monitor my baby's heart rate she sees angry red scratches on my legs around my knees.

'My cat,' I say, but she doesn't look convinced. As it sounds so unlikely I decide not to offer that my cat is obsessed with sitting on my knees when I am on the loo, and uses his claws for stability.

The midwife gazes at me with concern in her eyes.

She asks if my partner is supportive and I say he is, but that he has his own shit to deal with. His mum has now been diagnosed with a degenerative mental illness and she won't take her meds. She calls him every day asking when he is going to visit and, recently, she has taken a turn for the worse. Adam's work is suffering as a result of being pulled in different directions and I tell myself I should be more understanding because his mother is frail and vulnerable and ageing rapidly but, honestly, she was a pain in the arse a long time before she got ill. Then there's my own mum and dad, who I want desperately to call me to see how I am. To ask after the baby. But they don't. The silence is painful.

'Do you need to see a counsellor?' the midwife asks.

I tell her thank you, but no. I've never had a counsellor in the past, when I have probably needed one, so I definitely don't need one now. 'I'll be fine,' I say, with no real conviction.

In the back of my mind when she asks this question is Alice, the girl who'd phoned me to let me know that Max wanted me dead. I've discovered that this appalling human being is now training to become a counsellor. It's hard to believe that she has designs on messing with people's heads and that she'll be allowed to. How on earth could she ever acquire the requisite skills to counsel others? With Alice in mind, I've come to the conclusion that I don't trust any of 'em. Counsellors. Therapists. Psychiatrists.

'Thank you, but no,' I say again, firmly.

No Comment

I was asked to go back to the police station to answer more questions. My solicitor said that they would probably drop all charges if I told them who the silent partner in the brothel was and gave them information about drugs and dealers. Fat fucking chance. By that time, however much I disliked Max and the girls who were still working in the brothel, I hated the police so much more. At least with criminals I knew where I stood.

I found out through Tony – whose finger was on every pulse, and who only ever had my best interests at heart – that a drug dealer had also been making threats about me. Max was the least of my worries. And I was worried. There were a few shadowy figures that I thought could easily kill if their freedom was at stake. I just hoped that they knew me and knew that I would never, ever mention their names.

Beyond the lurking threats and the general anxiety about what would happen to me, what it really came down to, for me, was this. What the police were doing wasn't right. They were supposed to be the good guys. Naive of me, perhaps. Too much *Inspector Morse*, clearly. But with my eyes now wide open, there was no way I was getting into bed with the police.

I told my solicitor that I wouldn't tell the police anything about anyone. He sighed.

This time, I no commented almost everything.

The investigating officers had trawled through my note-books with care and had found the crumbs they wanted amongst the vast amount of information at their fingertips: from creative stories and poems, to the notes I had made when I was working in my promotional roles, to my acting contacts, to my sex-work contacts. All my ideas, from stage-play adaptations to my dreams and fears and fantasies ... here was a disordered map of my entire life. I hated to think of them probing my thoughts and dreams. The feeling of violation made me nauseous.

Among it all were the notes I had made about how I would

run a brothel. What uniforms I would have. What sex toys I would provide. What I would call it. What themed rooms I would have. I also had non-sex-work business plans. One idea was a shoe business that I'd bought a domain for. Another was how to keep beach towels on sun loungers if there was a strong wind. I had even visited the patent library in Birmingham to see if anyone had already had a similar idea. But the police weren't interested in all that.

Then, having picked up one of these notebooks one afternoon, there was my friend Tony's doodling about how to be a criminal. I hadn't minded him scribbling down his own ridiculous ideas. Suits, particularly financial suits, like to imagine a different life, one in which they aren't bored of numbers and the grind of a desk job, no matter how well paid. In some cases, to get some enjoyment out of life, they fill the rest of their time with booze. Or food. Or drugs. Or hookers. Dipping their toes into another world gave them a kick. Tony had written something along the lines of 'move money to Jersey, get another identity'. Drunken, coked-up doodling was all it was. And whatever Tony had jotted down in a moment of wishful thinking, it was clearly not my handwriting, and they had three books to compare it to.

They probed me about it, intrigued by the idea that I was the kind of person who had multiple identities, all around the world. I was, in their eyes, a highly skilled criminal. One who wrote down all her wicked plans in her notebooks – for anyone to find. Thank goodness I had no story ideas about killing someone.

After the interview I got my notebooks back. They had

copied all the information they needed and were done with them. As was I. I ripped them into a thousand pieces when I got home. I was in such a rage. I never wanted to write anything, ever again.

Pussy Parlour

I have it. The best business idea I have ever come up with.

I am so obsessed with my cat that I convince Adam to drive an hour away so that we can visit a cat cafe. I have been to a few and some are dreadful, full of irritating children who think that the more they poke a cat, the more likely the cat is to play with them. But some cat cafes are cool, with good coffee, great cakes and happy cats. I spend the entire journey back excitedly talking about how we should open one.

'Imagine! A real cathouse!' I enthuse. 'And perhaps we could have a brothel or dungeon through a secret door! It's the perfect cover, the police would never guess what was going on!'

Adam's sigh is long and weary. It's the sigh of a man who has been here before. He puts his foot down.

Knowledge is Power

For the first time in my life, I found myself with a social worker, which was deeply ironic given all the anguish I'd been through at secondary school and then with Tom. A woman who was connected with CLASH had assigned herself to me after hearing what had happened. She took me to places that supported women in all sorts of situations, charities and outreach programmes designed to help in any way they could. They provided food and sanctuary and stress-management classes and arts and crafts and whatever we needed to get through our own individual hell.

I had never felt I was one of those women. Many had been homeless, many had addiction issues and had been to prison. They couldn't afford to eat and, although the police had stolen my money, I could afford food, if not my rather extreme rent costs. But here I was. At one place, a nun did reflexology on my feet and I felt a wave of love and emotion for the wonderful work that these women were doing. But the moment of peace didn't last long. Fighting back in any way I could was how I was going to survive, not by having my feet massaged.

I became obsessed. Any time I wasn't working I was gathering intelligence, researching the police who had arrested me and the anti-trafficking organization that had raided the brothel with the police. I wanted to know everything about them, in the same way that they now knew so much about me. I amassed pages and pages of information, little clues that I had followed through different social media platforms, through Google. If a person is angry and determined enough, there's a lot of information to be found – and knowledge is power.

The anti-trafficking organization had handed out leaflets to us all at the raid and I had kept hold of mine. They had had the nerve to list NHS outreach numbers on the leaflet and when I told Natalie, whose work for an outreach programme had led me to the ECP, she was livid.

'We would *never, ever* work with an organization like that! We would *never, ever* work with the police on a raid! Our clients would never trust us again!'

Her anger matched mine. And two very angry women is a formidable combination.

I'd also found out that the anti-trafficking organization was linked to a Christian group and that my arresting officer, Kate, was a member of their church. I took all my research and gave it to my solicitor.

Suddenly, overnight, the anti-trafficking website disappeared. I didn't know if it was my solicitor or Natalie who had made that happen. Either way, it was gone. And I was delighted. An eye for an eye, and all that.

A Dress for Any Occasion

The police called two days after my second interview and told me that they were going to charge me. I'd expected it, as the notebooks and my words in the first interview had completely fucked me.

When I next had a day off from my promotional job, I put on my nicest, most colourful dress and went to the police station for the third time. Natalie smiled when she saw the summery, floral number I was wearing.

'You look lovely!' she told me.

I wanted to look fabulous. More, I *needed* to look fabulous.

They were trying to turn me into a victim, but I was determined to remain defiant and strong. They had no idea how strong I could be. They didn't know me at all.

Bill collected me from the waiting area and took me back to the custody desk where I had been separated from my belongings just over a month before. He formally charged me with assisting in the management of a brothel. He said that they were dropping the arrest for Railcard fraud. I almost laughed at that, but couldn't quite. I managed to keep things light; I was charming and jovial. I would never let him or any one of them know the hell I was going through. I would never let them know how they had ruined my life.

Bill reminded me of my bail conditions, which said that I couldn't go back to work at the brothel where I'd been arrested. He said, 'Like you would want to go back there anyway!'

I thought about the men I'd effectively been forced to work with since my arrest, who thought that they could demand anal for a tenner. Thought that they could push their fingers into my cunt. That they could follow me on my train journey home.

With all the grace I could muster, I said, 'Of course not.' But I was thinking, *First chance I get, I'm going back there.* I wanted my regulars back. I wanted to earn proper money again. I wanted to do what *I* wanted to do in the room. Last of all, but most importantly, I wanted to look them all in the face – Max and each of those women who had left me to rot – and show them that I was a fucking phoenix. And then, when I had earned what I needed, finished paying off my loans and saved some money for my own place, I was going to move on and never see any of those fuckers again.

Mine That Milk!

Another thing I didn't know, which my midwife informs me of, is that pregnant women make milk before birth. I feel as though I have lived under a rock my entire life, when the reality is anything but. Still, I have to wonder what I actually learned at school, apart from how to deliver a perfectly aimed headbutt. I listen with genuine amazement as she hands me some syringes to collect the milk that, I discover, is called colostrum. She explains that it takes a few days for the milk to come in properly after the birth, so it is useful to have some colostrum on standby at the hospital. It takes about three nights of squeezing my tits before a yellow liquid emerges. It becomes a nightly ritual, an unexpectedly fun game for me and Adam.

'There!' he shouts.

'There!' I squeal.

Excitedly he catches and collects the liquid from my nipples with the tiny syringes. We fill them all up, store them in the freezer, and order some more from the internet.

I tell my midwife proudly what we've been up to when I next see her. She is horrified.

'You aren't supposed to start that yet! You could have brought on labour!'

Given the size of me, I can't believe that that would necessarily be a bad thing. How on earth is it possible to pass a basketball through an egg cup? But making this colostrum for the baby? That I can do.

Curiouser and Curiouser

I found out from my solicitor that Max had never had his house searched and that he hadn't been charged for managing. Instead, he had been charged with allowing the premises to be used as a brothel. I also learned that the police had seized twenty wraps of cocaine from his bedroom there. They hadn't charged him with that either. How on earth could the man who had been running the place the entire time, the man who had copious amounts of cocaine stashed away in his bedroom, which was clearly not only for his own use, the man who had admitted he was the manager, the man who was in situ all the time while I was wearing an Easter bonnet and singing to the elderly . . . how was he getting away with everything? He was even back at the brothel, working again, and I heard from Tony that business was good. Meanwhile I was scrabbling around for ten-pound extras listening to lines like 'Don't you want to taste my cock?' and 'Be nice to me and I'll be nice to you' and the old chestnut 'Have you ever tried to get a proper job?'

As I waited for my court hearings, I became angrier and angrier.

Eve's Not Here Right Now

The staff in my local curry house are delighted to see my enormous bump when I go in to pick up a takeaway. 'At last!

You have a child! Many congratulations!' The owner, Nadir, pumps my hand up and down enthusiastically, an enormous grin on his face. 'Free poppadoms!' he declares to the man who is about to scoot off and fetch my order from the kitchen. This overfamiliarity would have irritated me at any other point in my life. Hell, it would have grated only a month ago. But now I seem to be swimming in love hormones, and I grin a grin that matches Nadir's and tell him how happy we are.

Back at the house, Adam and I sit on our sofa with piled plates on our laps – mine is well towards my knees as I haven't seen my lap for a while now – and prepare to eat our food.

'Enjoy this because after the baby comes we will have a table. Like grown-ups!' I say, finding from somewhere within a mum voice I didn't know I possessed.

As we eat, the cats try their usual tactics to get their paws on our food; even though they've been fed, they always want more. Their strategy is that one will approach from the front and mewl loudly. Then, while we are distracted, the other will attack from behind. Usually I'll chase them both from the room, but one will always have a piece of something from our plates in their mouth.

But a weird thing has happened recently. The cat's meowing is scratching a pleasure zone in my brain. It's completely bizarre and the closest sensation I've previously had to this was listening to ASMR, whether that's plastic spoons rippling over a microphone or a set of perfectly shellacked fingernails tapping rhythmically, like the pitter-patter of soft raindrops. I can't get enough of the cats' sounds. All the sounds. From the deep, resonating purrs, to the different notes of meowing they both hit. Is this normal? I wonder.

I willingly hand them some chicken, hoping that they'll stick around for a bit longer.

The Three Cs

My solicitor called me into his office so that we could go through the evidence the Crown Prosecution Service had handed over. Everything from my phones and computer and notebooks had been printed out. Everything they thought they could use was now easily visible on the page. Everything else, the stuff they weren't interested in, was overwritten in heavy black ink, redacted. There was a lot of black. Including all the texts I had sent every week to my boss saying things like, 'Can I please work Mon, Tue, Wed?' or 'I can only do Thurs and Fri this week. Is that OK?' Also redacted were Max's responses, which generally said 'Fine', but also on occasion, 'Yes. If you suck my cock.' It was banter and he didn't mean it, but it wouldn't help the CPS to have pesky texts available as part of my defence.

My solicitor read out the texts one by one and I explained them. Some were from my regulars. Some were chatting with the other girls. In among it all there was a troubling one. One Friday night Max had left us in the shit – who knows what had happened to him – and the girls who normally carried keys and dealt with the safe weren't in. So, it was down to me to collect a key, open the doors and get everything in order. The text I'd written went something like this:

'That fucking asshole has fucked off and left me with no booze, no bog roll and no coke.'

My solicitor peered at me over his desk and over his glasses waiting for an explanation. 'No Coca-Cola?' I said, perkily.

Then there was a text from Tony which, as a client, simply said, 'Cock. Cocaine. Champagne.'

I got the picture. A text from a drunk punter was included and counted as evidence against me, but, 'Can I please work Mon, Tues, Weds?' was out. Redacted, redacted, redacted. The reason given was that they were from my 'personal life'.

We could have requested they removed the redactions, but I was advised that it would be pointless. After all, right there in front of us were the messages from when I managed the handful of days in my failed daytime venture and that one night, when Max had failed to show. It was enough to show I had been 'assisting in the management of a brothel'. As the law stood, I was fucked.

The question remained that if I was 'assisting', who was doing the job proper? Who was the main manager? But there seemed to be no interest in that line of inquiry. They certainly weren't pursuing Max or the big boss. The only person who had been charged with managing was me. I couldn't figure out the motivation. What was the point of coming for me like this?

All the pictures on my phone had been printed out too – shots of my friends, my promotional work, my acting, my family. My life. It felt to me as though the police and the authorities were crawling around inside my head, that they were taking a part of me. A part I would never get back.

As I flicked through the wad of A4 paper, I paused. It was a cock.

It had been sent to me by a man I had met while promoting and had then been on three dates with. We had kissed on the last date, but that was it. For me there was no spark so I had politely expressed regret and let him know that I wouldn't be seeing him again. He had responded by sending the picture of his dick and a monologue spread over three texts of the things he would like to do to me. Tie me up. Put a tube up my ass and insert a rodent. The kind of really well-meaning, balanced stuff of life that makes a woman appreciate the mild brothel creepers and the lovely Matthews and Tonys in her life.

Sister

After my sister got over the shock of my arrest and upcoming trial dates, she was brilliant. As was Patrick. I had always clashed with him because of his views on race and women, but he had had his own run-ins with the law and so had the same hatred for the police that I did. We bonded. As for my sister, we became closer than we had been for years. There was still judgement. She was, after all, our mother's daughter. But as long as I didn't talk about the conditions in the brothels I was working in, as long as I spoke about my court case and stayed far away from sex, we were great. We spoke on the phone all the time and I really appreciated her support. I was convinced the police were recording our calls as I would sometimes hear an echo on the line I had never heard before, but she would calm me down and make me laugh. I loved her for that. And I loved that our relationship had taken this turn after years of squabbling. It was about time.

Enter, Domination!

I spent almost two months grafting in those grim brothels, working as an independent hooker and plugging away at my promotional work too, and it felt like a lifetime. But just before I left London, having run out of brothels that might work for me, I took a job at one last place. I was too knackered to give much thought as to how it might differ from the others. But it turned out this one was very different. It offered mistress services and would train up any successful applicants. Many dommes who I have met since learned their craft there. I threw my hat into the ring. I was a trained actor, after all, with a track record of kink in my personal life. If I couldn't manage to be a convincing dominatrix then it really was time to give up.

On my first training day I met the woman who would be schooling me in the art of domination. She was down to earth and pleasant; I liked her. The madam – let's call her Cheryl – not so much. She was in her sixties and dominated her staff. She was tough. Her opening gambit was to let me know that I needed to lose weight, change my hair and wear more make-up. I took it on the chin. More make-up and a haircut I could do. But nobody makes me lose weight if I don't want to. Not after Tom.

On my first day I was given an A4 page of closely typed text and told to learn it. It was a series of instructions. I would be tested.

'On your knees and never look at me unless I give permission.'

'Only speak when I allow it.'

'Any deviation from my instructions will result in . . .'

'You are my toy, my plaything, to be used or discarded however I see fit.'

And so it continued.

The script was a crutch for women who had never dominated men before. I very quickly learned it by heart – it wasn't Shakespeare, after all – and then, after a couple of weeks, never used it again. There was no need. I prefer flow in a session. And a script prevents that as only one participant knows the words. For me, a session was much more like improv. Let's see what happens, it's more fun that way.

The owner had only one woman working each day, and so we each had one day a week to make money. As a new girl I was allocated either Saturday or Sunday, which were always much slower than a weekday as it's less easy for a married man to visit. The room rent the madam took from us was outrageous; £350 a day and then, once we had made a certain amount, she would take an additional 10 per cent. The woman who trained me told me that, years ago, she had never left with less than £1,000 in her pocket. But times had changed. Just as there had been an increase in the number of hookers there had also been an increase in the number of dominatrices. Which meant less business. Cheryl knew that there were many women ready to take our places so, although there were fewer punters, she kept the room rent the same. There were one or two days when I left with less than £100 in my purse. Another time I left owing money, which got added to my rent the following week.

I found being around a proper madam, at a time when I was being done for what she *should* have been done for, gruelling. All the more so when one day I realized that Cheryl had never worked as a hooker. A man had made an appointment on a rare double domme day, and the other woman and I moaned when we found out who the client was – neither of us wanted to take him. He had an enormous cock, and he always wanted a hard fuck.

'Why are you moaning?' the madam said. 'You are lucky girls!'

Only a woman who had never had multiple cocks in her vagina on a daily basis would make a comment like that.

I was determined to make it work. I loved domination. I loved learning how to strap-on fuck, fist, whip, cane and flog. I loved electrics, bondage, candlewax and so many of the other activities I still do in my sessions today. Anyone can have a go at any of those things – you really can try it at home – but a professional dominatrix knows how to do everything safely. They know which wax to use and how to apply it. They know where electrics shouldn't be applied. They know how to secure a man with rope, but not mark him or cut off his circulation. They know how to get the bottom ready for anal play and how to prostate massage so that a man can have a more intense orgasm. I learned it all with relish. The role-play came easy to me and was my favourite part. I felt as though I was acting again, which of course I was. I would even get butterflies before meeting a new client, a less intense feeling than when I used to stand in the wings, ready to go on stage. But a good feeling.

It was wonderful to feel good again.

An early client, who was macho in his personal and working life, said he wanted to be tied up and teased. But I soon realized that he didn't want that at all. There are always clues to look for, and you have to tune in to get it right, but you didn't have to be Sherlock to realize he wanted it up the arse. I saw his face change when I said, 'Look at you, all tied up and vulnerable. I could do anything to you, and you couldn't stop me.' His cock was getting harder as I lightly touched his arse with my fingers. I repeated 'anything'. My fingers lingered. His cock was now dripping. A finger the first session, then two sessions later he was dressed in a bright pink tutu and corset while, holding tight to his blond pigtails, I fucked him from behind. 'I'm a dirty slut! Fuck this dirty slut!' he shouted.

And I am very good at this, I thought.

The Waiting Game

I left London, packing up the flat, wondering if I'd ever be able to have a set-up like that again. In some ways it was very comfortable to be back full-time up north as I was far away from the police and the brothels that had made life so miserable. Patrick had arranged for a joiner to find an exact match for the old front door, and I cleaned up the flat and tidied everything away, but it didn't feel the same any more. It was as though the police were everywhere; I couldn't put out of my mind that they had touched everything. I could feel their presence.

I was still working my one day a week at the domination place in London. Those were long days, when I would catch a train at 6 a.m. and jump on a coach back late at night. I managed to accrue a little stash of cash, £2,000, from that work and the graft I'd put in at the previous brothels after loans and my northern rent had been paid, but I was terrified of putting it in the bank just in case the police froze my account. And I certainly wasn't going to keep a brick of notes under my mattress again. I gave it to my sister to look after. I felt safe that it was there, with her, and that I could access it when I needed to.

That done, I tried to keep as busy as possible and to do things I liked and which took my mind off the upcoming court dates, but it was difficult. I ran, I lifted weights, I walked, but it wasn't enough. Neither was my one day a week in London enough to take me out of myself. My head felt too full, but at the same time I felt empty, as if I was slipping away. I wanted to find myself again, but I was too angry to really know what I wanted. My easy laughter and smile felt like a long time ago.

When a friend asked me to get involved in a local amateur production of a musical, I gratefully agreed and this did bring me some joyful times. I loved the music and seeing how amateur performers, young and old, got so much out of what they were doing. I threw myself into it and there were brief moments when I was on stage when I could pretend everything was OK. That everything was going to be fine.

And then the bailiffs turned up at my dad's workshop, heavy-handed, threatening and frightening, and demanded money from him, or they would take away all his tools, leaving him unable to earn. Frantic with worry, Dad called my sister, who he believed was the sister more able to help him financially. Without asking me, she gave my £2,000 to the bailiffs.

When I found out I was broken as I knew I would never get it back, but what could I say? I was back to square one.

Face to Face

My solicitor got my bail conditions dropped so, technically, I could go back to work at the brothel. I could also see Max. Of course, I wasn't so daft as to go back to work before my court case as I was afraid the police would raid again and arrest me on even more trumped-up charges. But I did want to see Max. I wanted to look him in the eyes and ask him why he had asked Alice to call and threaten me.

We met outside Euston station. I looked good, deliberately so, while he looked even more dishevelled than usual. In a local pub he babbled small talk about my journey, the weather, how good I looked. He insisted on buying the drinks.

'Too fucking right,' I said through gritted teeth, as I accepted a large gin and tonic.

My plan was to get a little tipsy while encouraging Max to get absolutely smashed, knowing how loose lipped it made him. He was clearly nervous of me and his armour was to put on his usual show of bonhomie. Max was incredibly charming and funny when he wanted to be; we had always joked in the brothel that the men really came to chat with him and not to see us girls at all. That afternoon, he was on sparkling form. I wanted to put him through a window, of course, but there was a part of me that really cared about him. In some ways, I loved him; all the more so since working for a series of truly awful men. It was an extremely confusing relationship.

When I worked at the brothel I had seen the other women take care of Max and initially I wondered why they felt the need, then after a while I was able to see what they saw and over the two years I worked there, I joined in. We would hide his beer and tell him when he was too drunk or too high and that it was time he went to bed. We'd put an arm around his shoulder and shuffle him off to his room. He was dying before our eyes. But as long as he returned home to his lovely house somewhere in middleclass-shire with a huge wad of notes on a Sunday, his wife was happy, no questions asked. Our worry was that one night he wouldn't make it home, or maybe he'd get there but wouldn't make it back to work again. Max's lifestyle was not sustainable.

As the drinks slipped down, he talked. He told me that it would suit his case very much if I got the blame, and as the police had come down on me far harder than they had on him he thought it was working. The pity and the fondness I had harboured in my heart evaporated in that moment. I bit my tongue and clenched my fists, my nails pressed hard into the palms of my hands. I pointed out as evenly as I could that I typically spent three or four months a year touring shows for the elderly. I said that he had been running the business for ten years, so how could they possibly accuse me of managing the place? The only reason they were going after me so hard was for my £7,000 – the cash they had taken from me on arrest plus the savings in my safe.

The mists of alcohol lifted and clarity finally dawned on him, a sudden realization that he should feel bad for me, as his fall guy, taking the brunt of it all, not pleased with himself. He feigned pity. 'Of course, you must come back to work! You must be working at some god-awful places!' he said. He wasn't wrong about that.

I said it was a possibility, but only after my trial was done. 'But I wouldn't mind dropping in to see the girls.'

He would tell them that he had seen me, and I didn't want them to think I was too scared to face them. Better to speak to them myself. I wanted to set them and the story straight.

Two Fingers a Day

Apparently if a pregnant woman puts two fingers in her vagina every day and pulses, this exercise of strengthening the pelvic floor helps with labour. I am sceptical until I read the comments on YouTube from the new mothers who say it really helped them. But how to put two fingers in when your tummy is as big as a barge? I employ Adam for the job – his fingers, my pulsing. Each night we now have our ritual of colostrum collection, as I am close enough to my labour date that my midwife has signed off on it, followed by vaginal pulses. It's a whole new world.

I feel as though everything is moving in the right direction with the baby, but that it might take a couple of years for Adam to fancy me again. I think Robbie Williams got it right. He said, after seeing his wife give birth, 'It's like seeing your favourite pub burn down.'

The Lion's Den

On the short walk from the pub to the brothel Max called someone on his mobile and said he needed them there, now. I caught the words 'support me'. I had no idea who he was speaking to. He was giggling hysterically as we walked through the doors, as though the whole thing was a big joke. I was finding it more difficult to muster a smile.

The place was as I remembered it. Whatever chat there had been died away as all eyes turned to the door. Most women then looked away, unable to hold my gaze. I spotted Tara and pointedly said hello to her. She'd been my good friend but she hadn't been in touch at all since the raid. She pretended she didn't know me and turned her back.

The doorbell rang and in strolled one of the few men I had ever been scared of, a drug dealer called Dave. Clearly Max had called Dave to 'support' him, and Dave had come quickly.

Rage is a funny thing. If a person gets angry enough, they aren't scared any more. You pass through rage and into defiance. With the adrenalin pumping, it can be dangerous, but it's effective. This is where I was. And, intimidating as he could be, I had always liked Dave. He was straight down the line with no bullshit. He was also great in the sack and had never asked for a discount. You can be apprehensive of someone, even scared of their reputation, but also know that unless you cross them there will never be an issue. But Dave thought I had crossed him, and that was a problem. I knew that I hadn't been able to control what people had been saying behind my back for the past couple of months, but face to face I could tell them the truth. This was my moment, so I was pleased rather than concerned that Dave had arrived. He would believe me, because I was as straight as him.

The three of us went to the back of the property and into the small room that housed the toilet, the only place where you might get some privacy. And then we talked. Max, more sober now, tried to weasel his way out of his part in it all, but it was hopeless. He was caught. 'I never told everyone that you were going to take us down . . .' he told me, at which point Dave turned on him.

'Yes, you fucking did. You told everyone she had sold us all out. That the girls would be out of a job and that you and I and —,' he mentioned the big boss's name, 'would go to prison.'

I felt a flood of enormous relief. It really couldn't have gone better. I'd engineered it to a T – with a bit of unexpected help from the hapless Max. I was in the clear. I wouldn't get killed. Perhaps I could stop looking over my shoulder now.

I had already decided that I was going to come back to the brothel when I was out the other side of the court cases and recoup what I had lost. I would reconnect with my regulars and swap numbers so that when I left for good they would provide me with a steady income. No more shitty flats. No extras. No menus. And, most importantly, I thought, I would pick up where I had left off teaching kids about Shakespeare and entertaining little old dears at nursing homes.

Dave made Max tell the women the truth – that I hadn't said anything to the police about how the brothel was run, or who owned it. Then to hammer it home, as the women still looked confused, he told them that their jobs were not in any jeopardy because of anything I had done or said. Max, shuffling and stumbling, apologized to me, saying something along the lines of 'It's time for her to come back in from the cold. Whenever she wants to work in the future she can.'

And feeling more triumphant than Boudicca the first time she saw off the Romans, I left the brothel with my head held high.

Court

A court date finally came through for the POCA hearing at the magistrates' court, the proceeds of my crime being the £7,000 that had been taken from me. Policeman Fred informed my solicitor that they had applied to detain my cash for a further three months while inquiries into my criminal case were ongoing. I knew exactly what they were doing by stalling. They wanted my criminal court date to come before the POCA court date because, with a guilty conviction, they would have more chance of keeping my money. The court date stood, but the police's application would be considered.

As I took in the criminals milling around outside court in

their grey tracksuit bottoms with their furious chain-smoking and their loud, aggressive mouths I thought, *I am not like them!*

The magistrate clearly agreed. 'When will your client arrive?' he asked my solicitor.

'I'm here!' I sing-songed from the row behind my solicitor, and a moment of confusion passed across the magistrate's face. I had dressed very carefully that morning like Alicia Florrick, The Good Wife herself, and had put on a sharp skirt suit. My hair was neatly tied back. Make-up minimal. The magistrate had clearly thought I was part of the legal team, not at all the brash tart he was expecting. Of course that's what he was expecting. The surprise on his face was almost comical. But I was in no mood to laugh.

As we expected, the police request was granted. Fred walked out of court looking smug. I wanted to smack him right in the chops, but instead, as our paths crossed in the foyer, I managed to say with a winning smile, 'How wonderful to see you again, Fred.' Never let bastards see your real feelings. Never let them have the power of knowing that they have got to you.

The whole thing was an elaborate performance, a bit like being in a play. And I knew better than most how to perform.

Box Ticked

I hear through an old theatre friend who used to work in the sex industry that a writer we know has secured funding from the Arts Council to write a play about sex work, despite having never been a sex worker herself. I wouldn't dream of applying for funding to write about the trans struggle or to explore issues around racism. But sex workers? Anyone can have a punt. It wouldn't be so bad if this woman was an ally, with good intentions. But the woman in question is in the End Demand camp, so we know that whatever she writes it won't accomplish anything for sex-worker rights. If she finds an audience, it can only do us greater harm. I would imagine she wrote on the application form that she wanted to give marginalized people a voice, but surely there should be a box to tick that states whether you want sex workers to live or die? Imagine a member of the BNP or the National Front receiving Arts Council funding to put a play on? It just wouldn't happen.

Of course, I am all for free speech and believe that writers should be able to write about lives they haven't lived, but if that writing does a group of people harm it becomes rather more complicated. There's a debate to be had, not simply a financial hand-out.

But sex sells. Plays and television about the sex industry sell. For us to get our own work on the screen or the stage, to get our own stories told, we are required to out ourselves. That's not an option. Instead, we have to watch non sex workers sensationalize our lives and wring as much as possible out of our life experience. Occasionally these writers may do an obligatory interview with one of us to tick another box to say they have done their research. But I've found they're not interested in telling the truth of our stories; they just need a story that makes eyes open wide and keeps bums on seats.

It's why we are left with the two extremes: the posh hookers and dominatrices who work from five-star hotels or the drug-addicted women on the street. People outside the industry are incapable of seeing anyone else – and the vast number of women like me, who aren't one or the other, don't get our stories told. The 'happy hooker' or 'misery memoir' stories increase the level of stigma the rest of us face every day because the public believe in them both. By believing that it's one or the other the stigma makes us more vulnerable. We are not seen as real people. It makes it harder for us to access healthcare, it makes it easier for the police either to ignore us if we are in danger or to harm or criminalize us. And it makes it easier for the johns to abuse us. If the john doesn't think we're real, three-dimensional people who matter, then it's an open invitation to misbehave, to threaten, to harm, to kill.

I ask the writer if she would like to watch one of my domination sessions, to help her get a little closer to reality.

She declines.

It's a Court Date

I had last seen Max at the magistrates' court. His criminal case was linked with mine, the two of us in the dock together, as it were, and he had seemed high and disoriented. The same old Max, then. In contrast, his solicitor was a pit bull, shouting at everyone from the magistrates themselves and the court usher to the clerk and even his own client. He wanted to separate our cases so they could pin everything on me, and they couldn't do that with Max and me in the dock together. The magistrate agreed, so from then on I was on my own, which, considering I knew Max was as guilty as sin, wasn't a bad thing. I thought some daylight between us might help my case. Now, after waiting for what seemed like for ever, my criminal court date was suddenly upon me.

The night before my trial I cried for the first time since I'd been in the cell. Wracking, heartbreaking sobs that I couldn't control and which I thought would never end.

My sister came with me to London to support me, which surprised me. I knew she would find the whole thing very difficult. Not just the seriousness of the proceedings and the possible outcome for me, but also being around hookers and the sex-work allies, including Natalie and Maggie. Maggie, who would talk about giving head in the same sentence as 'pass the salt'. I knew my sister would find her impossible to communicate with. But there was also a part of me that thought it would be good for her, shake her up a little and enable her to see that there was a different world out there with people leading very different lives, while still being good people, great people, with the same wants and needs as her. Money, food, shelter and to be healthy and happy and for our families to be healthy and happy. Don't we all want that?

My sister was dressed casually in jeans, while I had again put on a nice frock, which meant the security team at the courts were much more pleasant to me than they were to her. They assumed I was a lawyer and she was the criminal. The whole thing was, if nothing else, a very salutary lesson in stereotypes.

Standing slightly outside of myself, I found the experience

completely fascinating and curiously entertaining, as though I was watching a television programme. We'd each been assigned roles and were playing them rather well, I noted. Then I would snap out of it and realize that it was real, that it was my life, and I could very easily be sent to prison. The fear would flood back in, making my blood pound in my head. When I had a moment, I would google my name to check that nothing had been released to the press; fortunately, I wasn't interesting enough to garner any attention. I was lucky this was all happening in London. In my local area a hamster on a roof is a front-page headline. I was grateful that my family and friends didn't need to know and didn't need to worry.

The police were also in court to follow the case's progress. Bill, who'd charged me, was there in such a badly fitting suit he looked like a criminal. And even though this was my criminal case, Fred – whose priority was the POCA case – came along to watch too. And, alongside them both was my arresting officer, Kate. I guessed it was all fun and games for them: the pleasure of seeing the chase through to its conclusion, the jaws of the law wrapped around some poor soul's jugular, inflicting as much pain as possible. But I couldn't help but continue to wonder how the Metropolitan Police could be so hard up that my £7,000 would make such a difference to them. Why did they want it so much? Was it to teach me a lesson and to put me firmly in my place? Because surely such a paltry amount wouldn't make much of a dent in all the compensation they were having to pay out for continually employing racists and rapists? Why did my criminalization matter so much to them?

This Is Going to Hurt

The information I am gathering to prepare myself for labour has ratcheted up a few notches. I am asking any mother I know, anyone who has been through it all, from Adam's friends to my plasterer's wife, the same questions. 'What was your birth plan?', 'What medication did you take?', 'How long was the labour?' And, obviously, 'How much did it hurt?' I can't stop myself – having had my head in the sand for a long time, I now need to know everything.

I dive into YouTube in an enormous way. It has tips and advice on every aspect of pregnancy, from conception to birth. What I should eat, what I shouldn't eat, what exercises help make the delivery easier, the difference between being twenty and forty when you're carrying a baby, effects on your body after birth, and of course the actual birth. I become completely obsessed with what I find, and also quite nervous. I am not soothed by the gentle and gentrified tones of the women who have had three or four children and want to impart their knowledge from their Habitat homes in Hampstead. Instead, I watch an episode of *One Born Every Minute* And it absolutely terrifies me.

The only person I am not asking about childbirth is my mum.

This frantic period of information gathering is the one time during my pregnancy that I am relieved she is ignoring my phone calls. Early on in the pregnancy she told me on at least three occasions that she had been cut from her arse to her vagina when she gave birth to me. That is the main problem with talking to drinkers; they repeat themselves. And that verbal tic is annoying enough if they're talking about a doctor's appointment or doing the shopping, but it is bloody scary if you have a belly full of baby and they're forcing you to think again and again and once again about being cut open with some garden shears.

I listen and learn and try not to avert my eyes. There isn't long to go now.

On Trial

During one of the breaks in court, I went to the loo, and Kate followed me in. Luckily, Maggie saw her and followed closely behind. When I came out of the cubicle Maggie was standing next to the sinks and indicated, with a finger on her lips, that I shouldn't speak. Then she briskly walked me out of the room as we heard another toilet flush behind us. She told me that despite there being plenty of other toilets in the building, Kate had very deliberately followed me into that one.

I wondered what I would have done if I had been alone, face to face with her. What I would have done if she had asked me, as she had in the police car, 'Are you OK?' I thought about the seven months I'd endured of disgusting brothels and the struggle to have enough cash for rent and food. I thought about the bank loan interest that was increasing month after month and would continue to increase until I got my £7,000 back. The humiliating phone calls first to my accountant and then to HMRC to explain why I couldn't pay my tax bill. The stress of keeping it all from my parents and from most of my friends.

This hell all stemmed from that moment seven months ago in the brothel when I hadn't appeared like a victim, when I hadn't been apologetic, repentant or subservient enough towards Kate, and refused to grant her the respect that she thought was her due. That's why she'd arrested me, I was sure of it.

What would I have done with her faux sympathy? There's no question that putting my thumbs through her eyeballs would have given me tremendous satisfaction. Maggie had saved me from fucking up.

Back in the courtroom there was a glimmer of hope. The CPS had not sent their evidence to my solicitor on time and the three magistrates were considering throwing the whole case out. As the prosecutor and my solicitor argued, I sat there, waiting, with a knot tightening in my stomach. Then the court clerk spoke up. He pointed out that the allegations against me were too serious to be dismissed as they involved the exploitation of other women. His words fucked me over as badly as any man had ever fucked me over.

The case was back on.

I knew then that they would find me guilty. After all, assisting in the management of a brothel is easy to prove when *all* the women working there are assisting. We were all chipping in in our own way, not least because Max was so useless. There was the brief venture into the daytime brothel; the long days of waiting for just one client in an attempt to escape the chaos of the nights. There were the texts from me asking other women to work with me. There was that text from the one Friday night when I'd been in charge.

So, I pleaded guilty. Because, as the law stands, I was guilty.

As my solicitor read out a statement, I listened with a curious detachment. The woman they were talking about sounded as though she'd had a dreadful life. Domestic violence at the hands of her first long-term boyfriend when she was a teenager. Terrible debt that she'd fallen into for all the right reasons but couldn't be repaid however hard she worked. How prostitution was intended as a short-term job to pay off debt and was never going to be for ever. I realized at some point that my solicitor was talking about me. But there was more. Stories I hadn't shared with my solicitor because they were too personal. A mum who had spent a great deal of my life loathing me. A descent into self-harm every time I felt powerless, whether that was at school with the cruel bullies or during my relationship with GP Tom who had raped me at night.

I wondered how that woman was still alive. How she hadn't topped herself at some point. Not bodging it with the pills she'd taken as a teenager, but doing it right. Perhaps a knife across the throat or hanging herself in some secluded wood. Yet I was still standing. And, yes, I felt unstable as I leaned against the wooden dock to stop myself from falling down. But the nightmare would pass. It always did.

I glanced over at the cops and was surprised to see that Kate had left the courtroom. Bill had his head down, as if he didn't want to hear what my solicitor was saying. Fucking listen, I thought. Listen and know that you are the piece of shit, not me. Understand that the police are shit. That the courts are shit. And that this is a shitty system and an unfair world in which we live.

The chief magistrate then asked me to stand. I could barely focus as she gave me the lightest possible sentence that she could for the crime, a twelve-month conditional discharge. The sense of relief that I wasn't going to prison was profound. But my second thought followed fast. I now had a criminal record and, for the rest of my life, that would hang over me. My previous 'good character' was gone and on any enhanced DBS check it would state 'managing or assisting in the management of a brothel'. The words 'sexual offence' would be clearly marked in black and white. Most people don't want to be in Gary Glitter's gang but there I was. No more singing to the elderly. No more teaching kids. Nothing that involved performing to the vulnerable. I could perhaps continue the hopeless pursuit of theatre roles and an acting career, but masochism isn't my thing. And I was damned if I'd do any more promotional work and put up with the kind of shit I had in the past. I now belonged in the margins and would stay there. I knew that my criminal record would affect everything from then on in my life, from booking home insurance and holidays to getting above-board jobs. I knew that I would never be allowed into America. To add insult to injury, Max, who already had pages of convictions against his name, who was a career criminal, looked like he was going to get off with another line of ink against his name that wouldn't change the direction of his life one jot.

I went back to working at the brothel. I reconnected with

my old clients and made a few new regulars. And I spent a lot of time not thinking about my future. I focused on making money instead. Because that's all there was now.

A Woman with Balls

Over the years I've met and spoken to at least ten politicians. I've had a Zoom chat with another and interacted with a few more on email (including a very patronizing conversation with Stella Creasy), and I have emailed at least fifty more to no avail. Yvette Cooper is one of only two politicians who have actually listened to me and then done something. In 2015 I was invited to speak to her as the Home Affairs Select Committee were gathering evidence about sex work. She heard my story, letting me speak without interruption, and seemed shocked. But, more than that, she believed me. She was attentive and I could tell that what I was telling her had the potential to bring about change. She asked me if having a criminal record prevented me from getting other work and I said 'Of course!' I will never pass a standard or enhanced DBS check now, which means no more performing to the elderly as they lie dying and no theatre-in-education work, which has the potential to change children's lives.

In her evidence-gathering exercise, Yvette also spoke to an NHS outreach programme for sex workers, National Ugly Mugs and the Terrence Higgins Trust, all organizations who fight for sex-worker rights. And, of course, Maggie was there. She told me before the meeting to keep my sleeves rolled up so

Yvette could see I had no track marks. 'Really,' she said, with a deadly serious face.

After the meeting I felt we had achieved something. The NGOs had statistics and data which showed that criminalizing sex work in Sweden had made everything more dangerous for the women over there. Women had been evicted from their homes, deposits had been kept by landlords and some sex workers had lost custody of their children. And I had my own story, of course, which showed that the current English laws weren't working either. From speaking to sex workers and NGOs, the committee made a series of recommendations. The first was a change in the law 'so that soliciting is no longer an offence and so that brothel-keeping provisions allow sex workers to share premises'. They saw the impact criminalization has on sex workers' ability to leave prostitution, and called for a law to delete 'previous convictions and cautions for prostitution' from sex workers' records. And they stated that 'trafficking for the purposes of sexual exploitation is an important and separate issue from prostitution between consenting adults'.

That was huge for us, and a similarly sizeable blow to the anti-trafficking organizations and the police who cite trafficking as a reason to raid brothels. Trafficking is the main argument our opponents attack us with because who can fail to be moved when they see a picture of an underage girl, trafficked against her will, lying on a spunk-stained mattress with a bucket of her own piss beside her? People seem to be unaware, however, that there are already laws in place that deal with traffickers and the exploitation of people. The committee making the distinction between the two made me feel hopeful that things would change. Not for me. It was too late for me. But for other sex workers. It meant that they would not have to go through the same shit. Their potential futures would not be eradicated.

But then the Conservatives decided that they wanted to do their own research.

God Botherers and Nincompoops

In 2018, six years after the raid on the brothel and three years after the Home Affairs Select Committee made their recommendations, the English Collective of Prostitutes was informed that the Conservative Party Human Rights Commission was gathering evidence to argue against the Home Affairs Select Committee's findings and a meeting was being convened. The Conservatives weren't happy and wanted some evidence to support the belief of the chair of the Commission, the Evangelical Christian MP Fiona Bruce, that we should implement End Demand. The very thorough work that Yvette Cooper and her team had done – all the evidence gathered over months from discussions with sex workers, NGOs, academics and the like – was thrown out in favour of one day's work during which the Conservative Commission would bring in the evidence they wanted. A proper kangaroo court.

The ECP asked me to go along with them, which I was keen to do, so I prepared a statement about why I had been selling sex, about the raid and the consequences for me personally. It took most of the night to put it all together; it was imperative that I was a credible witness. The ECP often asked me to attend different events debating prostitution laws as I was a good example of what harm the criminal justice system was doing to us, and was willing and able to speak up for decriminalization. Up to a point. I never used my real name and I refused to speak if there were going to be cameras or an audience.

I was up unreasonably early and jumped on the Tube to Westminster in a slightly nervous flap, only to find that they had changed the time of the meeting. They'd moved it earlier, not that it mattered as the Commission spent so long talking to the End Demand lot that those of us speaking on behalf of sex workers only had thirty minutes in total to talk, not long enough to put across a great deal of our thinking.

The Commission itself was made up of some very open-minded individuals: a number of devout Christians and people who were being paid to run anti-trafficking organizations. This was a group of people who had only had orgasms to procreate. As I began to speak about what happened to me, I could see their eyes glaze over. They weren't the least bit interested in the details of my life as a sex worker, or in me as a person; they had their own agendas to service. It was a total waste of my and the ECP's time. I couldn't understand what the point of the meeting had been and how, rather than going forwards, we seemed to be moving backwards.

Why wouldn't they listen to the women the law was failing? Why wouldn't they listen to sex workers? And why bother having a committee at all when you already know what you're going to decide? Surprise, surprise, then, that the end result was a recommendation that the End Demand model be implemented. Sexually frustrated prigs are nothing if not predictable.

Adam

When I first saw Adam, he was standing near the brothel door wearing a long coat. He was wide eyed and looked nervous, like he was ready to bolt. I looked at him, not to gauge how good looking he was. I looked at him to see if he had the potential to contribute towards my rent that week. 'In or out? In or out?' Max roared at him, almost scaring him off completely. So I quickly took over and passed him a beer. And just like that the verdict was 'in'.

We went to a room and talked. I had a strong sense that here was a good guy. I have no recollection of what else happened that night, of the details. What I remember is his manner and the fact that he was really, really funny. I was pleased when he came back to see me the next week. And the one after. Soon we arrived at the point where he would wait while I was with another client and then we would go off together.

I became fond of him. I really enjoyed shagging him and talking to him, and he was beginning to enter my thoughts when I wasn't working. That hadn't happened before. I took his number just in case the place got raided again. Besides, I was so close to leaving the brothel and working independently and I could see that he was someone who was going to stick around, that there was a place for him in my future. I was saving all the time and, having had my first taste of domming, I was looking for a perfect place to install a dungeon. I had it all mapped out.

One night I walked up the stairs from the bathroom to the communal space and there he was again. He was more drunk than normal and, when he saw me, he got on his knees in front of the amused Romanian working girls and told me he wanted to marry me. I laughed it off and said, 'Absolutely – I can't wait.' Then, as ever, we went downstairs to a room.

Seven years later Adam proposed for real.

Perhaps it was easier for Adam because by the time we were officially together I was just domming and no longer shagging. But, still, it takes a strong man to see his partner getting dressed up for someone else. And it's not lost on either of us that society would look at my ex, the respectable GP, and at Adam and think one a catch and the other a user of women. But people are never that simple. Life is never that simple.

I adore him and he adores me, and I like the fact we met in a brothel. It's far more interesting than if we had met on fucking Tinder.

Tipping Point

I am one month away from my due date. Other than to let me know that my cousin's husband died, my mum has been very silent. I thought we were back on track after that family moment, but she has retreated again. When I was younger she would punish me by not coming to watch me perform in my college plays or she'd buy me nothing for Christmas or my birthday. That hurt. Now, as an adult, her punishment of choice is silence. I honestly thought she wouldn't and couldn't keep this going until I give birth – her granddaughter is at stake here. I crack. I call and say to Mum, 'Why is it either me always calling you or Dad calling me? Why do you never call me?' She denies it and says I am wrong, that we have spoken, that it's my pregnancy brain forgetting things. I come off the phone gaslit, but also with a sense that things will be better now that we have connected, however poorly. We are on the home stretch now. Surely Mum will start to make an effort and I will stop being so stressed about our relationship.

Dungeon

After my trial came Max's. Unbelievably, the police thought that I had no hard feelings towards them and would help them gain a conviction. Policeman Bill had been in touch with my solicitor and wanted to know if I would give evidence against my manager at his upcoming trial. I impolitely declined. I was back at the brothel and keeping my head down as best I could. I had a goal and I had to keep that in mind: earn cash and build up my burgeoning domination business. The police could go fuck themselves.

I diligently studied dommes' websites to see how they marketed themselves and how I could be different. I chose a name that no other domme had and found a guy who could build my website. And, finally, I found my dungeon through Max and his dodgy contacts – sometimes it's best to keep your enemies close.

I could tell straight away that the place had the most amazing potential, despite its unpromising location underneath an NCP car park in central London. It was huge – two massive rooms that I would need to decorate. I'd light it and fill it with kit – the small things like floggers and rope and the big stuff like a cage and a bench – either buying it or scavenging it. Even when empty, it was incredibly atmospheric. I was being charged over the odds for rent, always the way when the landlord knows that you work in the sex industry, but it also meant that there wouldn't be any inspections. There was an understanding.

Through my growing list of contacts I found a woman who was in need of a dungeon to work from. She said she would give me some kit in exchange for sometimes using my place and that seemed like a reasonable deal. I was still nervous about the police. I was on their radar and sharing a premises was potentially problematic, but I thought the Met would have trouble proving sex was happening in the new place, not least because the other woman's session activities consisted of sploshing, which is throwing custard pies at men, and riding on their backs as they make donkey noises.

Then, from another domme who was retiring, I got a cage, a cross and a bench for about £300. Many new dommes come on the scene and buy all their new kit at Fetters, an expensive BDSM shop, spending tens of thousands of pounds. But even when I was setting up for the first time I knew that that was crazy. You don't know if the job is going to be long term for you and, even if it is, you can't know that you will get enough customers to make it work, and to pay back such huge sums.

I was cautiously excited. I had a dungeon to paint and a marketing campaign to get on with. This time, I decided not to jot it all down in a notebook.

Arise, Saviours!

With my swollen feet up in an attempt to improve circulation, and a cup of tea in my hand, I read an article about investment banker and so-called philanthropist John Studzinski's birthday bash, an event that has attracted such magnificent luminaries as Gordon Brown and Theresa May. Studzinski's name rings a bell, so I go off down a rabbit hole, looking back at my previous research on anti-trafficking organizations, information I'd necessarily begun to immerse myself in when I was arrested.

I am right. Studzinski, the wealthy investment banker and philanthropist, is the Founding President of Arise Foundation, an anti-slavery and anti-trafficking NGO which used to be run by an odious chap called Luke de Pulford, who I have had the displeasure of running into once or twice at parliament. It suits the anti-trafficking organizations to call us all prostituted women as inflated numbers will secure funding from government for their so-called cause. And if the government is not giving the anti-trafficking organizations enough, there is always a billionaire like Studzinski, a man so religious it's said he has a chapel in his Chelsea house, on hand to help.

Luke de Pulford likes to show his face, both metaphorically

and physically, whenever there is a new attempt to erode sex workers' rights. He was on the committee when I gave evidence at the Conservative Party Human Rights Commission and, more recently, spoke at the 2018 debate on Commercial Sexual Exploitation, which was an attempt to prevent hookers from advertising online – essentially a UK version of FOSTA-SESTA. At the time, a few of my sex-worker colleagues and I had to sit in the gallery and listen as the MPs spoke at length about how we were too traumatized to be trusted to speak for ourselves. When the MP Victoria Atkins referred to us as sex workers, Jess Phillips immediately piped up to insist that we should be referred to as prostitutes. The writer Kat Banyard, the author of *The Pimp Lobby*, was in parliament for the sexual exploitation debate as well. Her book, a so-called feminist manifesto in favour of sexual equality, tells us that prostitution should be eradicated. Banyard now works as an adviser to another supporter of End Demand, the MP Dame Diana Johnson, who shamelessly used the murder of Sarah Everard to push her anti-sex-work agenda during the debate on the Police, Crime, Sentencing and Courts bill. She said: 'If Ministers are serious about protecting women, they must recognize that exchanging money, food and accommodation for sex is a form of violence . . . Violence against women is endemic, but also preventable. In remembering Libby Squire, Sarah Everard and many others, we need deeds from this Government, not words.'

It is not our fault that men kill women.

These people all like to turn up and pretend they care about women's rights, but the reality is that they only want to support women who are exactly like them. If they truly cared about eradicating prostitution they would be focusing their attention on poverty, the reason most sex workers enter the industry. It's deeply ironic, then, that sex workers have so little chance of ever winning the argument for more rights because the side that opposes us is bankrolled by billionaires.

With the bit between my teeth I pull up the website of Arise Foundation and see with absolutely no surprise that Lord Hogan-Howe – a man who was Commissioner for the Metropolitan Police, the UK's most senior policeman, when I was arrested – is a trustee.

During that time, he 'oversaw a massive reduction in murder rates and crime overall, as well as successfully policing the London Olympics. He is passionate about ending human trafficking and modern slavery', it says in his biographical note. You bet he is. And if a few harmless hookers get criminal records in the crossfire, who cares? No wonder he ignored the letter of complaint that Andrew Boff of the London Assembly sent on my behalf after my experience with the police. Boff was wonderful and, years later, I still think of him warmly. There are few politicians I have met who listen and want to do something about sex workers' rights. He was one of them. An actual saviour. I only wish there were more like him.

Where's Saint George When You Need Him?

My phone rings and I am thrilled to see it's Mum calling. 'Your mum isn't very well,' Dad tells me.

'Oh no.' I am genuinely concerned. 'What's wrong with her?'

'She's upset about the row you two had.'

I can hear my mum in the background prompting him, as though he's a ventriloquist's dummy. And I suddenly realize that, in a way, that's exactly what he is and has been since his stroke made him totally dependent on her. I'm on the back foot because a second ago I was thrilled to hear from her and the next I am the cause of another of my mother's illnesses. I say to Dad it wasn't a row, that I had simply told her she should be showing some interest in me and her future grandchild.

Dad counters, saying that they have looked over their call logs and can see that they have called me multiple times. I say, '*You* called me, Dad. Never Mum.' And, with her voice still in his ear, he says that isn't true. And my brain is swimming as I start thinking that perhaps he is right. Perhaps, between all my crazy hormones and the insomnia and pain and stress, I am wrong.

And then she isn't in the background any more, she's on the phone, clear and articulate, not ill at all but just waiting to make her attack. I cling to my defensive words like a life raft, but I can feel them drifting away from me. I mumble and stutter.

This is the woman who seems to blame me for everything that has gone wrong in her life and yet will happily sponge off me, taking my money without a second thought. This is the woman who speaks to me with a different tone from the one she uses for my sister. The woman who believes that she should be respected as though she's the fucking godfather, without there being any reason for that respect to be shown. To try to make sense of it all I think back to that time she was too drunk to realize that Dad needed to go to hospital. I think about how my sister, the daughter she adores, didn't visit him on another of his many hospital stays, even though she lives so close, while I travelled up and down the country to check in on him. I think about how it's because I gave them cash over the years that they didn't lose their house when times got tough. I am a good daughter. I am.

Mum fires words down the line about how rude I am. And I simply don't understand. I throw my phone at Adam and tell him to speak to her. Please. Because I am done. I am screaming, and crying and flailing around the kitchen in exasperation like a madwoman. And yet I still want my mum's approval. I still want her love and for her to support me. I want her to have my back. I want her in my life. More than anything, I want her to be my daughter's grandmother.

Porsha

My last ever brothel client turned out to be a double with another girl who I'd met years before at the Archway brothel. Then, I had been leaving my day shift as she was about to start a night shift. I'd noticed that she looked terrified.

I'd asked the maid, 'What's with the new girl?'

'First shift.' she said, barely looking up from her newspaper.

'Ever?' I asked, and the maid nodded.

I dropped my bag and coat and ushered the girl behind a curtain so that I could give her a few pointers.

'Do not let them fuck for the full half-hour. Start them on their front and massage for ten minutes or so until they are writhing around and ready, as then they will finish quicker. Lastly, and most importantly, appear confident. That way the johns are less likely to try it on. They will take any opportunity to try it on.'

A couple of years later she ended up working with me at Max's. It was only after a few shifts that I recognized the woman who was now calling herself Porsha. The Archway place had broken her in. Gone was the terrified rabbit and in its place was a confident, sexual, hardened creature with a love for cocaine. Her first shift she took on two drunk young men by herself; something I have never done at work. She also managed one of our regulars, Ernest the rapist, better than I did, better than anyone could. Ernest appeared to be the perfect gentleman, with his polite manner and tailored suit, until he was in the room with you. Max wouldn't bar him. Money is money after all.

When I went back to Max's brothel after my criminal conviction Porsha was still there. She'd survived the police raid – though as she'd been with the client doing coke I'm not sure how. They'd both been naked when the police had stormed into their room, so who knows where they'd managed to hide it. Now there were more drugs than ever circulating around the place, which was another good reason to leave. A new woman was selling, including a drug called mephedrone. I tried it and didn't like it. I couldn't see the point of it. MDMA makes me want to touch and be touched, while coke makes me confident and horny, though it's difficult to orgasm. But despite mephedrone being a stimulant, it just made me feel dozy.

In the early hours of my last ever shift with Porsha, I did a bit of coke while our client and Porsha did coke and mephedrone too. After the session she gave me the last bit of mephedrone and a rolled-up fiver that we had used to sniff the coke. Unthinkingly, I shoved it into my bag. Then I fell asleep.

Mid-morning, I roused myself, showered and dressed and stepped blinking onto the London pavement and into a clear, bright, gorgeous day. I strolled to the bus stop, intending to go to my new dungeon, where I'd be sleeping from now on. There were finishing touches to be done. But as I stood waiting a plod appeared alongside me, just inches from my face.

'Can I ask where you have come from?' he asked.

Nearly There

I am to be induced a week early, which means I have less than two weeks to go now. I rationalize that what isn't done isn't going to get done before my little girl comes along, but that's OK. I have worked my arse off during the last eight months, renovating and moving into a new home that's ready to welcome our baby. I've written a play and hundreds of thousands of kinky words for my clients, with a few spanked bottoms thrown into the mix. I'm now putting things that are out of my control to one side. I block my parents and choose not to engage with them or my mother-in-law. We all have choices, after all. Mine is that baby comes first.

I am forty and in addition to my 'geriatric' age, an induction has been prompted by my last scan, which showed that my baby's growth has slowed. That finding came during a particularly stressful time, and I wonder if I should have blocked my parents earlier. I feel all the better for it.

The induction means that my birth plan has gone out of the window. No relaxing birthing pool for me. Instead, a tablet shoved up my vagina until my cervix is ready. Then a love hormone injected into my arm to start contractions. The hospital bag is ready. My baby's cot is ready, and her pram is ordered. I have come a long way from thinking about her as a parasite to thinking that carrying a baby is the most beautiful and wonderful thing in the world.

I cannot wait to meet her.

The Edge

The policeman steered me away from the gawping grannies at the bus stop and took me around the corner, where I could now see plod number two leaning against his police car.

I was panicking. I remembered hazily that Porsha had given me the rest of her wrap . . . Why had she done that? She had never done that before. And why the fuck had I taken it when I didn't even like mephedrone? Had the police been waiting for me to come out of the brothel? Had they been there for four hours waiting on little old me? As the questions kept surfacing I realized with a dazzling clarity that if they could get me for drug possession it would improve their chances of keeping all my cash in the pending POCA case.

Plod number two asked me my name and I refused to give it. I said, 'I think you already know.'

Then he said he was going to search me for drugs.

I gave them my bags and turned out my pockets. Where had I put it?

Then the bombshell. 'I am arresting you for the possession of class A . . .'

I looked at what he was holding and laughed with disbelief. He had found the rolled-up fiver, that much I could see, but the other thing in his hand wasn't the wrap. It was discarded chewing gum that I had folded in a tissue and put back in my bag.

Plod number two looked confused by my reaction and then realized his mistake.

'Is this . . .?'

'Chewing gum. Yes.' I tried not to smile. 'The fiver was a tip from my last client. And it was a slow night so I only have a couple of hundred, so you can't get me for proceeds of crime this time. Anything else you would like to do me for?' My confidence had come flooding back.

And with that they had to let me go.

Alone on the street I called my solicitor, who then called the station to bollock them for harassing me. I flushed the wrap, which they'd somehow missed in a tiny pocket of my work bag, in the first toilet I found.

I couldn't help but wonder how, when I never left the brothel with drugs on my person, they'd known that was the day to wait for me?

I remembered how a cop had asked me to be a confidential informant, and I wondered now if they had asked other girls too. Porsha. Bloody Porsha. It would explain why they hadn't done her for coke possession.

It was the final push I needed to break free and concentrate on building my own business. I never went back to the brothel.

Mum. Dad. I Have Something to Tell You . . .

Two year on from the bailiffs' visit and I was attempting to advise my dad about his business after he had once more been forced to start again. Times had changed and his client base, who he had relied on mainly via word of mouth, were old and dying. His tradesman contacts were similarly either dead or retired. He needed a marketing campaign that was in step with the times; he needed to embrace social media and he needed a website. I was angry about what had happened to him, cross that he had once again been too trusting. His biggest client, a man Dad had thought was his friend, had gone into liquidation while owing him money. This man had known what he was doing. He had put everything in his wife's name and dissolved the business so there was nothing that Dad could do to get his money back. It's called phoenixing, and people like this guy do it time and time again: set up a business, build up debts and then dissolve it. The law allows them to get away with it.

Getting angry wouldn't help. We had to move on, and I was going to help Dad to do that. I was sick to the back teeth of giving my parents cash. As it was, I had already paid the wages of one of Dad's staff who had lost his job overnight, and covered their monthly mortgage a few times. My time and my business experience were invaluable. After all, I had just put everything in place for my new business, quickly, efficiently, creatively. So although I knew Mum didn't think much of me and my opinions, I thought that Dad would have some respect, would see that I knew what I was talking about.

As I started outlining my thoughts about strategy, while we were out and about doing some shopping, he interjected that he needed to ask my sister what she thought as she was 'the money'. He thought my sister had business skills as she was running the office side of Patrick's business, and the pair of them seemed to be doing well with all their conspicuous consumption, spending money on designer clothes, holidays and expensive cars.

The words stung like a punch. 'Actually, Dad,' I said, 'most of that money from my sister – that £2,000 you needed urgently – was from me. I've been working as a dominatrix and I make very good money.'

It was out. It hadn't even been that difficult. It was a simple statement of fact. But the effect was as though a brick wall had suddenly sprung up between us.

'You need to talk to your mother,' Dad mumbled. He put his foot down and drove us home in silence as fast as he could, desperate to remove himself from the conversation.

At home I found Mum in the bath. I sat down on the loo beside her, and told her what I'd told him. I was nervous, but I was also amped up with adrenalin. It was time. Her face went slack jawed for a moment and then she said, 'You don't do any of that strangling stuff, do you? Because I heard that was dangerous.'

It was clear neither of them wanted to know all the details. But, as I handed over a few thousand more, my last offering, I imagined how I could use my job to my advantage whenever they pissed me off. 'No beef for me, thanks Mum,' I'd say, when we were gathered around the table for lunch. 'I've got to make sure I can poo in the morning because hard sports Joe is coming. Last time he took what he couldn't eat away in some Tupperware! Gravy, Dad?'

Three Days to Go

To bring on a natural labour and avoid an induction I have tried curry, but Adam scoffs that a chicken korma – the hottest I can handle – couldn't possibly have the desired effect. I'm still prepared to try sex again, even though it's traumatic for both of us, with me wincing as he frantically lubes me up, followed by the sensation of having something incredibly sharp shoved into me. Perhaps raspberry tea is the answer.

I go for a sweep at the hospital, the midwife prodding my insides to get the cervix to soften. I ask her why the sweep and sex hurt so much, and she says it's because everything has become more sensitive and engorged down there. I'm not sure I want to dwell on this. The sweep process means you then have a 50/50 chance of going into labour naturally between twenty-four to forty-eight hours afterwards. I'm keen to go into labour naturally, as I have a feeling my induction is going to take days. It often does, my word-of-mouth research tells me. Plus, if I'm away from home that long, I'll miss my cats. When one of my cats wakes up, he cries for me and will search the house until he finds me. I can't bear that he will wander from room to room and not be able to find me. And it troubles me that when I do eventually come home he'll have competition for my love and my time.

I am more than ready for my labour to start now. I have packed a new John Grisham and a Linwood Barclay. I will take my computer and some earplugs. In addition to the many bedside TVs in competition with each other in the ward there will be visiting relatives, which normally means screaming, shouting, running children. I really don't like screaming kids very much. I try to put that thought from my mind. But the 'What have I done?' question keeps coming back.

I Fought the Law . . .

My solicitor was getting increasingly pissed off with Fred, the officer in charge of my POCA case. I was glad that someone else could now see what a nasty little prick he was. To explain his behaviour I assumed that he must have spent thousands on hookers, and that this was his revenge. Or possibly that his wife had realized what a bell end he was and had left him. Either way, he really had it in for me and his misogyny seemed to run deep. He was hellbent on keeping my £7,000. It was a fortune to me but a drop in the ocean for the Metropolitan Police, who have the rich pickings of people's safety deposit boxes to raid.

After I had pleaded guilty to my criminal charges, I was sure Fred was creaming himself, certain that my cash was coming his way soon. But the way I felt about it, he would have to prise the money from my dead hands before I gave it up.

The issue that was still being batted back and forth was whether or not the seized money had been intended for use in unlawful conduct. Asked that question by my solicitor, Fred hedged his bets and said he'd like to leave it for the court to decide, a conclusion my solicitor described as 'outrageous'. At court it had been accepted that my involvement in the management of the brothel was minimal, not meaningful in any way, and was over only a very short period of time. By refusing to relinquish my money and continuing to suggest that I was profiting from my involvement, Fred's stance was tantamount to disagreeing with the court's verdict.

By this point, Max had been found guilty of allowing a premises to be used as a brothel, which was, in my opinion, a lesser charge than I had had to plead guilty to. As for dealing and managing, he had got off scot-free. Unbelievably, Max was in the process of appealing, and even more hard to comprehend was that he asked me to be a witness on his behalf. I had to be careful about what I did next as I wanted to keep my new dungeon. So, I spoke to his barrister and said I was extremely happy to testify that he had been the best boss I'd ever had. After which conversation, funnily enough, they dropped me as a potential witness.

If the police were still under the impression that I was going to testify for Max at the appeal, they would apply to postpone my civil trial once again and keep hold of my money for a while longer. I was desperate for my cash so I could pay off my bank loans, pay HMRC the tax I owed and simply continue with my life, which felt as though it was on hold. But I was making money. I could survive. My solicitor informed the police's barrister that I wasn't going to give evidence. And so I waited.

Almost There

My induction date arrives but there is a backlog of appointments at the hospital. They say they will call me as soon as they have a bed for me. The waiting game is excruciating. I wake in the night terrified because I'm experiencing a new sensation, which I can only describe as a kind of grinding that starts near my vagina and then travels to my lower back. It goes on for a few minutes and then stops. It doesn't hurt but I am scared nonetheless. I get up, with some difficulty, and waddle into the bathroom to peer in the mirror at my bump, which looks the same. But when I press on the area below my chest it feels looser, less full. And I realize I feel better. It is easier to breathe. There's more movement in my hips. She has moved down.

More of a Whimper Than a Bang

The battle for my money ended not with the fight to the death I was prepared for, but with a pathetic shuffling of bits of paper. I spent a lot of time crafting a long statement, which my solicitor passed on to the Met's solicitor. I particularly liked the ending: 'The police have turned me into a full-time whore by keeping the money I earned lying on my back.' It wrapped up: 'If that isn't state-controlled pimping, I don't know what is.' It was a strong enough argument for their solicitor not to fancy challenging me and my solicitor in court, so he offered a settlement. They would keep £3,000 and I could get the rest back.

'Tell 'em to fuck off,' I said to my brief.

The next figure came through. They would keep £1,500. I laughed, and wondered how much the police were having to pay their solicitor for all this toing and froing. Again, the answer was no.

The next offer arrived. This time, they wanted to retain £800 on the basis that I had not paid Max his cut from the days that I'd worked as the manager. So, effectively, they wanted me to pay them a manager's cut of my earnings. The offer came with a parting comment from the Met's solicitor that he wanted to get back to pursuing 'real criminals', which I appreciated.

My own solicitor advised me to think carefully about this final offer, and I did. Much as I wanted to face Fred in court, I knew that if I had on the bench a radical feminist, a Christian, a misogynist or any other person who thought I was scum, I would lose all of my money and still have to pay my solicitor close to £2,000 in fees. I settled. I hoped that my £800 went towards buying the bastards a bad curry at Christmas. And from time to time I google 'Is Fred dead?'

The money they nicked from me was money I'd earned the hard way; it was every profiterole I'd turned, every blowjob I'd given, every pool of puke I'd mopped up in a nightclub.

Pain and Pleasure

Time has lost all meaning. All there is, is pain. Pain so overwhelming that I don't understand it. I have read that contractions hurt like nothing else and the women I've probed for information have mentioned, almost in passing, that labour and childbirth would hurt. But this? I'm underprepared. The contractions come in waves that build and increase and grow, and I scream until the pain subsides again. It radiates along my back, starting in the middle and working its way down to the bottom of my arse, like sciatica. It's pain that makes me kick against the bottom of the bed and moan to a God I don't believe in.

I get into the bath, and rock on my hands and knees, humming between ragged breaths the tune of 'Row, Row, Row Your Boat', over and over, in the hope of distraction. I can't sit. I can't stand. And as I struggle to get out of the bath my waters break. Not a gush, but a steady stream of warm liquid that trickles down my thighs. I pull the help cord and the midwives come. I feel that perhaps my body, after being uncooperatively slow, is now moving too fast. Women say that the body knows what to do but, with this medical intervention, mine seems confused.

The midwives take me back to the ward and I lie in my bed, the backpain tearing through me. I'm sweating so much I throw off all my clothes until I'm down to my knickers and bra. I ask the midwives if Adam can come to me now but I'm told that, due to Covid, he can only join me in the delivery suite.

'When will that be?' I ask.

There's no clear answer, only that I am next in line.

I ask for gas and air.

I'm told it's only available in the delivery suite.

I'm in a holding pattern of terrible pain and asking the same questions as old midwives depart and new midwives come on shift. I'm given the same answers. No partner. No gas and air. I desperately try to put my TENS machine on my back myself but perhaps the pads aren't in the right place or perhaps I'm not pressing the right buttons at the right time and perhaps I am too sweaty for the pads to stay stuck. The machine is fucking useless. It's Adam who knows how to use it and I think help-lessly about how carefully he read the manual at home so that he'd be able to help me.

I beg and plead and then scream for more pain relief and it finally works. A midwife brings me a gas and air cannister. I breathe and breathe and breathe into it and at some point it runs out. Someone tops it up. My contractions are coming every few minutes now. How can a person feel all this and still be conscious?

I hear the midwife say, 'This isn't fair. She has been like this for hours.'

I've never experienced life as fair, so perhaps this is just how it was always meant to be.

'Don't stop breathing into the gas and air,' I am told. I'm certainly not going to stop doing that. Somehow, I manage to sit up.

I am now completely naked and the midwives attempt to put a sheet over me. But I really don't give a fuck if the whole hospital sees my fanny. I push the sheet aside as I squirm with the pain and, like a comedy sketch, they try to tuck it in around me again. But there is nothing neat and tidy about this.

Rabbits

I remember a time before my arrest when all four of us were in the old family kitchen. I was sitting at the table with Mum, my sister was perched on the worktop and Dad was making us drinks. Wine for me and Mum, cider for him and Coca-Cola for my sister. Back then we all got on. My sister didn't know I was back whoring and hadn't yet started up with my ex, my mum was only drinking a glass or two of wine a few nights a week, Dad hadn't yet had his stroke and was healthy. I was happy. We were all happy.

Mum was making some rabbits for a craft fayre, and as she was on a deadline we were all helping to stuff them and laughing because they were the ugliest rabbits we had ever seen. In a single moment we were all roaring with laughter at Mum's latest crazy endeavour in that small room filled with cigarette smoke, and I was hit with a realization that this would never happen again. We would never, all four of us be this happy and complete as a family as we were at that moment.

My laughter paused and I took a sip of my drink as I eyed the three of them. They were my family and, for better or worse, I would love them and cherish the good memories until either dementia or a coffin took me away. My dad. My mum.

My sister. None of us perfect by any stretch of the imagination but I'll tell you something. No family has ever laughed like ours.

The End

Adam is waiting for me outside the delivery suite. His face contorts with concern when he sees me. Mine crumples into pure relief that he is here. At some point the anaesthetist arrives and explains the side effects of the epidural. I do not give a fuck. Just dose me already, I say. And, just like that, there is no more pain. It's as if everything comes into focus. Everyone is so nice. So competent and professional and, with their help, the next fifteen hours pass in a drug-fuelled blur of midwives and handovers and examinations and drips and antibiotics. It's all very calm, but then we're told that baby and I have an infection and our heart rates are both too fast and irregular.

My body isn't cooperating. It has been my bread and butter. My lifeline. It has done everything I have required of it all my life. Standing for twelve hours on a factory line, fighting when I needed it to, shagging when I needed to. Dancing through life and experiencing everything that I wanted and many things I didn't. But never giving up. But now my body is being pushed past its brink, past its capabilities, and it's not working properly. It seems my body can't give birth to this baby. However many times they pump oxytocin into me my cervix won't dilate. I get to six centimetres and then stop, my body exhausted, labour stalled. I just want the baby to be OK and I know now that the longer she is in my body the more chance there is she will suffer.

The team around me – a group of people that seems to have grown – can see from the machine that my contractions have stopped. A C-section is mentioned, and consent forms appear, with a new doctor explaining the side effects. I sign. I'll do anything. I just need her to be OK. The theatre is glaringly bright and full of people. I am introduced to them all and told what they each do; but I can't take anything in. I am terrified.

An older woman, the anaesthetist's assistant, insists I wear a mask, even though my Covid test has come back negative only a few hours ago. My midwife comes over and tells me that, if I am too hot, she will remove it. That I don't need to wear it. She shoots a pissed-off glance at the older woman and I love her. Every single one of these midwives is the most glorious strong protector, both warrior and angel.

They place a blue curtain between me and down below, and then they begin. The anaesthetist checks my body for feeling, spraying my legs, my tummy, my tits with some kind of cold, ethereal liquid from a cannister. He is handsome, I notice, and I wonder how I can be thinking this when I am so bloody scared.

I'm told that my baby should be out within ten minutes. But she isn't.

I'm not sure when the atmosphere in the room changes. I can hear the drainage hoover sucking up blood. A noise that goes on and on. Adam's face is etched with worry. Beyond my blue curtain I hear someone say that there is a 'problem'.

'Talk to me. Say anything,' I say. And Adam starts talking.

I try to concentrate on the words spilling out of him and not to feel the heavy pressure inside my body as though someone is massaging my heart just beneath my chest. And I try not to hear the sucking vacuum and the gurgle of blood. But my thoughts drift and I wonder when they will get her out and whether she will be OK.

Then, at last, there is the glorious snuffly sound of a baby.

She is put next to my face and I look at her through my drowsy haze. I can't believe how beautiful she is. She looks back at me, as if to say, 'You'll do.'

I have lost two litres of blood. But none of that matters. She is OK.

I can't stop looking at her. Her eyes, her lips, her nose, her neck, drinking in every part of her. I have never in my life been filled with such hope and love and completeness. My midwife tells me off and says I should go to sleep. But I can't stop looking at her. My heart feels open with the purest love that nothing, absolutely nothing else can come close to. I will die for her. I will kill for her. And I know already that being a mother is the most amazing experience of my life.

Everything that has happened has brought me to this moment. I understand that if I hadn't gone through hell at home and at school and felt the need to escape, that if I hadn't gone to drama school and got into terrible debt, that if I hadn't sold sex and ended up with a criminal record, and if I hadn't been in the brothel the night Adam had stopped by, none of this would have happened. All of these life paths and choices have brought me here, to this moment.

And it was all worth it.

I watch the sunrise as my daughter feeds from my breast.

I look down at her face. The pureness, the innocence, the beauty that take my breath away.

I feel hope.

I feel happy.

I feel peace.

EVE'S GLOSSARY

Actors: Middle- and upper-class typically unemployed irritants who know what is best for working-class sex workers.

Anti-trafficking organizations: Organizations that purport to combat human trafficking but generally ignore Vietnamese nail salons and Chinese cockle pickers in favour of making sex workers' lives harder.

Brothel creeper: Your dad.

CBT: Cock-and-ball torture, involving punching, kicking, nettles, chilli, candles, Deep Heat, electrics, clothes pegs.

Consent: When adults give each other permission to do things to each other, whether money changes hands or not.

CP: Corporal punishment, which is physical punishment intending to cause pain. It includes spanking, caning, using a slipper, a crop, a tawse, a whip, a flogger, a wooden spoon, and anything you like really, generally on a bottom.

DBS check: Disclosure and Barring Service, which prevents convicted hookers from teaching Shakespeare to kids, but didn't stop Ian Huntley from being employed as a school caretaker.

Dominatrix: The wife experience. No shagging and much nagging.

ECP: English Collective of Prostitutes, a collection of people who fight for the rights of sex workers.

End Demand: A campaign to stop men from buying sex. As likely to work as Prohibition did in America in the 1920s and 1930s.

Escort: A word used to describe our job if we don't want to own shagging for cash.

Evangelical Christian: A religious person who is pro-life unless you are a hooker.

Feminization: Dressing and training a man so that he acts like a woman. Specifically, walking and talking like a woman, not doing the fucking dishes.

GFE: The girlfriend experience, which means kissing and fucking and being nice to the client.

GUM: Genitourinary medicine, involving very helpful sexual health checks.

Hard sports: Defecating on a person, generally into their mouth. No curry the day before the session. No man ever requests soft sports.

Hooker: Also a harlot, whore or working girl, a person who rents their body for the service of sex.

Independent: A hooker or a dominatrix who doesn't have a manager.

POCA: Proceeds of Crime Act, involving the confiscation of assets. An easy way of raising funds for police Christmas parties.

Prostitute: A term we sometimes call ourselves but mostly used by SWERFS (see below).

Sex worker: A person who works in the business of making someone horny.

Sex worker-exclusionary radical feminist: A woman who believes in the rights of all women apart from sex workers.

Tie and tease: Tying up a person and teasing them with fingers, tongue, hair, feather duster, your cat, anything you like really if they are blindfolded.

Water sports: Urinating on a person, generally into their mouth. Asparagus should not be consumed beforehand unless you really hate your client.

NOTES AND SOURCES

p. 16: **any wannabe young hooker . . . is kidding herself**: Lucy Platt and Teela Sanders, 'Is sex work still the most dangerous profession? The data suggest so', article on website of London School of Hygiene and Tropical Medicine, https://www.lshtm. ac.uk/newsevents/expert-opinion/sex-work-still-most-dangerous-profession-data-suggests-so, 16 August 2017. Accessed 29 August 2023.

p. 16: **You might think that street sex workers . . . in police raids**: Stewart Cunningham, Teela Sanders, Lucy Platt, Pippa Grenfell and P. G. Macioti, 'Sex Work and Occupational Homicide: Analysis of a UK Murder Database', *Homicide Studies* 22:3, (2018), pp. 321–38, available at https://researchonline.lshtm.ac.uk/id/eprint/4647626/1/Sex%20Work_GOLD%20VoR.pdf. Accessed 29 August 2023.

p. 28: **It took *The Five* . . . were sex workers**: Hallie Rubenhold, *The Five: The Untold Lives of the Women Killed by Jack the Ripper* (Doubleday, 2019) is a brilliant book. I have never read a book that has made me so angry about the shit that working-class women have to endure. It's unbelievably well researched and vital reading, I think, for every scumbag who thinks a woman who is subjected to violence 'had it coming'.

p. 47: **Unlike Jamie Dornan . . . touched his wife and baby**: Charlotte Wareing and Katy Forrester, 'Jamie Dornan needed a shower after visiting a SEX DUNGEON to prepare for Fifty Shades of Grey', *Irish Mirror*, 2 January 2015, https://www.irishmirror.ie/showbiz/celebrity-news/jamie-dornan-needed-shower-after-4824796. Accessed 29 August 2023.

p. 113: **Confused that a council . . . might backfire**: See Mark Cardwell, 'Senior Birmingham council officer paid more than £420k in a year – among the highest-paid in the UK', *BirminghamLive*, 9 April 2021, https://www.birminghammail.co.uk/news/midlands-news/senior-birmingham-council-officer-paid-20352966. Accessed 13 September 2023.

p. 158: **Tell that to Eva Marree Kullander . . . parental custody by the courts**: See https://en.wikipedia.org/wiki/Eva_Marree_Kullander_Smith. Accessed 13 September 2023.

p. 158: **in the countries that have implemented it . . . marginalized and stigmatized**: Department of Justice, 'Assessment of Review of Operation of Article 64a of the Sexual Offences Order (Northern Ireland) 2008: Offence of Purchasing Sexual Services', September 2019, available at: https://www.justice-ni.gov.uk/sites/default/files/publications/justice/assessment-of-impact-criminalisation-of-purchasing-sexual-services.pdf. Accessed 28 August 2023.

p. 159: **Amnesty is with us . . . infuriated all our opponents**: Amnesty International, 'Amnesty International policy on state obligations to respect, protect and fulfil the human rights of sex workers', (POL30/4062/2016), 26 May 2019. Available at: https://

www.amnesty.org/en/documents/pol30/4062/2016/en/. Accessed 28 August 2023.

p. 159: **I'm not sure . . . Harvey Weinstein God**: 'Meryl Streep thinks Harvey Weinstein is "God"', YouTube, Bazaar Daily News, https://www.youtube.com/watch?v=xTlydbdS0Hc. Accessed 28 August 2023. In fairness, Streep was unaware at the time of Weinstein's abuse and has since spoken out about it: https://www. huffingtonpost.co.uk/entry/meryl-streep-harvey-weinstein_n_ 59db5d87e4b072637c45420e. Accessed 9 January 2024. As an actress who admits when she is wrong, my hope is that perhaps she'll read this book and her opinions on sex work will also change.

p. 159: **While people who had never walked . . . criminal penalties for sex workers should be removed**: See Niina Vuolajärvi, 'Criminalising the Sex Buyer: Experiences from the Nordic Region', LSE Policy Brief 06/2022. https://www.lse.ac.uk/women-peace-security/assets/documents/2022/W922-0152-WPS-Policy-Paper-6-singles.pdf. Accessed 28 August 2023.

p. 194: **You don't have to be Albert Einstein . . . bad idea**: See Open Society Foundation, 'Criminalizing Condoms', 2012. Available at: https://www.opensocietyfoundations.org/publications/criminalizing-condoms. Accessed 23 September 2023.

p. 207: **The police keep . . . over to the Home Office**: 'What happens to money seized by police in the UK?', Ashcott Solicitors website, https://www.ashcottsolicitors.co.uk/what-happens-to-money-seized-by-police-in-the-uk/. Accessed 5 September 2023.

p. 212: **In America . . . or to the street**: FOSTA stands for (Allow

States and Victims to) Fight Online Sex Trafficking Act, and SESTA stands for the Stop Enabling Sex Traffickers Act. Both are US Senate and House bills which became law on 11 April 2018 and were intended to shut down the websites that facilitate trafficking: See Liz Tung, 'FOSTA-SESTA was supposed to thwart sex trafficking. Instead, it's sparked a movement', *ThePulse* podcast, 10 July 2020. Available at https://whyy.org/segments/fosta-sesta-was-supposed-to-thwart-sex-trafficking-instead-its-sparked-a-movement/. Accessed 28 August 2023.

p. 213: **If we argue too articulately . . . string a sentence together**: In a discussion on BBC's *Business Daily* on 18 April 2019, the writer Julie Bindel, talking to sex worker and academic Christina Parreira on 'Should Prostitution be a Normal Profession?', wrote Parreira off as 'the least typical of any woman in prostitution', and with that comment refused to accept that there are plenty of women like Christina – smart, informed and in control of their lives – working in the sex industry. See https://www.bbc.co.uk/sounds/play/w3csy77g. Accessed 28 August 2023.

p. 213: **If we argue too aggressively . . . and need protecting**: 'Fiona takes part in debate on "Helping Vulnerable Women in Prostitution"', Fiona Bruce's website, 6 July 2018, https://www.fionabruce.org.uk/news/fiona-takes-part-debate-helping-vulnerable-women-prostitution. Accessed 30 August 2023. The MP Fiona Bruce almost always votes against laws that promote equality and human rights. See: https://www.theyworkforyou.com/mp/24857/fiona_bruce/congleton/divisions?policy=6703. Accessed 28 August 2023.

p. 265: 'The first was a change in the law . . . consenting adults':
The Select Committee's full findings are at https://publications.
parliament.uk/pa/cm201617/cmselect/cmhaff/26/2606.htm.
Accessed 4 September 2023.

p. 273: **If Ministers are serious . . . we need deeds from this
government not words**: Hansard, House of Commons Debates,
vol. 691, 16 March 2021, col. 206, https://hansard.parliament.uk/
commons/2021-03-16/debates/1BD30E62-8C44-4DCC-BBBA-
0BA42E8D61E0/PoliceCrimeSentencingAndCourtsBill. Accessed
14 September 2023.

p. 274: **If they truly cared . . . most sex workers enter the industry**:
The English Collective of Prostitutes has put together a very
readable and thorough study of the correlation between sex work
and poverty called 'Submission to the United Nations Special
Rapporteur on Extreme Poverty and Human Rights', available at:
https://www.ohchr.org/sites/default/files/Documents/Issues/
EPoverty/UnitedKingdom/2018/NGOS/English_
CollectiveofProstitutes.pdf. Accessed 28 August 2023.

p. 274: 'Oversaw a massive reduction . . . ending human
trafficking and modern slavery': See https://www.arisefdn.org/
anti-slavery-about-us for more on Arise Foundation and Lord
Hogan-Howe. Accessed 31 August 2023. However, Hogan-Howe
appears no longer to be an Arise trustee at the time of going to
press.

p. 284: 'It was a fortune to me . . . safety deposit boxes to raid': See
'Where do I store jewellery and cash? Not in a safety deposit box',
MPR Solicitors website, 20 April 2015, https://www.mprsolicitors.

co.uk/site/blog/criminal-department-news/where-do-i-store-my-jewels-and-cash. Accessed 28 November 2023. Also Adrian Levy and Cathy Scott-Clark, 'The raid that rocked the Met', *Daily Mail*, 24 October 2009, https://www.dailymail.co.uk/home/moslive/article-1222777/The-raid-rocked-Met-Why-gun-drugs-op-6-717-safety-deposit-boxes-cost-taxpayer-fortune.html. Accessed 31 August 2023.

HELPFUL ORGANIZATIONS

There are some amazing organizations and charities that work incredibly hard to help people who are involved in the sex industry and/or the criminal justice system, as opposed to the de Pulfords of this world who, as far as I can see, go from charity to charity helping bugger-all people apart from themselves and their billionaire overlords. I'd like more people to be aware of them.

English Collective of Prostitutes

https://prostitutescollective.net/

National Ugly Mugs

A UK charity working with sex workers to do research, to design and deliver safety tools, and provide a support service: https://nationaluglymugs.org

Terence Higgins Trust

The UK's leading HIV and sexual health charity: https://tht.

org.uk. Their statement on sex work is here: https://www.tht.org.uk/our-work/about-our-charity/our-position-sex-work

Synergy Theatre Project

A charity that uses theatre to create a fairer world, helping people involved in the criminal justice system to discover alternative pathways: www.synergytheatreproject.co.uk/

Q&A WITH THE AUTHOR

Firstly, tell us why you wanted to write the story of your life and experiences as a sex worker?

I have been working in the sex industry now for over two decades and it felt like it was time to write about my life – I realized just how much I have to say. I have been involved with activism since my arrest – going to protests, posting on social media, writing to politicians and meeting them when given the opportunity. But it feels as though nothing ever changes for sex workers and I hoped that by sharing my story I might open a few eyes, not only to what life is really like for us but to make people aware that sex workers are people too. We're human too. We laugh, we cry, we have families, hopes and dreams.

When a literary agent got in touch and said she liked what I was writing, it felt like a huge opportunity to reach more people than I can when standing with a banner outside parliament, and tweeting or blogging into a shadowbanned void. Sex workers are incredibly vulnerable members of society on so many fronts and we rarely have a voice so, despite it being hard for me to look back at some of the difficult things I have been through, I seized the opportunity.

What I want readers to know is that the most privileged and powerful people in society – our politicians – keep attempting to put in place laws that will make our lives even harder than they already are. And because the law sees us as disposable, we are even more vulnerable than we might already be with clients. We run the risk of being robbed, raped and killed. When we attempt to speak we are ignored, dismissed as being either mentally ill and damaged or too privileged – by which I mean too educated – or too middle class or too wealthy, for our words to be trusted.

When we're arrested for trying to work, the criminal records we're given lead to us being unable to exit the sex industry as we won't pass a standard DBS check. That means jobs such as cleaning, teaching and caring are put out of our reach. We're caught in a cycle. Then there's the POCA (Proceeds of Crime Act), which the police uses to rob us in the brothels we work in. Stealing off sex workers when most of us are just trying to live, pay off debts and feed our families really pisses me off. At the heart of it is this question: Who knows what is best for us more than women, such as me, who have worked in this industry for decades?

To tell my own story feels like I'm taking back a degree of power. Societal change in attitude towards sex workers feels like a huge goal to aim for, but that is what I hope to achieve with the book. I've succeeded if someone who has read *How Was It for You?* sees a newspaper headline with the word 'prostitute' and thinks of that person as a human being and not only a sex worker. Or if they question the motives of a politician they hear talk about sex workers being victims.

And when an article is published in a major newspaper that dismisses us as pimps, the reader might wonder what the journalist's own agenda might be, and consider who pays their wages.

Sex workers have so many enemies to contend with and obstacles to overcome, but we will keep fighting. As I see it, we have no option. And this book is my small way of contributing to that fight. It's our experiences that change our character and form our opinions. The more experiences we have in life, the more shoes belonging to other people you're able to slip on throughout the journey, the more we're able to really see others and empathize. My experiences have made me softer in some ways, but also harder and more resilient. I am much more guarded around both men and women and it takes a lot for me to trust someone. Sharing that vulnerability felt like an important thing to do.

How do you feel about the way sex workers are portrayed in the media, both historically and now? Are there any fictionalized accounts that you connect with?

I love watching British crime drama, which is strange as you might think I've had my fill of cops – in all senses of the word. But whenever a storyline with a sex worker appears I brace myself. Sex workers are almost always depicted as victims. And, perhaps surprisingly given the quality of the dramas being produced, there has been very little change in the way British crime dramas have portrayed sex workers over the past few decades. Occasionally I hear the words 'sex worker' rather than 'prostitute', which is a bit of a break-through (and well done to *Silent Witness* for that) but otherwise the storyline is generally the same: woman who's had a hard life turns to drugs, alcohol and prostitution (their words, not mine) to survive. The closest to real life I have seen in a fictional account is in the 2017 drama *Harlots*, which I loved. Based on a book by Hallie Rubenhold, and set in a brothel in the eighteenth century, it carefully depicts the workers as three-dimensional women who have dreams and loves and genuine friendships. I recognize the camaraderie that you do occasionally find in brothels and which I really enjoyed when I did brothel work.

Ideally our own stories – written by sex workers – should be adapted for TV and film to prevent writers who have never stepped into a sex worker's brothel or dungeon from creating stereotypical portrayals that play into a harmful narrative. But stigma prevents us from waiving our anonymity. Besides, I'm not sure that production companies want to put the reality of our lives on TV, when so many punters are only looking for 'juicy' stories. The reality of our lives can be domestic and mundane. But, for me, that's what makes sex workers' lives interesting: we're just ordinary women. I understand why this truth might not appeal to everyone. But the issues around politics, the police, domestic violence and class that I confront head on in *How Was It for You?* are important. I think every story about sex workers needs to be as honest.

When you write your own story, so the wisdom goes, you take control of the narrative. Was that important to you?

It took forty years, the birth of my child, the loss of a parent, the disastrous and humiliating attempt at a new career and writing the story of my life to begin to sort my shit out. It was only after *How Was It for You?* was published in hardback in June 2024 that I finally realized that my anger and stress had manifested into something that was damaging my life and holding me back. I decided to seize my narrative with both hands, and change its trajectory.

Since the birth of my child, I have always wanted to be the best mum I can possibly be and to do what I need to be less stressed. I started working out and took up a martial art, something I had wanted to do since my early twenties but, as a woman, thought it wasn't my place. Now, in my forties, I'm not wasting any more time and I really don't give a fuck what others think – something you may have picked up on in the book. It's teaching me self-discipline and inner calm. I feel less angry and it has helped with my stress levels. And I've discovered that domination and martial arts have something else in common other than consensual violence: you cannot go into either the ring or the dungeon angry. You need to be in control.

I'm mostly in control of myself, now. And I'm able to rationalize that I can't control other people. My feeling is that the people who hurt you in life have to live with themselves, and that's their problem. Rather than feeling anger towards them, I feel sad for them. They're having to live with their story; and it's not a great reading experience. I feel incredibly lucky to have the life I have now. I feel as though I have a second chance and I am going to get the most out of every day.

One thing in particular that readers have found surprising is the animosity within the sex workers' community itself. Why was it important to write about that in your book?

My aim was to humanize sex workers and I have done that as truthfully as I can. Within every industry it's completely normal not to like all our colleagues, and the sex industry is no different in that regard. We do judge each other: what services we offer, what we charge, our working conditions. I am judged, and I judge in turn; it's very difficult not to compare and contrast.

I have seen various working practices that are impossible to overlook and I wanted to write about them here. Blackmailing clients is a problem as it affects other sex workers by making it harder for us to collect the personal information needed for deposits. Clients who are half expecting a negative experience isn't good for business and it makes us less safe. I don't like thieves, and I've seen a great many of those. I really don't like women who pimp out their younger relatives who are miserable to be doing the job, who I've seen crying between johns. I find it gross when women who don't offer sex look down on those who do, all the while insisting that they are not sex workers themselves. They are. And I really don't like the woman who got me arrested.

But just because we don't all like each other does not mean that we don't all want the same thing. Safety at work. And decriminalization is the only way to achieve that.

For someone who has never worked in the sex industry: what do you think is the one thing that would surprise them the most?

That the most successful sex workers like men. We like their company, we are interested in what they have to say, and we can talk to them for hours without our eyes glazing over. Some sex workers, however much they are being paid, really don't like men and it shows. They rarely stay in the business for long.

What experiences have you had in life that make you so alive to the potential problems of publishing this book?

I only became politically aware after my arrest and subsequent conviction, at which point I began to read everything I could about class and sex work. I could immediately see that there was no space in the media for a working-class sex worker who can occasionally string a sentence together. People like their sex workers either posh and sexy – the classic 'call girl' who rubs shoulders with the elite – or leaning up against a cheap car with a needle in her arm. They like the familiarity of what they have seen on TV – which is the problem with those one-dimensional depictions – and my views and story were always going to divide opinion as I don't place myself in either of those two camps. I'm neither a victim writing a misery memoir nor am I keen to write solely about the sexy situations I have been involved in, penning soft porn for someone else's vicarious tit-illation. It may surprise some people to learn that I won't do anything for money. This is the book I needed and wanted to write, and I'm very proud of it.

For years, I really believed that through my activism and

speaking to politicians about my experiences with the criminal justice system I could somehow make a difference. But I didn't. Trying to make my voice heard was like having walls appear in front of me at every step, with no chance of scaling them and no way around them. The one exception was meeting Yvette Cooper. That's when I felt like progress was being made. She recommended that women should be allowed to work together in brothels without fear of prosecution. Then the Tories, who were in power at the time, decided that she was wrong. It felt like all those conversations, in which I'd had to rake up painful memories, were for nothing.

From those experiences, and the fact I had never heard a voice like mine in the media, I could see that despite having found a publisher it might be difficult to market the book, and my anonymity wasn't going to make it any easier. Right-wing newspapers, we all thought, wouldn't cover it because many are anti sex work and anti porn. And left-wing papers are, perhaps surprisingly, going the same way. There have been many more articles in *The Guardian* about criminalizing the purchase of sex since Labour won the election. Even the media outlets that really do care about working-class voices, such as *Spiked*, are anti sex work and porn.

One chance for breakout success for a book like mine is to get a celebrity endorsement, but we are in the midst of cancel culture and livelihoods get lost for speaking up for anything seen as controversial. While a few big names requested to see a copy of the book, we then didn't hear a peep from them. Perhaps none of them wanted to take the risk of saying anything supportive. But that is an easy criticism for me to make from my position of anonymity. Brilliantly, Jo Brand doesn't give a fuck about being cancelled.

But even then I didn't think that our ads would get shadow-banned and censored, that the book – and its provocative hardback cover – would make so many gatekeepers quite so nervous. Perhaps one day – and I still live in hope – there will be room for voices like mine.

The book has proved to be very divisive. What would you say to those who have criticized you for some of the things you've, very honestly, shared?

First and foremost it is great to have any review. I will always defend free speech, even when I am being called something unpleasant. If people are afraid to air their real views, then it gives more oxygen to our very dangerous cancel culture.

But, of course, I don't agree with some of the criticisms levelled at the book, and at me personally. Accusing me of being anti working class because I don't work a minimum-wage job any more pisses me off. I don't think I am better than a factory worker. But I do think we are all better than the piffling amounts we get paid for so many so-called working-class jobs.

What I have found really odd about some of the responses to the book is that so many women have accused me of internalized misogyny. Especially odd are the reviewers who then go on to say they expected more titillation from the book, which is a hilarious contradiction. I take issue with the internalized misogyny label because to like all women would mean living in some kind of Stepford dystopia, where women do not have the power to be either unpleasant or to be disliked. The enforcement of women liking all women takes away the power to have our own opinions. I am very happily full of opinions. And I am not going to like every woman simply because she has a vagina any more than I will dislike every man because he has a cock.

I have been criticized for being too angry, but why are women not allowed to be angry? Submissive and silent are two things that women should never be. We continue to suffer too many injustices and we need to keep fighting for our freedoms. This attempt by other women to shame me and reshape my life story as a tale of nihilism, and the desire to do harm to another woman in a less powerful position than journalists occupy, is the worst possible example of internalized misogyny.

Some of the reviews have said that I'm unlikeable. Well, most of my family think I'm unlikeable, so I can't argue with that.

Who do you hope is reading this book?

I think any author would say 'everyone'. Emily Edwards was kind enough to say exactly that – 'everyone should read this book'. But it's younger people in particular that I'd like to reach. They're the ones who are optimistic and open-minded enough to want to build a fairer society in the future. They strike me as desperate for change.

We need a new brand of politics and my generation has shown we aren't going to deliver that. People want politicians to be open and honest about difficult subjects and to talk to people on the sharp end of our social issues. Talk to the poor and the working class about the economy, talk to the renters and the homeless about the housing market and to sex workers about sex work. While politicians only ever seem to think in the short term, I think the younger generation is looking to make positive long-term changes, partly because they have to. If *How Was It for You?* finds its way into their hands, and they take from it a better understanding of someone else's life, then that can only be a good thing.

What are some of the responses to the book that have pleased you the most?

Some of the reviews have been lovely. I've been called lots of nice things. 'Intelligent' always surprises me. 'Funny', I love. When reviewers talk about how it has changed their previously held opinions, well that was my aim. I want this book to enlighten and entertain. And I really don't mind if I also piss some people off!

ACKNOWLEDGEMENTS

I would like to thank a few people for their help, support and patience and, without whom, this book would never have happened.

My agent, Silé Edwards, for her belief in me and my story. Without her, the words would have remained in one of my many notebooks.

My editor, Andrea Henry, who I hope has removed the words that could get me sued, and made the remaining words so much better than I ever could have imagined.

Gillian Stern, who came in for the final edit, sprinkled fairy dust and made the manuscript stronger.

All the team at Picador, who have been lovely and worked hard to make *HWIFY* happen.

My partner, Adam, who is the funniest man I have ever known.

My daughter, who makes everything worth it.